Restoring BROKEN People

Dr. Rod Buzzard

Putting Together the Pieces of Our Lives

"The Spirit of the Lord is upon Me,
Because He has anointed Me
To preach the gospel to the poor;
He has sent Me to heal the brokenhearted,
To proclaim liberty to the captives
And recovery of sight to the blind,
To set at liberty those who are oppressed;
To proclaim the acceptable year of the LORD."
Luke 4:18-19

I

Light for Life Ministries, Inc.
P.O. Box 494311
Port Charlotte, FL 33949-4311
239-247-5431

Email: lightforlife@light4life.org
Web site: www.light4life.org

II

Contents

Introduction

Default or Design

In the winter of 2007 I found myself in charge of a recovery group in the church that I was pastoring. It was not my intention to ever be involved in recovery, but through some circumstances that prevailed, there I was.

At first I didn't really understand why I was in that position. There were others more experienced than I in our area. Although I had been certified as a young pastor by the Indiana Mental Health Association to be a substance abuse counselor, my life's work had been that of a pastor. So, I felt that someone who had struggled with drugs and alcohol would be a better fit for the job.

But, in looking back, I realize that in God there are no mistakes, but divine appointments. These appointments are given for our learning, strengthening, healing, and growing. As I reflect, I see the hand of God working with me to make me more of the servant that He wants me to be and to position me for the work that He wants me to do.

So, default or design. The natural man says it was default, but God's Word tells me that it was by His design I found myself in that place. Through the experience God has given to me a new burden for those who are bound up and need or want to be set free. He wants to make new creatures out of ship-wrecked lives. So, this is an effort to offer some tools that can be used to help those who are broken hearted find healing and those that are bound up to be set free.

Restoring

At the age of 20, I was called to start a ministry in Auburn, Indiana. It was an exciting time in my life as I watched God lead and miraculously supply to make it possible for those who were broken hearted to come to know God and His love. That began a 30-year journey in that community for me. It was incredible to watch God faithfully touch one life after another and to bring freedom and abundance into their hearts.

Auburn was the world headquarters for the Auburn, Cord, and Duesenberg Automobiles of the 1920s and 30s. The town flourished under the blessing of that industry. Those cars were way ahead of their times. Some of them had rack and pinion steering, front wheel drive, and many technological bells and whistles that would make us marvel today. The Duesenberg was an exclusive and luxurious automobile that could only be purchased by the very wealthy. So the saying became, "That's a Duesy!"

Sadly, the company went bankrupt in the mid-30s and when it did, the town went down with it. Times became so bad that a generation didn't even want to remember the great Auburn, Cord, and Duesenberg Company. The world headquarters and showroom was closed and boarded up for years along with its engineering and design offices. Those beautiful cars ended up in the junkyards of the world and seemed destined to rust out and be buried in the annals of forgotten memories.

Then, about the time I came to Auburn, a man felt that those cars had potential. He began to promote classic festivals and auctions and the World's Largest Classic Car Auction was born through his efforts. Soon, restoration shops sprang up around town. Many of the men in our church were being blessed by the efforts to restore those autos. What was left as junk soon became beautiful and blessed a whole new generation.

That is what God wants to do for people. All problems with addictions, compulsions, and destructive behaviors have their roots in a broken heart. Jesus came to heal the broken, to restore people, and to set the captive free.

12 Steps

The 12 Steps of Alcoholics Anonymous have helped untold millions of people deal with their addictions and compulsions. Why do these steps help and heal people? When I researched the history of these steps, I discovered that they were born in prayer and Bible Study. God's Word and the leading of the Holy Spirit inspired the steps. Two men were searching for sobriety and joined a Bible Study and prayer group called the Oxford Society. They were meeting to find a closer relationship with God. To accomplish that, they met several times a week to study the Bible and to pray together. These men found freedom from their addiction through this experience and then wrote down the steps that brought them to an ongoing sobriety.

Jesus Sets Us Free

So, let me take you back to my story. After going through the tremendous lessons of *Celebrate Recovery*[1], there was a greater hunger on the part of our group to know more. Many of these people had been sober for 10 or more years, but had not been in the church or involved with Bible study. They wanted to continue connecting the dots between

2

Introduction

the 12 Steps and the Bible. That is where this book came from. In an effort to feed them, these lessons were written from God's Word and my heart. It is an effort to reflect what the Holy Spirit was teaching our group through those days of growing.

Jesus said that we would know the *Truth* and the *Truth* would set us free. The Truth is not a set of facts, but a Person. The *Truth* is Jesus Christ Himself. Knowing Jesus Christ personally and having a daily relationship with Him sets the captive free. *Walking in Him daily brings restoration. He makes us into new creations.* (*2 Corinthians 5:17*)

God wants us all to be free of the things that bind us up. God wants to keep us free. The Bible says that we are to *"stand fast therefore in the liberty where Christ has set us free and be not entangled again with the yoke of bondage"* (*Galatians 5:1*).

Jesus, the Healer

In *John* chapter 9 when Jesus came upon a man who was blind from his birth, the disciples wanted to know if it was his sin or his parents' sin that caused him to be blind. Some people are all about blame and shame. It seems to be the warp of human nature that even though we are all made of the same stuff and struggle, we want to find fault with others. That was the spirit of the age when Christ was on earth and sadly it is still with us today.

But Jesus didn't buy into the spirit of condemnation, He said, *"You're asking the wrong question. You're looking for someone to blame. There is no such cause-effect here. Look instead for what God can do. We need to be energetically at work for the One who sent me here, working while the sun shines. When night falls, the workday is over"* (*John 9:3-4*, The Message).

The ministry of the Lord is to heal the broken hearted. People are broken hearted for so many reasons: sickness, divorce, loss of loved ones, absent father or mother, abuse, unresolved conflicts, betrayal, misunderstandings, addictions, compulsions that we are born with, etc. The list goes on and on. The Lord is not interested in finding blame to put us down; He wants to work on us, in us, and through us to bring healing. That is why one of His names is "Jehovah Rapha" which means "The Lord our Healer or Physician".

The Lord is not interested in putting us, but wants to lift us up. Let's face it; we have all made a mess of things one way or another. We

3

are all made of the same stuff and in the same boat. Thankfully, Jesus wants to get into our boat and heal us. He wants to navigate our boat into better waters. All we have to do is let Him.

This book is offered as a tool to help people find the truth and freedom that Christ offers to them. God wants us to be free. It is His will and desire that we come to Him. He will not cast out any who come to Him. Just one touch from His hand will change you and transform you into a person who can follow Him and be used for His glory.

Jesus, the Liberator

Twice in *Luke 4:18-19* Jesus proclaimed that He came to this world to liberate people who are held captive and oppressed by the enemy. The enemy of our souls uses many things to bind us and oppress us. Drugs, alcohol, inappropriate sex, overeating, anorexia, bulimia, rage, control, depression, inferiority, superiority, laziness, workaholism, self-righteousness, pride and the list goes on and on. These things are tools in the hands of the spirit that now works in the children of disobedience (Satan). *Ephesians 2:1-3* says that we are born into a world controlled by this spirit who wants to keep us bound up and blind to the truth.

God, in His love, has come to set us free. Jesus came to set us free from any and every thing that keeps us oppressed and bound up. *He who is in you is greater than he who is in the world. (1 John 4:4).* There is no work of the enemy that can stand against the power of Jesus Christ. He, by His Spirit, can touch you and make you free in Him.

Once we are set free, we have to stay free. In Galatians we are told that *we can begin in the Spirit and end up in our old ways (Galatians 3:1-3).* So because we continue to battle the old ways that are a part of our DNA, we have to daily fight the battle to stay free. *Galatians 5:1* says to, *"Stand fast therefore in the liberty by which Christ has made us free and be not entangled again with the yoke of bondage."*

When we look at it, everyone needs recovery and we have to work at it for the rest of our lives. We need to take communion every day. Communion is a time to remember what Jesus did for us and to examine ourselves. Jesus died on the cross to set us free and to heal us from every disease. He died for our forgiveness and to restore us to God. Every day we need to take time to remember this and to ask the Lord to show us if we have become bound and oppressed by our flesh, the world, and the devil. These 12 Steps help us to enter this process and to work on a daily relationship with the Lord Jesus Christ.

Twelve Steps and Their Biblical Comparisons

1.   We admitted we were powerless over our addictions and compulsive behaviors, that our lives had become unmanageable.

"I know I am rotten through and through so far as my old sinful nature is concerned. No matter which way I turn I can't make myself do right. I want to but I can't" (*Romans 7:18,* The Living Bible, TLB).

2.   We came to believe that a Power greater than ourselves could restore us to sanity.

"For God is at work within you, helping you want to obey him, and then helping you do what he wants" (*Philippians 2:13,* TLB).

3.   We made a decision to turn our lives and our wills over to the care of God.

"And so, dear brothers, I plead with you to give your bodies to God. Let them be a living sacrifice, holy-the kind he can accept. When you think of what he has done for you, is this too much to ask?" (*Romans 12:1,* TLB).

4.   We made a searching and fearless moral inventory of ourselves.

"Let us examine ourselves instead, and let us repent and turn again to the Lord" (*Lamentations 3:40,* TLB).

5.   We admitted to God, to ourselves, and to another human being the exact nature of our wrongs.

"Admit your faults to one another and pray for each other so that you may be healed. The earnest prayer of a righteous man has great power and wonderful results" (*James 5:16,* TLB).

6.   We were entirely ready to have God remove all these defects of character.

"Humble yourselves in the presence of the Lord, and He will exalt you" (*James 4:10,* NASB).

7.   We humbly asked Him to remove all our shortcomings.

"But if we confess our sins to him, he can be depended on to forgive us and to cleanse us from every wrong. [And it is perfectly proper for God to do this for us because Christ died to wash away our sins.]" (*1 John 1:9*, TLB).

8.   We made a list of all persons we had harmed and became willing to make amends to them all.

"And just as you want people to treat you, treat them in the same way" (*Luke 6:31, New American Standard Bible*, NASB).

9.   We made direct amends to such people whenever possible, except when to do so would injure them or others.

"So if you are standing before the altar in the Temple, offering a sacrifice to God, and suddenly remember that a friend has something against you, leave your sacrifice there beside the altar and go and apologize and be reconciled to him, and then come and offer your sacrifice to God" (*Matthew 5:23-24*, TLB).

10.   We continued to take personal inventory and when we were wrong, promptly admitted it.

"So be careful. If you are thinking, "Oh, I would never behave like that"- let this be a warning to you. For you too may fall into sin" (*1 Corinthians 10:12*, TLB).

11.   We sought through prayer and meditation to improve our conscious contact with God, praying only for knowledge of His will for us and power to carry that out.

"Let the word of Christ richly dwell within you, with all wisdom teaching and admonishing one another with psalms and hymns and spiritual songs, singing with thankfulness in your hearts to God" (*Colossians 3:16*, NASB).

12.   Having had a spiritual experience as the result of these steps, we try to carry this message to others and to practice these principles in all

our affairs.

"Dear brothers, if a Christian is overcome by some sin, you who are godly should gently and humbly help him back onto the right path, remembering that next time it might be one of you who is in the wrong" (*Galatians 6:1*, TLB).

Serenity Prayer
God grant me the serenity to accept the things I cannot change;
courage to change the things I can; and wisdom to know the difference.
(Although known most widely in its abbreviated form above,
the entire prayer reads as follows:)

Living one day at a time; enjoying one moment at a time;
Accepting hardships as the pathway to peace; taking, as He did, this sinful world as it is, not as I would have it; trusting that He will make all things right if I surrender to His Will; that I may be reasonably happy in this life and supremely happy with Him forever in the next. Amen.

Denial

Denial is the root of our compulsive behaviors. When we do not face the truth about ourselves, we become addicted to our behaviors that bring self- destruction. Adam and Eve did this with God in the Garden of Eden. They denied their guilt and blamed their behavior on others. Denial is based on the fear of rejection, which is shame. Why deal with denial?

> **D -** Disables our feeling
> **E-** Energy lost
> **N-** Negates growth
> **I-** Isolates us from God
> **A-** Alienates us from our relationships
> **L-** Lengthens the pain[1]

God loves you and will not reject you if you come to Him humbly and honestly, admitting that you need Him and want Him to help you.

Alcohol and Drug Use in America
(Statistics area from a survey taken in 2006)[2]

1. 125 Million Americans aged 12 and up drank alcohol in the last 30 days. (50.9%)

2. 57 Million Americans (23%) participated in binge drinking at least once in the 30 days prior to the survey.

3. 17 Million Americans (6.6%) were heavy drinkers.

4. 20.4 Million Americans (8.3%) aged 12 and up were current (past month) illicit drug users.

5. 22.6 Million Americans were substance dependent or abusers (9.2% of the population aged 12 or older).

6. 3.2 Million abused both alcohol and illicit drugs.

7. 4 Million people aged 12 and up (1.6%) received treatment related to the use of alcohol or illicit drugs.

Twelve Steps and Their Biblical Comparisons

12 Symptoms of Addictions and Compulsions

1. A pattern of out-of-control substance usage or behavior for a year or more.

2. Mood swings associated with usage or behavior.

3. An increasing pattern of usage or behavior over time, combined with failed effort at control.

4. The presence of major or milder forms of depression.

5. Impulse control problems, especially with food, sex, drugs, or money/spending/gambling.

6. The use of the substance of behavior to reward oneself or to reduce anxiety.

7. Obsessing about and doing the drug/behavior (becomes the central organizing principle of life).

8. Experiencing consistent negative consequences due to the substance or behavior.

9. Alternating pattern of out-of-control behavior with over-controlling behavior.

10. A history of emotional, physical, sexual, or spiritual abuse.

11. A family history of addiction, rigidity, divorce, or disengagement.

12. Marked feelings of loneliness or abandonment, shame, or self-worthlessness.

Restoring Broken People

People

A. This is all about PEOPLE.

B. Every home in America is affected either directly or indirectly.

C. Satan has come to steal, kill, and destroy (*John 10:10a*).

D. Jesus has come to give life more abundantly to PEOPLE (*John 10:10b*).

E. PEOPLE are created by God and are important to Him. God loves everyone and has a plan for each individual life. God wants to restore all who are broken, bound up, and held captive by the enemy. There is hope in God for everyone.

F. Three Things we must do to Restore Broken People

   1. Reach out with unconditional love.

     The Father waited for the prodigal son to return.
     The Father reached out to the bitter elder son to forgive.
     (Luke 15:11-32)

   2. Release the anointing of the Holy Spirit that delivers and heals.

     No one can be truly free without the work of the Holy Spirit.

   3. Remain available because it is an ongoing war, not just a battle.

Jesus taught us that the demon goes out and looks for another host. When it finds none it returns with seven others and if it finds its former house empty and clean, it returns with the seven others. The end of that person is worse than the beginning. (*Matthew 12:43-45*)

Step 1 ~ We admitted we were powerless over our addictions and compulsive behaviors, that our lives had become unmanageable.

"I know I am rotten through and through so far as my old sinful nature is concerned. No matter which way I turn I can't make myself do right. I want to but I can't" (Romans 7:18, TLB).

Recovery begins when we admit the truth.

Cambridge Dictionary[3] defines "admit" in two ways:
*Admit **(ACCEPT)** *To agree that something is true, especially unwillingly: He admitted his guilt/mistake. She admitted (that) she had made a mistake. At first he denied stealing the money but he later admitted (to) it. I wasn't entirely honest with him, I admit, but I didn't actually tell him any lies.*

*Admit **(ALLOW IN)** To *allow someone to enter a place: Each ticket admits one member and one guest. Men will not be admitted to the restaurant without a tie. To allow a person or country to join an organization: To allow someone to enter a hospital because they need medical care.*

Recovery begins when we allow the light to come in through the curtains. We admit. We agree to the truth even though we don't want to because it means saying we were wrong. Recovery begins by admitting to all of the truth. It requires humility and we tend to resist that because it often feels humiliating. But God doesn't want to humiliate you. He just wants you to be honest with yourself so you can be healed. He wants to bind up your broken heart and to lift you up, but in order for that to happen you have to open the door to your healing by admitting the truth about your circumstance.

Three Things that Keep Us from Recovery

Rejecting the truth when we hear it

"My people are destroyed for lack of knowledge. Because you have rejected knowledge, I also will reject you from being priest for Me;

because you have forgotten the law of your God, I also will forget your children. (Hosea 4:6).

The truth is:

- God loves you and has a wonderful plan for your life.
- God became a man in Jesus Christ and died for you so you can be totally forgiven of all your sins.
- If you give your life to Christ and make Him your Lord, He will help you and heal you.
- God can use the wrongs committed against you to bless you. They are stepping-stones to God's blessings.
- Those who have wronged you have done you a favor because God promises to give you double for all that you suffer wrong.
- God does not expect you to live under abuse and mistreatment when you have the power to change your situation.
- God will deal with those who have wronged you. He wants you to forgive them so you can be healed.
- When you don't forgive you take the bait and Satan has entrance into your heart to control you.
- God can and will deliver you because "greater is He that is in you than He that is in the world." When you admit Christ into your life you have the greatest power in heaven and on earth living in you.
- Jesus Christ. He is the way, the truth and the life. When He lives in you, you have the Truth living in you.

Releasing control of our life to the wrong things

"Wine, women, and song have robbed my people of their brains" (Hosea 4:11, TLB).

We can be addicted to many things such as sex, pornography, food, self-pity, self-righteousness, drugs, alcohol, power, control, a desire for peace, fun, people, children, parents, mates, and many other things.

Anything that we allow to control us in place of God is an idol.

Chapter One ~ Admitted

All things are good if they are used in the boundaries for which they are intended. But when we use them to take God's place in our heart, we become a prostitute. We sell our self for and to those things and our brain is robbed.

"My people ask counsel from their wooden idols, and their staff informs them. For the spirit of harlotry has caused them to stray, And they have played the harlot against their God" (Hosea 4:12).

The only thing that can control you and make you healthy is a loving and caring Higher Power who knows all about you and wants to lead you into those things that you were created to do and be. Jesus Christ is that Higher Power. He is the One who can make sense out of life.

Giving Him daily control of our heart, our thoughts, our goals, and our desires is the path to recovery.

Refusing to listen to the truth

If we had a deadly disease and someone had the cure, we could listen and receive it or we could refuse to listen and let the disease eat us up. The same is true of recovery. Human nature is a disease that will eat us alive. It is sinful, selfish, and self-destructive. We find all kinds of excuses not to listen.

- They don't understand because they haven't been through my circumstance.
- They don't really care.
- They don't know what they are talking about.
- If God loved me this would have never happened.
- I don't have a right to get better. I deserve this.
- It's someone else's fault because they didn't treat me right, so I don't need to change. I am not responsible.
- If I can get to my addiction, I can forget the pain and survive a day.
- If I quit my addiction, I won't have any friends or fun.
- They are no better than me. Why should I listen to them?

Our excuses keep us from listening to the truth that will set us free. To start recovery, we must be willing to "listen." It means we have to become humble and teachable.

It is our decision, but if we will make this decision, freedom will come to our soul and Jesus Christ will give us beauty for ashes. God wants to help us and heal us. Remember, Jesus came to "heal the brokenhearted." It starts with admitting we need to be healed.

Prayer:

Dear God,

Today I make Jesus Christ my Lord. I admit that I cannot do life on my own. I admit that I have made a wreck of my life. I admit that You love me and want to help me. I admit that You died for my sins and have forgiven me. I admit You into my heart. I receive You as the truth and give You control of my heart today.

In Jesus' Name,

Amen.

Putting it to Work

We encourage you to write out the following things and to discuss them with your sponsor or accountability partner.

1.   List some times when you have not been completely honest with yourself or with others.

_____
_____
_____
_____
_____

2.   Discuss why you find it difficult to be honest about your shortcomings and difficulties.

_____
_____
_____
_____

3.   Memorize the following scriptures:

"...If you abide in My word, you are My disciples indeed. And you shall know the truth, and the truth shall make you free" (*John 8:31-32*).

"Therefore if the Son makes you free, you shall be free indeed" (*John 8:36*).

"If we confess our sins, He is faithful and just to forgive us our sins and to cleanse us from all unrighteousness" (*1 John 1:9*).

4.   What do these scriptures say to you?

_____
_____
_____
_____

Restoring Broken People

Step 1 ~ We admitted we were powerless over our addictions and compulsive behaviors, that our lives had become unmanageable.

"I know I am rotten through and through so far as my old sinful nature is concerned. No matter which way I turn I can't make myself do right. I want to but I can't" (Romans 7:18, TLB).

Hitting bottom is the beginning of healing from those things that control and destroy us. This always involves pain. We need to remember that pain is something God uses to warn us of danger. Just as pain keeps us from burning our fingers off when we touch a fire, God allows pain to let us know that we are in danger of being destroyed. *God never wastes a hurt.*

All of us can relate to David when he said in *Psalm 6:6-7 "I am weary with my sighing; every night I make my bed swim, I dissolve my couch with my tears. My eye has wasted away with grief; It has become old because of all my adversaries"*(NASB). Pain is something that we all share in common. But denying it will destroy us.

Denial is the enemy that keeps us bound up by the things that are destroying us. Being humble enough to admit that we are frail and imperfect and that we need help is the beginning of our healing process. Our weakness will become our strength when we admit it and begin to look for help to overcome it. The Apostle Paul admitted his weakness.

"For I know that nothing good dwells in me, that is, in my flesh; for the willing is present in me, but the doing of the good is not. For the good that I want, I do not do, but I practice the very evil that I do not want. But if I am doing the very thing I do not want, I am no longer the one doing it, but sin which dwells in me" (Romans 7:18-20, NASB).

The Love of God

The love of God is amazing. God knows everything about us, good and bad, but He has already decided to love us and help us if we will turn to Him. The story of the Prodigal Son clearly teaches us this truth.

And He said, "A man had two sons." "The younger of them said to his father," 'Father, give me the share of the estate that falls to me.' So he divided his wealth between them. And not many days later, the younger son gathered everything together and went on a journey into a distant country, and there he squandered his estate with loose living. Now when he had spent everything, a severe famine occurred in that country, and he began to be impoverished. So he went and hired himself out to one of the citizens of that country, and he sent him into his fields to feed swine." And he would have gladly filled his stomach with the pods that the swine were eating, and no one was giving anything to him. But when he came to his senses, he said, 'How many of my father's hired men have more than enough bread, but I am dying here with hunger! I will get up and go to my father, and will say to him, "Father, I have sinned against heaven, and in your sight; I am no longer worthy to be called your son; make me as one of your hired men."' So he got up and came to his father. But while he was still a long way off, his father saw him and felt compassion for him, and ran and embraced him and kissed him. And the son said to him, 'Father, I have sinned against heaven and in your sight; I am no longer worthy to be called your son.' But the father said to his slaves, 'Quickly bring out the best robe and put it on him, and put a ring on his hand and sandals on his feet; and bring the fattened calf, kill it, and let us eat and celebrate; for this son of mine was dead and has come to life again; he was lost and has been found.' And they began to celebrate" (Luke 15:11-24, NASB).

Notice that the Prodigal:

Was a taker- There are two kinds of people, givers and takers. Both types of people can become destroyed by their nature.

Takers like this man are destroyed by selfishness and self-centeredness. He was out of control and soon was out of everything that he wanted and needed. **Givers** can often become out of control by being too indulged with feeling like they need to fix everyone. The father in this story was a giver, but he knew how to let his son go and suffer the consequences of his own actions so that he would learn from his mistakes.

Hit bottom- The day came when the path created by his own choices led him to a dark and lonely existence. It was there that he came to his senses and realized that his father wasn't so bad and that it was time to get back to where he belonged.

18

Was willing to admit he was wrong- He admitted to himself and then he admitted to the one that he hurt. All of our sin is against God. It grieves Him because He created us and, like any good Father, He has plans for us for our good and for us to be blessed. He made us to be a blessing to Him and all of creation. When we go another way and waste ourselves on other things, God is grieved. We have wronged Him.

In order to start the healing process we have to humble our self and become willing to admit to our self, to God, and to those that we have hurt where we have been wrong. We don't do all these things all at once, but we begin by admitting we have hit bottom and that God has a better plan. *"Therefore humble yourselves under the mighty hand of God, that He may exalt you in due time" (1 Peter 5:6).*

Was loved and accepted- by the Father. God wants us to know that He loves us unconditionally. No matter what we have done or wanted to do, God has chosen to forgive us and has made the way for that forgiveness through Jesus Christ. God sent Jesus *to die for our sins to pay for them once and for all (Hebrews 10:11-18).* When we call on His name, He takes away our sin and makes us a part of His Royal Family in Heaven. He gives us His Holy Spirit who constantly lets us know that God loves us unconditionally. ***Scientists have now discovered that unconditional love has the power to actually change a person's DNA.***[4] God wants to give us victory over our habits and the nature that brings self-destruction. God wants to give us a new nature. God says that He will make us into a new creation by the power of His Spirit living in us.

"Therefore if anyone is in Christ, he is a new creature; the old things passed away; behold, new things have come" (2 Corinthians 5:17, NASB).

God will not reject us. He loves us and wants to deliver us and give to us strength and power to overcome our enemies, habits, addictions, and compulsions.

Perhaps you hit bottom a long time ago and you have already taken the step of admitting to yourself, God and others that you were wrong and need help to change. If so, that is great. We celebrate God's work in you. Perhaps you are just now doing that. Perhaps you haven't yet, but you need to. If so, we celebrate the fact that you are reading this book and considering that choice.

Bottom is a choice!
You can choose how low you have to sink before you turn back and find the help that you need to be free.

Just as the father received the prodigal, so God the Father will receive us when we turn to Him. You can do this by receiving Jesus Christ as your Savior.

Have you accepted Jesus Christ as your Lord and Savior? If not we suggest that you do so. When we open our heart to Him, He comes in to our heart and lives there by His Holy Spirit. He will help us everyday to become what He created us to be by constantly reminding us that we are His children and that He loves us. He will give us the power to overcome our addictions and compulsions that have destroyed us. He gives us another chance.

Making Him Lord means that He becomes the center of our life. We give Him control over our decisions and attitude. As the prophet Ezekiel said, Jesus becomes the "wheel in the middle of the wheel" (*Ezekiel 1:16*).

Just pray to receive Christ
Here is a suggested prayer, or you can use your own words. The Key is that we open our hearts. God looks at the heart, not the words.

Dear Lord Jesus Christ.

I admit that I am a sinner and need Your help. I believe that You died for my sins and rose from the dead.

I receive You today as my Lord and Savior. I receive Your death on the cross as the payment for all of my debts owed to you. I receive Your forgiveness for all the wrongs that I have committed. I receive eternal life from you as a free gift. I receive Your new life for me and will follow You as my teacher and guide.

Thank You for your promise to forgive me and to help me live in a way that glorifies You. Thank You for Your promise of eternal life with You because I have believed in You as my Lord and Savior. I am trusting that You will give me the wisdom and power I need to bring my life under 'Your' control. Thank You for Your help and love.
In Jesus' Name, Amen.

Record Your Decision

If you have prayed this prayer or one like it sincerely from your heart, then the Lord has heard you and He has come into your heart. Whether you feel it or not, it has happened. God does not lie. Jesus promised that He would come into your heart and He has done it. You will begin to see the evidence in many different ways in the days to come.

This is your Spiritual Birthday. Jesus said that when we receive Him, we are "born again". You were born the first time in the natural, now you have been made alive in the Spirit. We celebrate your New Birth with you along with God and His angels in Heaven. Congratulations!!!

If you have received Jesus Christ as your Lord and Savior today, then we encourage you to record today as your Spiritual Birthday.

Today,

_____
Date

I received Jesus Christ as My Personal Lord and Savior.
According to His Word,
He has come into My Heart and
Now lives in me by His Spirit.
This is the beginning of my eternal life with Him!

Putting it to Work

Respond to the following questions in writing and then discuss them with your sponsor/accountability partner.

1.   Think about where bottom was or is for you. Write a sentence about it.

_____

_____

_____

_____

_____

2.   Do you want God to help you change and become a new creation? If so write a sentence to God of your desire to have a new life in His family and to live with Him each day of the rest of your life.

_____

_____

_____

_____

_____

3.   What is the number one thing that you want the Lord to help you change in your life? Describe this with some detail.

_____

_____

_____

_____

_____

4.   What are you willing to do to make this change take place?

_____

_____

_____

_____

Chapter Three ~ Powerless

Step 1 ~ We admitted we were powerless over our addictions and compulsive behaviors, that our lives had become unmanageable.

"I know I am rotten through and through so far as my old sinful nature is concerned. No matter which way I turn I can't make myself do right. I want to but I can't" (Romans 7:18, TLB).

In the previous chapter, we spoke of denial and its power to keep us bound in our addictions and our compulsions. I think that *DENIAL* is summed up by these words spoken by Archie Bunker, lead character in the 1970s American TV sitcom, *All in the Family.*

> **Edith Bunker**: *"I was just thinking. In all the years we been married, you never once said you was sorry."*
> **Archie Bunker**: *"Edith, I'll gladly say that I'm sorry - if I ever do anything wrong."* --- Norman Lear[5]

We laugh, but sadly this illustrates the denial that destroys all of us at some point in time.

Now we are focusing on being **POWERLESS**.

Powerless – From Webster's Dictionary:
Devoid of strength or resources (powerless victims)
Lacking the authority or capacity to act (was powerless to help) [6]

In order to begin our healing and recovery we must admit that we are powerless and need help. We don't like to do this because there is something in us that wants to be in control. *Frankly, we want to be our own God.*

But sadly we don't have the power and wisdom to be our own God. We drive ourselves insane trying to be something or someone that we are not. We carve out what we think God, or a god, is and try to be that thing. For Pharaoh, King of Egypt it *"was being the monster in the River Nile and believing that he was the god who made the river"* (Ezekiel 29:3). For us it might be thinking we are some Clint Eastwood *character or some version of a beauty queen. Maybe we think that we are*

God's answer to women or the newest goddess to walk the runways. It is all self-deception that leads to insanity.

The Holy Spirit tells us in the Word of God that human nature is given to foolishness that makes us crazy. Listen to these words.

"Claiming themselves to be wise without God, they became utter fools instead. And then, instead of worshipping the glorious, ever-living God, they took wood and stone and made idols for themselves, carving them to look like mere birds and animals and snakes and puny men" (Romans 1:22-23, TLB).

We all do it. We have all done it. We have all tried to play the part being our own "god" and have gone our own way. Somehow we think that we know better than God does and that we can make our own way and our own world that will be a better place. But in reality we are just making a mess and driving ourselves, and those around us, nuts. Listen to what God says about all of us.

"There is none who understands; There is none who seeks after God" (Romans 3:11).

We are all in this boat. We all try to play God and end up looking pretty silly doing it. God sees it and understands it, but He wants to help us and heal us. That is what restoration is all about. He wants us to come to Him. He is cool. If we will admit that we are powerless, He gives us the power that we need to become like Him.

The Bible tells us that we can receive power from God.

"But you shall receive power when the Holy Spirit has come upon you;" (Acts 1:8).

The key to receiving this power is that we have to give our total selves to the Lord as His students and learn from Him. We have to listen to Him and trust Him. Jesus told the disciples what to do to be powerful people. *He told them to "go to Jerusalem and wait for the Holy Spirit" (Acts 1:5).* So we have to do the same thing to receive God's power in our lives.

Wait – means to seek with all our heart. It means to trust in and lean on God totally. The disciples went to Jerusalem and for 10 days they prayed together in one place in one accord. Then on the day of Pentecost the Holy Spirit arrived and changed them. They went from fearful individuals hiding behind doors to people with power sharing the love of Christ with the world.

God wants to give you that kind of power to help you overcome your addictions, co-dependencies, and compulsions. You don't have to depend on other things when you trust in and lean on the Lord. This is illustrated in the story of a Soldier in the Bible.

Now when Jesus had entered Capernaum, a centurion came to Him, pleading with Him, saying, "Lord, my servant is lying at home paralyzed, dreadfully tormented." And Jesus said to him, "I will come and heal him." The centurion answered and said, "Lord, I am not worthy that You should come under my roof. But only speak a word, and my servant will be healed. For I also am a man under authority, having soldiers under me. And I say to this one, 'Go,' and he goes; and to another, 'Come,' and he comes; and to my servant, 'Do this,' and he does it." When Jesus heard it, He marveled, and said to those who followed, "Assuredly, I say to you, I have not found such great faith, not even in Israel!" And I say to you that many will come from east and west, and sit down with Abraham, Isaac, and Jacob in the kingdom of heaven. But the sons of the kingdom will be cast out into outer darkness. There will be weeping and gnashing of teeth." Then Jesus said to the centurion, "Go your way; and as you have believed, so let it be done for you." And his servant was healed that same hour (Matthew 8:5-13).

The Centurion:

1. Loved and cared for his servant
2. Was powerless to help his servant
3. Understood being under a Higher Power
4. Surrendered control to his Higher Power
5. Was taken care of along with his servant by The Higher Power, Jesus Christ.

That is what exercising real faith is. It is submitting to and surrendering to The Higher Power, Jesus Christ, and trusting Him to do for you what you cannot do for yourself. You yield to Him and play by His rules and He takes care of you.

Putting it to Work

Review these questions and write down your answers then discuss them with your sponsor or accountability partner.

1.   List some instances when you were powerless and used addictions or compulsions to deal with your powerlessness?

_____
_____
_____
_____
_____
_____
_____

2.   Why do you like being your own god? What kind of feeling or pay off does it give to you?

_____
_____
_____
_____
_____
_____
_____

3.   How did your attempts at being your own "God" turn to disaster? Name some of the consequences.

_____
_____
_____
_____
_____
_____
_____

Step 1 ~ We admitted we were powerless over our addictions and compulsive behaviors, that our lives had become unmanageable.

"I know I am rotten through and through so far as my old sinful nature is concerned. No matter which way I turn I can't make myself do right. I want to but I can't" (Romans 7:18, TLB).

Addictions and Compulsive Behaviors

By the design of our being we were created to be *interdependent* on the rest of creation, the Creator, and on others. God made the sun to provide the energy, nutrition, and vitamins necessary. Water was given for continued life. Plants and animals were made for foods. We are interdependent on the creation. The creation needs man to facilitate and maintain creation, and man needs the creation to exist.

When God looked at man, God said that it is not good that man dwell alone so God extracted out of man the woman to be a perfect counterpart to Him. That means that Adam and Eve were made to be interdependent on each other. Man has something that the woman needs, and the woman has something that the man needs. This is obvious in sexuality, but it is also true in the mental, emotional, social, and spiritual aspects of life.

Genesis 2:18

When God created man and woman, that interdependence was in perfect balance, but that all changed in the Garden of Eden. After Adam and Eve disobeyed God, a nature or bent towards sin and rebellion entered into them and the human race. *The Bible says that by one-man sin entered into the world that brought death (Romans 5:12).*

The problem is that we are in the process of dying, but we were not created to die. So everything is out of balance. By birth, we are no longer connected in a balanced way to the things that we were created to inter-depend with.

The Bible goes on to say that *the consequence of sin is death (Romans 6:23).* We were born separated from God and from the people and things that we need to feel whole and balanced. This separation feeds a need to be wanted, accepted, and to feel good about our self.

So, we are set up for addictions and compulsions that feed those needs. The problem is that the addictions and compulsions that this world offers take over and go out of balance. They enslave and make our life unmanageable. Those addictions can be anything from drugs and alcohol to self-righteousness and a need to control others.

The Bible says that *whatever you yield yourself to, you become a slave to that thing (Romans 6:16).*

The question is not, "to be a slave or not to be a slave", but "whose slave will you be"? Bob Dylan wrote the song, "Gotta Serve Somebody." The song says, *"It may be the devil or it may be the Lord but your gonna have to serve somebody."*

Mercy and Compassion

When God looks at our state, the Bible says that, *"He has pity on us like a father on a child" (Psalm 103:13).*

He has put together a rescue plan to deliver us from this tangled web of sin and death. He became a man to die for our sins so we could come to Him and be re-connected. Jesus died as a righteous man for the sins of the world. All of our sin was placed on Him. When He died He felt the penalty of our sins through separation from the Father, but then He rose from the dead. Now He says if we will believe in His death and resurrection and call on Jesus as our Lord and Savior, He will forgive us and re-connect us to Himself. He forgives us of all our rebellion and sin. *"As far as the east is from the west, So far has He removed our transgressions from us" (Psalm 103:12).*

Power to Overcome

God re-connects us and then asks us to yield to Him. God will not make us follow Him. He only wants those who are willing. When we do, He makes us His laborers of love and leads us into a life of wholeness and wellness in Him. The result is that we become the balanced person that He created us to be. He restores a sense of security in us and we don't need the thing that we were addicted to. The Bible says, *"You become the servants of God and righteousness" (Romans 6:18).*

You're gonna have to serve someone. The question is *who do we want to serve and what outcome do we want?* If we serve our addictions and compulsions, the outcome is an unmanageable life that is never in balance and ends up separated from God and creation forever *(Romans 6:20-21).* If we choose to yield our self to Jesus Christ, then we end up with Him managing our life and keeping everything in balance.

Chapter Four ~ Addictions and Compulsions

When we let Him have control of our life He gives us a sense of His *love, joy, and peace (Galatians 5:22-23). He restores us to Himself and His creation forever and in His perfect love all fear is cast out (2 Corinthians 5:18; 1 John 4:18).* Romans 8:15-16 says, *"For you did not receive the spirit of bondage again to fear, but you received the Spirit of adoption by whom we cry out, 'Abba Father'. The Spirit Himself bears witness with our spirit that we are children of God."*

The Holy Spirit connects us to God as sons and daughters. God makes that so real to us that we cry out, "Abba Father" which means "Dear Daddy". He is the Father who is always good, always loving, who really loves you and thinks you are wonderful. He knows you are because He made you and said that you are *"fearfully and wonderfully made" (Psalm 139:14).*

God makes us a part of His family. *The Lord Jesus Christ is our brother, the firstborn among many brothers (Colossians 1:15; Hebrews 2:11-12).* **He places us in His Family which is comprised of all those who have put their faith in Him. Everyone who receives Him receives the Spirit of Adoption and we become interconnected.** Wow! God restores us so we can be what He created us to be -- a whole and fulfilled person in Christ Jesus.

Part of our recovery is to connect with others who have the Spirit of Adoption. We do that by finding a church that teaches the Bible is God's Word and encourages us to pray daily and to grow in the Lord. We connect with those who are finding victory day by day over the addiction and compulsions that we struggle with. We find someone to be our sponsor or accountability partner who has the Spirit of Adoption in them who will pray for us daily, hear our confession and be confidential, and who will help and encourage us to stay focused on the Lord and His power to get us through each situation one day at a time.

We do that by staying plugged into the power source. God is our power source. We are admitting that *we are powerless, but He is all-powerful.*

When we yield to the Lord, He not only forgives us, but He also puts His Holy Spirit in us. He is the same Spirit that raised Jesus from the dead. That same Spirit gives us power over our addictions and compulsions (*Romans 8:11*). It is not just wishful thinking or a good attitude, but the power of the Creator living in us. It will flow in you like a river bringing life and power *(John 7:38).*

Restoring Broken People

The Choice is Ours
God will not force our will and the enemy can't force our will. It is our choice. How can we choose?

1. We decide to ask the Lord to take control of our life. From our heart, we ask Him to be our master, instead of our addictions and compulsions. We start every day by re-committing our life to Him. As long as we are serving our self, our addictions, or compulsions will take over and make our life unmanageable. When we yield to Him, He sets us free *(John 8:34-36)*.

2. We read something from the Bible every day. Begin with the Book of John. We ask God to speak to us from the Bible. The Bible is the Word of God. The same Holy Spirit who lives in us when we yield to Jesus Christ, wrote the Bible. *He helps us understand it and speaks to us through it (2 Peter 1:16-21)*.

3. Find a church that teaches from the Bible as God's Word and become involved in it. God made us to be inter-dependent. We cannot make it alone *(Ephesians 4:11-16)*.

4. Find a place where there are others yielded to Christ and draw strength and encouragement from them. Making meetings with a recovery group is essential. God tells us that, *"Though One may be overpowered by another, two can withstand him; And a threefold chord is not quickly broken" (Ecclesiastes 4:12)*. God didn't put that in the Bible for the sake of "rope." It is an illustration of our human existence. We do better when we share our life with others. We strengthen and help each other.

Pray this Prayer:
Lord Jesus Christ,
Today I want to have a life change. I know that I have to serve someone or something. I realize that serving my addictions, my compulsions, and myself only leads to insanity, insecurity, and unmanageability. I need You and yield to You today. Take control of my life. From my heart I desire You to be my Lord and Savior. I believe that You died to forgive my sins and that You rose from the dead. Thank you for all that you have done and for forgiving me and accepting me back into Your family. Amen.

Chapter Four ~ Addictions and Compulsions

Putting it to Work

Write a response to the following and then discuss your answers with your sponsor/accountability partner.

1.   Make a list of your addictions and compulsions. Be honest and list all of them that you can think of.

_____

_____

_____

_____

_____

2.   Think about those who are in your life who have received the Spirit of Adoption by making Jesus Christ their Lord and Savior. Make a list of those people.

_____

_____

_____

_____

_____

3.   If you have not done so yet, find a person to be your sponsor/accountability partner. This person needs to be someone who has gone through recovery training and who believes in Jesus Christ and is led by the Holy Spirit. Make a list of possible persons.

_____

_____

_____

_____

_____

Restoring Broken People

Chapter Five ~ Unmanageable

Step 1 ~ We admitted we were powerless over our addictions and compulsive behaviors, that our lives had become unmanageable.

"I know I am rotten through and through so far my old sinful nature is concerned. No matter which way I turn I can't make myself do right. I want to but I can't" (*Romans 7:18*, TLB).

Unmanageable

"I" is at the center of the words "sin" and "pride". As long as "I" am on the throne of my life controlling it, my life will be out of control. It makes my life chaotic and unmanageable. The Apostle Paul said the answer *is, "I am crucified with Christ, it is no longer I who live, but Christ lives in me; and the life that I now live in the flesh, I live by faith in the Son of God, who loved me and gave Himself for me"* (*Galatians 2:20).*

The fool has said in his heart, "There is no God."
They are corrupt, and have done abominable iniquity;
There is none who does good.
God looks down from heaven upon the children of men, to see if there are any who understand, who seek God.
Every one of them has turned aside; They have together become corrupt; There is none who does good, No, not one. (Psalm 53:1-3).

When we go our own way we are making our self to be "God". There are two kinds of atheists: *those who believe there is no God and those who live as if there is no God.* The truth is that you and "I" always make a mess of things when we do it our way. That is the meaning of sin. It means to miss the mark. The result of sin is always death, chaos, and destruction.

In the Old Testament the Bible says that an angel named Lucifer governed the Universe for God. But one day Lucifer decided that he wanted to be God and went his own way. In *Isaiah 14:12-14*, Lucifer says, *"I WILL"* five times. That is where we get into trouble. The result was that he took the universe into chaos. *Genesis 1:2* says *that the earth became without form and void or chaotic and darkness was on the face of the deep.*

This is a picture of what happens when we won't put God on the throne of our lives. We get puffed up in pride and make a mess of things. Since we are not God and don't know what we are doing, we don't have control over ourselves or anything else. It becomes unmanageable.

The King of Tyre was filled with this nature of Lucifer. He was so delusional that God spoke directly to him about his mental state.

> *"Because your heart is lifted up*
> *And you say, 'I am a god,*
> *I sit in the seat of gods,*
> *In the midst of the seas,'*
> *Yet you are a man and not a god,*
> *Though you set your heart as the*
> *Heart of a god." (Ezekiel 28:2).*

God warned this king that he was headed for a mess. When we choose to think that we are a god and can get along without the true God, out of respect and love He backs off and let's us try it our own way. This is the judgment of God. He allows us to judge ourselves. The other day I was trying to figure out who was causing my problems. Then I looked in the mirror and realized I was looking at him. Doing things our own way instead of letting God have His way creates most of our problems. I repented, asked the Lord to forgive me, and to help me to *"be still and know that He is God!" (Psalm 46:10).* He filled me with His peace.

He knows that we can't manage it, but God is not controlling and insecure. He let's us make a mess and then He picks up the pieces. If we let Him, He Restores Our Broken lives. So in this first step we have to admit that we have tried it our own way, tried being our own god, and we couldn't manage it. It is time to step down from the throne and admit that we need someone greater than us to take control.

Manageable

The only solution is to give control of my life to another who is my Higher Power, God. This is something that you have to do for yourself. No one else can do it for you and God won't force you to do it. But when you ask Jesus to take over your life and you place Him on the throne of your heart, He sends His Spirit to live in you. He won't take control until you give Him control. His Spirit begins to lead you. As you listen and yield to the Spirit, He frees you from your addictions and compulsive behaviors.

To change a habit you have to replace it!

Listen to what the Bible says.

"I say then: Walk in the Spirit, and you shall not fulfill the lust of the flesh. For the flesh lusts against the Spirit, and the Spirit against the flesh; and these are contrary to one another, so that you do not do the things that you wish. But if you are led by the Spirit, you are not under the law" (Galatians 5:16-18).

The result of doing our own thing and going our own way is chaos, hurt, jealousy, pride, deception, fear, strife, broken promises and broken relationships, etc. That is because our nature is sinful and corrupt. It will always produce corruption.

"Do not be deceived, God is not mocked; for whatever a man sows, that he will also reap. For he who sows to his flesh will of the flesh reap corruption, but he who sows to the Spirit will of the Spirit reap everlasting life" (Galatians 6:7-8).

The Fruit of yielding to the Spirit

When we yield to the Spirit it means we listen to Him and obey Him. The result is wonderful. Listen to what God says will happen:

"But the fruit of the Spirit is love, joy, peace, longsuffering, kindness, goodness, faithfulness, gentleness, self-control. Against such there is no law" (Galatians 5:22-23).

How do we yield to the Spirit?

1. Begin each day with prayer. We ask God to show us His will and we trust Him and His Word no matter what happens. Commit the day to God and cast your cares on Him.

2. Begin each day with reading the Bible. The Bible is God's Word. The Holy Spirit was in the men who wrote it. He is in each person who has made Jesus Christ their Lord and Savior. He will speak to us through the Bible and help us know God's will and the answers that we need.

3. Find a song, a scripture, or a thought from God to memorize and dwell on. As a man thinks so is he. If we will think on the things of God, we will be filled with the Spirit.

4. Do what God wants us to do. If we get busy doing the "do's", we won't have time to do the "don'ts". Remember that if we fail, God will forgive us. We confess our sins and faults quickly and receive the Lord's forgiveness. Then we get up and start obeying again.

Prayer:

Lord,

    I admit that my life is unmanageable because I have been doing things my own way. I know that You love me and want to give me a better life but You won't force it on me. Forgive me for my pride and arrogance.

    I want You to take over. Please be seated on the throne of my heart. I need You and want You to. Thank You. Help me to hear Your voice and to do those things that will please You and make me what You want me to be. Thank You for hearing me and helping me.

In Jesus' Name,

Amen.

Chapter Five ~ Unmanageable

Putting it to Work

Respond to the following in writing and then discuss them with your sponsor/accountability partner.

1.   Name some instances when you were acting like you were a "god" and things got messed up.

_____
_____
_____
_____
_____

2.   Discuss what unmanageable means to you.

_____
_____
_____
_____
_____

3.   How did your addictions and compulsive behaviors make your life unmanageable? Describe the cycle.

_____
_____
_____
_____
_____

4.   Make a list of things that you want to turn over to God and trust Him to take control of in your life.

_____
_____
_____
_____
_____

Restoring Broken People

Step 2 ~ We came to believe that a power greater than ourselves could restore us to sanity.

"For God is at work within you, helping you want to obey him, and then helping you do what he wants" (*Philippians 2:13*, TLB).

How do we *"come to believe?"* Can we prove God's existence scientifically or through philosophy? Do we have a relationship with a special person that leaves us believing or do we go to a certain church or place that makes us believe? How do we *"come to believe?"*

Believe – In the Hebrew is the word "'aman" (aw-man')[7]; which is a primitive root; properly, *to build up or support; to foster as a parent or nurse; figuratively to render (or be) firm or faithful, to trust or believe, to be permanent or quiet; morally to be true or certain.*

Moses asked God how the people of Israel would believe that God had really told Moses to lead them out of Egypt. We all have the ability to believe, but we need a stable supportive reason to believe. It is not just blind faith or just having faith in faith. It is not just positive thought. It is having the reasons, revelation, and evidence necessary to be able to trust and place our faith in somebody or something. Moses understood this. So even though Moses was experiencing God's Presence and hearing God's voice, He knew that the people he had to convince weren't there and they would need reasons to believe.

God honored Moses' request. God is reasonable and He understands how we are made and what makes us tick. So God provides for us the things that we need to believe. In *Exodus 4:4-5*, God gave to Moses handling instructions with a serpent, *"Then the LORD said to Moses, 'Reach out your hand and take it by the tail' (and he reached out his hand and caught it, and it became a rod in his hand), that they may believe that the LORD God of their fathers, the God of Abraham, the God of Isaac, and the God of Jacob, has appeared to you."*

To begin recovery, we must be able to feel secure that God is real and that He really did become a man in Jesus Christ. We must be able to feel secure that He died for our sins and rose from the dead so God can forgive us for all of our sins. We must be able to feel secure in the Bible as God's Word and not just man's ideas about God.

God understands that we need that support and evidence. Again in *Exodus 19:9* it says, *"The Lord said to Moses, 'Behold, I come to you in the thick cloud, that the people may hear when I speak with you, and believe you forever.' So Moses told the words of the people to the LORD."*

God told Moses that He wanted to give the people that security. God has not changed. He still wants to reveal Himself to us so that we are totally secure in His reality, His love, His gift of salvation in Jesus Christ, and His promise to use our life for His purposes.

Sobriety is not only the absence of addictive substances or things. It is the awareness that God is real, that you know who He is, and that you know He is your Good Father!

Sobriety means to know that we know that He is with us and that we are walking in His plan for our life. Believing brings a sense of security that comes from being able to trust someone who is supernatural and greater *than any person or force in Heaven or on Earth.* In *Isaiah 43:10-11* says it again, *"That you may know and believe Me, And understand that I am He. Before Me there was no God formed, Nor shall there be after Me. I, even I, am the LORD, And besides Me there is no savior."*

Believe – In the Greek language of the New Testament is "pisteuoo"; *to believe. It means to think to be true; to be persuaded of; to credit, place confidence in.[8]* Again, it is not blind faith, but is being persuaded for a reason. God knows just what we need to be persuaded. Jesus said to Nathaniel, one of the men who became a disciple,

"'Before Phillip called you, when you were under the fig tree, I saw you.' Nathaniel answered and said to Him, 'Teacher You are the Son of God; You are the King of Israel.'" (John 1:48-49).

I don't know what Nathaniel was doing under that fig tree, but when Jesus told Nathaniel that He knew about it, that was all that Nathaniel needed to be able to know and be persuaded that Jesus was the Son of God and the King of Israel. God knows just what we need to be able to believe.

In order to start recovery *we must be persuaded* of God's reality and His love for us. We must be persuaded of the truth of the Bible and that Jesus Christ really is God who became a man, died for our sins, and rose from the dead. *God knows this and is willing to persuade us* personally of His reality and love for us.

Chapter Six ~ Came To Believe

How does God persuade us?

Testimonies

Matthew 9:27-29 says, "When Jesus departed from there, two blind men followed Him, crying out and saying, 'Son of David, have mercy on us!' And when He had come into the house, the blind men came to Him. And Jesus said to them, 'Do you believe that I am able to do this?' They said to Him, 'Yes, Lord.' Then He touched their eyes, saying, 'According to your faith let it be to you.'"

These blind men were already persuaded that Jesus was God and could do anything. They had heard of what Jesus did for others and believed. Jesus did hundreds of miracles in His short ministry. He always did those miracles so that people would be persuaded that He was God who became a man to die for their sins and rose again to totally forgive all their wrongs. We start our recovery by hearing about how God helped others out of their addictions, compulsive behaviors, and co-dependencies. We believe, "If God did it for them, He can do it for me." God sends someone to us that we trust. We see the change in someone that we know had to have a miracle to get better, and they did.

Turns us loose of our past hurts

Matthew 18:6-7 says, "'But whoever causes one of these little ones who believe in Me to sin, it would be better for him if a millstone were hung around his neck, and he were drowned in the depth of the sea. Woe to the world because of offenses! For offenses must come, but woe to that man by whom the offense comes!'"

The word for offense means, *"to take the bait."* WRONG and INJUSTICE exists in the world because there are wrong doers and unjust people. These are people who do not do the will of God. The truth is that we have all done wrong and been unjust somewhere. We have all hurt someone. The wrongs of life cause great hurt.

Everything from sarcastic words, neglect, to violence or sexual abuse brings hurt and pain into our lives. Often we try to deal with that pain through addictions and compulsive behaviors.

We get hurt, afraid, angry, and bitter and then Satan has our heart and mind. We are under his control and begin to act out of the nature of that fallen creature. In our hurt we become hurtful to others and to ourselves.

Restoring Broken People

They say that a hurting dog is dangerous. Remember it is *hurting people who hurt people.* Often the abused becomes the abuser or the repressed self-abuser. It is the work of the enemy to take us captive and to make us his slave. Once we drink the poison of bitterness, we are diseased, weak, and bound up.

The only cure is FORGIVENESS!

Forgiveness is not for the offender. *FORGIVENESS is for the offended.* It is to set you free from the bait that you have taken that allowed you to be trapped by Satan. Jesus said, *"Satan comes to steal, kill, and destroy" (John 10:10).* He does it through un-forgiveness. Hanging on to past wrongs keeps you bound up.

Forgiveness sets us free. Jesus came to give us an abundant life. We decide we will not take the bait. Instead of fear we will trust God. Instead of anger we will have mercy knowing that we have hurt others as well. Instead of being bitter, we decide to get better and learn from the experience. Instead of allowing Satan to have control of our heart, we decide to let Jesus Christ have control of our heart. When we do, God makes His love real to us. He persuades us. He reveals Himself to us.

Touches us in our need and helps us

"Immediately the father of the child cried out and said with tears, 'Lord, I believe; help my unbelief!' When Jesus saw that the people came running together, He rebuked the unclean spirit, saying to it, 'Deaf and dumb spirit, I command you, come out of him and enter him no more!' Then the spirit cried out, convulsed him greatly, and came out of him. And he became as one dead, so that many said, 'He is dead.'" (Mark 9:24-26).

God can do anything. Nothing is impossible for Him. When we commit our ways to Him and trust Him, He comes through for us and our faith grows. *We come to believe.* God wants you to "*come to believe.*" He's ready, are you?

Prayer

Lord,
I believe, but help my unbelief. Please move in me and make Yourself real to me. Show me anything that I am hanging on to that keeps me from believing and trusting in You. ~Amen

Putting it to Work

Respond to the following questions in writing and then discuss them with your sponsor/accountability partner. Remember we are not here to make you believe, but to help you believe. Only God can give you the evidence that you need to believe in Him, but we believe that He will.

1.   Be honest and write down where you are on the issue of believing. Do you know that you know that God is real and that Jesus is God who became a man to die for you, then rose from the dead? Write down your honest feelings.

_____

_____

_____

_____

_____

2.   Have you harbored hurt and unforgiveness towards someone that keeps you from being able to sense God's love and forgiveness? If so, describe that hurt or those hurts.

_____

_____

_____

_____

_____

3.   Has God ever done anything in your life to make Himself real to you? Describe it?

_____

_____

_____

_____

_____

Restoring Broken People

Chapter Seven ~ Power Greater Than Ourselves

Step 2 ~ We came to believe that a power greater than ourselves could restore us to sanity.

"For God is at work within you, helping you want to obey him, and then helping you do what he wants" (Philippians 2:13, TLB).

How do we come to believe that a "power greater than ourselves" can do for us what we could not do for ourselves?

Get off the Throne

Why don't we? Here are several possibilities. We:

- *Are afraid that being vulnerable will open us to hurt.*
- *Enjoy power and don't want to give it up.*
- *Think we know better than anyone else how to make ourselves happy and whole.*
- *Think being in control makes us look important to others and they will respect us.*
- *Resist change and would rather hold on to the old familiar rather than risk something new.*
- *Have not yet come to believe that there is a gracious power greater than ourselves who wants to restore and heal us.*

What happens when we stay on the throne of our lives?

We walk a slippery slope and fall quickly into a downward spiral of self-deception and separation from God and others. We become full of shame and fear and turn to addictions and compulsive behaviors in an attempt to make ourselves feel better.

Let's look again at *Romans 1:21-32. "Because, although they knew God, they did not glorify Him as God, nor were thankful, but became futile in their thoughts, and their foolish hearts were darkened. Professing to be wise, they became fools, and changed the glory of the incorruptible God into an image made like corruptible man--and birds and four-footed animals and creeping things. Therefore God also gave them up to uncleanness, in the lusts of their hearts, to dishonor their bodies among themselves, who exchanged the truth of God for the lie, and worshiped and served the creature rather than the Creator, who is blessed forever. Amen. For this reason God gave them up to vile passions. For even their women exchanged the natural use for what is against nature. Likewise also the men, leaving the natural use of the woman, burned in their lust for one another, men with men committing what is shameful, and receiving in themselves the penalty of their error -which was due. And even as they did not like to retain God in their knowledge, God gave them over to a debased mind, to do those things which are not fitting; being filled with all unrighteousness, sexual immorality, wickedness, covetousness, maliciousness; full of envy, murder, strife, deceit, evil-mindedness; they are whisperers, backbiters, haters of God, violent, proud, boasters, inventors of evil things, disobedient to parents, undiscerning, untrustworthy, unloving, unforgiving, unmerciful; who, knowing the righteous judgment of God, that those who practice such things are worthy of death, not only do the same but also approve of those who practice them."*

We need to look at this list carefully and see where we transgress. I didn't say *if* we fall into this list, but *where* we fall into this list. Why? We all fall in some points somewhere. It is a description of what happens when we try to run our life without God. It is human nature or what the Bible calls sin nature. It is a description of man's nature without God. It is flawed and falls short of God's glory. So, where are we on the list?

We are all different and we show depravity in different ways. That is why the Bible tells us not to judge because in the way that we judge, condemn, and put down another, we are guilty of the same thing. As a matter of fact, that is why we judge.

Judging others soothes our conscience. We compare ourselves to others to make ourselves believe that we aren't so bad. We think about the wrong of others so we don't have to think about our own wrongs.

God is the only One who can judge these things and guess what? He doesn't want to judge you. He says that He put these things on Jesus and they are dead in Christ. He wants us to receive what Christ did for us and be forgiven. He wants to Restore us to the person He created us to be. He does not want to judge us.

Give God the Throne of Our Heart

T – Trust in the Lord with all your heart.
H – Humble yourself to God and others.
R – Rely totally on God to direct you and take care of you.
O – Offer your body as a living sacrifice to God.
N – Never turn back to the old selfish king (self) for help.
E – Eternal perspective – God sees what we can't.

Chapter Seven ~ Power Greater Than Ourselves

The angel Lucifer decided one day that he would no longer allow God to have the throne of his life. That one decision transformed him from Lucifer, Son of the morning, to Satan, the adversary, the accuser, and The Devil which means, false accuser and slanderer (Isaiah 14:12-15).

Think of that. One decision can transform your life. One choice can change your life forever. We have seen it with alcohol. One decision to drink and drive can land a person in a world of hurt or worse, can kill an innocent victim. One choice to use a gun to get money for drugs can put a person in prison until they are old. One choice to have sex can give a person a disease that makes them miserable for the rest of their life.

It works the other way too. One decision can turn your life around for the good. Today is the first day of the rest of your life. We can't change the past, but we can do something about our future. We can choose today to trust God and let Him use us for His glory. We can choose today to forgive those who have hurt us and be set free from bitterness, resentment, and rancor.

When you put Jesus Christ on the throne of your heart, He transforms you from a sinner to a saint, from darkness to light, from being condemned to forgiven from being bound to being set free, and from a member of the world to a citizen of the Kingdom of Heaven. We don't deserve this. He does it for us by His grace, which is His undeserved favor.

Proverbs 3:5-8 says, *"Trust in the LORD with all your heart, And lean not on your own understanding; In all your ways acknowledge Him, And He shall direct your paths. Do not be wise in your own eyes; Fear the LORD and depart from evil. It will be health to your flesh, and strength to your bones."*

God wants to heal, restore, and bless us, but He will not force His love and goodness on us. However, as soon as we are ready to trust Him and let Him help us, He loves us so much that He rushes into our lives to give us the help we need.

God's Way, Not My Way! One of the hardest things that I have dealt with in my own recovery is thinking that God needed to be on the throne to do things my way. That is not how it works. That is the same as being on the throne and turning God into some kind of computer that we program to do our bidding. We have to back down from keeping control and trust Him. We have to yield to Him and believe that He will have our best in His heart.

Letting God lead us is the prerequisite to being a child of God. *Romans 8:14* says, *"For as many as are led by the Spirit of God, these are sons of God."*

That is why Jesus said that we must become as a child to enter into the Kingdom of God. Receiving Jesus Christ as our Lord and letting Him have the throne of our heart allows God to make you His child.

John 1:11-13 says, *"He came to His own, and His own did not receive Him. But as many as received Him, to them He gave the right to become children of God, to those who believe in His name: who were born, not of blood, nor of the will of the flesh, nor of the will of man, but of God."*

God leads us by putting His Spirit into our heart –

He comes to live in us. We are the Temple of the Living God. He speaks to us and listens to us. His power lives in us.
"Don't you know that you are the Temple of God and that the Spirit of God dwells in you" (1 Corinthians 3:16).

It really humbles me to think that the God of all creation who made the heavens and the earth, who knows all things and holds all things together by His Word, would honor me by coming to live in me. It is so awesome and yet a little scary. Who am I to have that privilege? I don't deserve it, but He is so good and full of love that He does it by His grace.

His Spirit is a "power greater than us" that leads us day by day. He has it all under control and has it all figured out. He lives in us so we are never alone and never without God. He is always there to show us the next step. All we have to do is follow.

By speaking to us through His Word –

"All scripture is given by inspiration of God, and is profitable for doctrine, for reproof, for correction, for instruction in righteousness" (2 Timothy 3:16). The Bible is God's Word. It was written by the Holy Spirit. *"No prophecy of Scripture is of any private interpretation, for prophecy never came by the will of man, but holy men of God spoke as they were moved by the Holy Spirit" (2 Peter 1:20-21).*

When we read the Bible and ask God to speak to us through it, the Spirit makes it alive in our minds and hearts. Certain thoughts will seem to jump off of the page as the Holy Spirit shows us God's wisdom in and for our circumstances.

Chapter Seven ~ Power Greater Than Ourselves

By placing us in a community of believers –

God will lead us to a community of believers where God and His Word are used as the guide for life. God calls us "sheep" and says that we need to be in a flock of sheep that are cared for by a Shepherd that is called and chosen of God. God tells those that He chooses to –

"Shepherd the flock of God which is among you, serving as overseers" *(1 Peter 5:2).*

God will use the Shepherd through teaching and speaking inspirationally by the Holy Spirit to help you know God's will. God gives us Shepherds ...

"till we all come to the unity of the faith and of the knowledge of the Son of God, to a perfect man, to the measure of the stature of the fullness of Christ; that we should no longer be children, tossed to and fro and carried about with every wind of doctrine..." (Ephesians 4:13-14).

God is the power greater than us who leads us to the place we need to be so we can have a community of believers that will provide security and guidance in God's will and Word. God will use other sheep that have learned how to follow the Lord to give us a good example and help us walk in the right way.

That is why it is good for us who are in recovery to find the church that God has called us to and be faithful to attend as often as possible. Make sure it is a church that teaches from the Bible as the Word of God and proclaims that Jesus Christ is the only way to salvation and eternal life.

By opening and closing doors for us –

God is totally in control of all things. The Bible says that He counts the very hairs of our heads and knows where we are and what we need every day. God can cause people to favor us and they don't even know why. He knows how to limit the evil that touches us to only those things that will work in our favor to fulfill God's plan for us.

1 Corinthians 10:13 says, *"No temptation has overtaken you except such as is common to man; but God is faithful, who will not allow you to be tempted beyond what you are able, but with the temptation will also make the way of escape, that you may be able to bear it."*

Romans 8:28 says, *"And we know that all things work together for good to those who love God, to those who are the called according to*

His purpose."

So we came to believe in a power greater than ourselves. It is knowing God in both His greatness and His love that we can have peace when we are sober. We don't have to feed our compulsion or eat comfort food until we kill ourselves with sugar. We can rest in the Lord. He is bigger than anything. He is still on the throne. Even our stupid mistake will be turned for the good by His grace. Relax! He is the Power Greater Than Us!

Prayer

Dear Lord Jesus,

I am so sorry that I try to take Your job away from You. You are the Lord of all creation and the Lord of me. You are God and I am not. Today I ask You to take the throne of my heart. Take the controls. I want You to be the programmer of mind and decisions. I want You to lead me to do your will. I know that if I will trust You and give You the control, that You will heal and restore me. Thank You for Your promise and that You will keep it.

In Jesus' Name,

Amen.

Putting it to Work

Respond to these questions in writing and discuss them with your sponsor.

1.   Can you identify where you fall on the list found in *Romans 1:20-32*?

_____

_____

_____

_____

_____

2.   Can you identify the things that you tend to judge others that are found on the list of *Romans 1:2-32*?

_____

_____

_____

_____

_____

3.   List some ways that the Holy Spirit has led you in your heart to know God's will for your life?

_____

_____

_____

_____

_____

4.   Discuss some areas of your life where you need God to show you the answers?

_____

_____

_____

_____

_____

Restoring Broken People

Step 2 ~ We came to believe that a power greater than ourselves could restore us to sanity.

"For God is at work within you, helping you want to obey him, and then helping you do what he wants" (*Philippians 2:13,* TLB).

I used to pastor in Auburn, Indiana, the home of the Classic Automobile Industry. Auburn was the headquarters for the Auburn, Cord, and Duesenberg cars of the 1920s and 30s.

They were famous cars filled with innovations way ahead of their times. Unfortunately the company went bankrupt due to poor investing and the town went into poverty with the company.

When I arrived there in the 70s, all that was left of this great company was some empty buildings and rusting cars in the junkyards of America.

Then a man got the idea that those cars could be restored and become worth more than anyone had ever dreamed. He began to sell that dream to people around the world.

Some of the guys in the church I was pastoring started working in those restoration shops. I remember them asking me to stop by. They were so proud of what they did. They would show me a car that was brought from the junkyard. It was horrible, dirty, rusty, and good for nothing. But they would say, "We will restore this one and it will be worth a quarter of a million dollars."

They did it. Now those cars are selling for a million plus dollars because someone restored them.

Restoration

That is what recovery is all about. It is God taking someone that is wasting away in the junkyard of life, cleaning him or her up and making that individual into something more valuable than anyone else ever dreamed.

Why does God do this? He does it because He created us and loves us. God doesn't make any junk. He knows the person we really are and sees our potential. He desires to lift us up out of the dirt, the mud hole that we are wading in, and make us into a new creation. In His love He does not want to condemn us for our wrongs, but wants to forgive, cleanse, cover, and restore us to better than original condition.

Restoring Broken People

How can we be restored?

> **R-** Recognize the shame and fear that keeps us from help.
> **E-** Empty our self of our own ideas.
> **S-** Seek God's help with every decision we make.
> **T-** Turn to people that are being restored.
> **O-** Operate in the realm of faith.
> **R-** Receive God's forgiveness in Jesus Christ.
> **E-** Exchange our old lifestyle for God's new life style.
> **D-** Define our purpose as "living to glorify Jesus Christ."

R- Recognize the shame and fear that keeps us from help

Shame is the feeling of being rejected or the fear that we will be. We have all experienced this in either a family situation from a parent, sibling, or being the black sheep or at school and at play with friends growing up. Once we experience that rejection, we fear it. We don't want to go through it again. So we create defenses against the pain.

It might be to "control everything so we can't be rejected," or might be to "not get close to anyone so we can't be rejected," or it could be to "do anything the crowd wants so I won't be rejected." Being able to recognize it gives us the start we need to begin to be restored.

E- Empty our self of our own ideas

Often people never find restoration because they are so proud that they will not listen to anyone else. We especially tend to do this with God. One of the keys to being restored is that we listen to what others have to say, even when it is hard to hear. All of us have blind spots. Those areas that everyone else can see, but we can't see that need to change. This is where a sponsor or accountability partner can really make a difference in our recovery. Be willing to hear what others say to you and especially what God has to say to you.

S- Seek God's help with every decision you make

God really does care about you. He has a plan for your life and knows ahead of time the circumstances that you will face. He knows how to use everything for your good, even the bad things that will happen to you. His plan is the best plan.

Chapter Eight ~ Restore

T- Turn to people that are being restored

God has already put you in a place where He can surround you with the right people who will help you to be restored. Attending meetings and finding a church is important. No one is an island to himself. The Bible says, *"Two are better than one, Because they have a good reward for their labor. For if they fall, one will lift up his companion. But woe to him who is alone when he falls, For he has no one to help him up. Again, if two lie down together, they will keep warm; But how can one be warm alone? Though one may be overpowered by another, two can withstand him. And a threefold cord is not quickly broken"* (Ecclesiastes 4:9-12).

We need each other. When one is down, the other one lifts them up. We do not function well alone. Connecting with people who are moving forward in recovery is essential to being restored.

O- Operate in the realm of faith

When God works in our lives, it is usually in secret. Often we don't understand why things are happening the way they are? If we live in doubt and fear we will find ourselves back in the junkyard, wasting away. Faith operates in the realm of the unseen. It believes that God will keep His promises and that He will show us the way. When you go in for surgery, you have to trust that what a doctor will do will be for your good. Most of us don't understand, we just believe that the doctor will help us and the pain will be for the better. In the same way, to be restored, we have to trust God to use the pain to make us better.

R- Receive God's forgiveness in Jesus Christ

We all have done wrong on the way to the junkyard. We are probably there from the decisions that we made. God already knows about that, but has said that He loves us anyway. He has already forgiven us and wants us to receive His forgiveness. The Bible teaches us that praying with faith and confessing our wrongs bring forgiveness from God.

James 5:15-16 says, "And the prayer of faith will save the sick, and the Lord will raise him up. And if he has committed sins, he will be forgiven. Confess your trespasses to one another, and pray for one another, that you may be healed. The effective, fervent prayer of a righteous man avails much."

E- Exchange your old lifestyle for God's new life style

To overcome a habit, you have to exchange it for a new one. The definition of insanity is "doing the same thing the same way and expecting different results."

There are places that we go to that you can't go to if we want to be restored. They will bring us down. There are activities that we once participated in that we need to stop. There are magazines, movies, books, foods, or drinks that we consume that we have to stop consuming. But, they have to be replaced. A vacuum always pulls in its surroundings. We can't be restored being empty. We need a new lifestyle.

Jesus says that when a demonic spirit is cast out it looks for another house to live in. When it finds none, it will return to the house that it used to live in. If it finds that house swept, cleaned, but empty, it will enter back in to that house. Terrible! But that is not the end of the story. It will bring seven more spirits with it that are even more evil. The end of the person is that they are worse off than before *(Matthew 12:43-45)*.

We have to be filled with a new Spirit to recover from those things that have kept us bound up and broken hearted. Being filled with the Spirit is not an event, but a lifestyle. God tells us, *"And do not be drunk with wine, in which is dissipation; but be filled with the Spirit"* *(Ephesians 5:18)*.

The word *"filled"* actually means to be continually filled or filled and filled and filled and filled ... without end.[9] Just as alcoholism, drug addiction, overeating, and all our other addictions and compulsions are a lifestyle, so following the Lord is a Life Style. What does that Life Style look like?

God says it is *"speaking to one another in psalms and hymns and spiritual songs, singing and making melody in your heart to the Lord, giving thanks always for all things to God the Father in the name of our Lord Jesus Christ, submitting to one another in the fear of God"* *(Ephesians 5:19-21)*.

Being filled with the Spirit happens when we make a conscious effort to recognize God's Presence and to honor Him in our hearts and in our conversations with others. It means that we think about the Father, Jesus, and the Holy Spirit from the time we awake to the time that we go to sleep. It means that we are so filled in our mind with thoughts of God that we dream of the Lord and that we naturally share what He has done for us with others. It means that we love to be with His people, worship

Him in group settings. In this Life Style, God fills us with His Spirit. Then we are free because, *"Greater is He that is in you than he that is in the world"* (*1 John 4:4*).

D- Define your purpose as "living to glorify Jesus Christ"

We all live for something or someone. It may be our self or it may be some sport or drug or group of friends. Make Jesus Christ your defining point in life. Say to yourself and others, "I am living to bring glory to Jesus Christ". When we see our self as living for Him, we reflect His glory like the moon reflects the glory of the sun. We take on His likeness. We are restored to His Image that was created in us.

"Success is a journey, not a destination."
~Arthur Ashe

Putting it to Work

Respond to the following in writing and then discuss these things with your sponsor/accountability partner.

1.   How has God honored your faith? List some events that describe how God has moved in your life.

_____

_____

_____

_____

_____

2.   List the areas of shame, fear of rejection, and how they made you behave and feel.

_____

_____

_____

_____

_____

3.   Are there places in your thinking and emotions where the enemy has a foothold in you? List them and be ready to pray with someone about them.

_____

_____

_____

_____

4.   Describe the changes in your Life Style that are keeping you full of God and keeping the enemy out.

_____

_____

_____

_____

Step 2 ~ *We came to believe that a power greater than ourselves could restore us to sanity.*

"For God is at work within you, helping you want to obey him, and then helping you do what he wants" (*Philippians 2:13,* TLB).

Some things drive us insane. For example, instructions just make me crazy. Listen to some of the instructions found on different items.

Funny Instructions

- For a hair dryer: Do not use while sleeping.
- On a bag of Fritos: You could be a winner! No purchase necessary. Details inside.
- On a bath bar: Use like regular soap.
- On a frozen-dinner box: Serving suggestions-defrost.
- On a hotel-provided shower cap box: Fits on one head.
- On a package of tiramisu (printed on the bottom of the box): Do not turn upside down.
- On English bread pudding: Product will be hot after heating.
- In the instruction booklet for an iron: Do not iron clothes on body.

Just some funny examples of how crazy and inconsistent life can be. All of us can get crazy with life. It is a part of our humanity. Life just doesn't make sense. The more we try to put it into a box, the more the box seems to fall apart on us. Those experiences can leave us feeling helpless, out of control, afraid, and sick.

When you are sick you need the right medicine. In recovery we need discernment to know how to apply God's Word to our lives so we can walk in the love, power, and sound mind that God has promised to us. In order to understand sanity, we are going to contrast it with insanity. I found three examples in the Bible that help us discern sanity from insanity and what God tells us we can do about it.

Moses and Pharaoh

In the book of Exodus, we read that Moses had every reason to be insane. He was raised under Pharaoh's house, but was pulled towards

his family and people who were his slaves. In his rage he killed an Egyptian
and then was rejected by the slaves he sought to free. He could have been consumed by hurt and bitterness, but instead he chose to trust in the Lord.

I feel sorry for Moses. He spent forty years wandering the desert, eating nothing but bread off the ground and the occasional bird, and every day a million people would come up to him and ask, "Are we there yet?" Robert G. Lee

Sometimes that is how we feel. We try our hardest to do our best, but it isn't good enough. Our attempts to bless others are met with scorn and betrayal. We feel like "why even try when all the world wants to do is shoot us for caring". That is "stinkin-thinkin" that leads to insanity, addictions, and compulsive behaviors.

But Moses found another way. When left in the wilderness to tend sheep, Moses became aware of God's reality. He found out that the Lord wasn't just a religion or culture, but a real person who had a plan for him. Moses found sanity in an insane world by putting His faith in the Lord. Because Moses trusted God, God brought Moses through the Red Sea, the Wilderness, the rebellion of the people, and many other events. He is in heaven today with the Lord and was seen on the Mount of Transfiguration with Jesus. Let's contrast Moses to Pharaoh.

Pharaoh received revelation from God Himself of His goodness, greatness, and genuineness. Pharaoh grew up with Moses and knew the testimony of the Hebrews among them. Then when Moses went to Pharaoh with God's message, God proved Himself to Pharaoh with 10 plagues. Each was designed to show that God was more powerful than the Egyptian gods. The last plague was the death of the firstborn, which were worshipped as gods. Pharaoh being the firstborn of the land was worshipped as a god.

In spite of these direct revelations, Pharaoh insisted on being a "god" and defied the Lord. Like the Frank Sinatra song, "My Way", Pharaoh trusted in himself and did it his way. He drove himself insane doing things the same way, but expecting different results. He was in a rut and wouldn't let God teach him anything new. They say that a rut is just an open-ended grave. Pharaoh was in a rut and couldn't see what God was doing. He was drowned in the Red Sea with the armies of Egypt (*Exodus 1-28; Matthew 17:3; Hebrews 11:23-29*).

Chapter Nine ~ Sanity

Pharaoh just would not learn. That is the meaning of stupidity. It

is not that we are ignorant. It is that we insist on "doing it our way."

King David and King Saul

David was a shepherd boy who was the runt of the family. David's father continually sent David out to do the menial tasks of the family while the older brothers were promoted to stardom as warriors and heroes for Israel. But David learned to know and trust in the Lord as a shepherd boy. David learned to lean on God's power to care for, protect, provide for, and lead the sheep. When confronted by a bear and then a lion, David saw God's power to defeat those monstrous obstacles. God chose David to be King because David was a man after God's own heart. David was persecuted by King Saul. David didn't fight Saul but continued to serve Saul. Twice David had the opportunity to kill Saul, but didn't. David said that it was not right to touch God's anointed.

David was not sinless. David failed in some big ways. With Bathsheba, David committed adultery, murder, and political cover up. Later in life David let Satan fill his heart with pride by numbering the people - something God told David not to do. But when God confronted David with those sins, David was humble and honestly admitted the sins. God forgave David and promised to use David and David's descendants. Eventually, Jesus came to us from the house of David (*1 Samuel 16:11-14; 18-19; 24:3-7; 26:4; 2 Samuel 11-12; 24*).

King Saul was keeper of his father's donkeys. When God called Saul, he was humble and lowly. But when Saul became king, he became full of pride and felt that God didn't really mean for him to obey God.

When Saul was confronted with the disobedience, Saul made excuses and blamed the events on others. Saul became an insane individual. Saul was insanely jealous of David and began to bully David and tried for years to kill David even though David was serving and blessing King Saul. King Saul was wasted with hurt, pride, and bitterness. In the end, Saul looked to witches for help and ended up destroyed by the very enemies that God told Saul to destroy *(1 Samuel 9-11; 13-16; 18:6-11; 26:5-25; 31)*.

When God tells us to destroy an enemy, it is for our own protection. God says, *"Conquer an addiction, compulsive behavior, or a sin" to protect and bless us. God wants us to destroy these enemies of our flesh before they destroy us" (Galatians 6:7-8).* God is not trying to take away our fun or be mean; He is trying to protect us from the consequences and to help us. Saul didn't want to follow instructions. Instead he did it his way and destroyed himself and those around him.

Peter and Judas

Peter was a fisherman that the Lord called to be His disciple and eventually the lead Apostle of the early church. Peter was a hot-tempered individual who spoke too often and too quickly. But Peter was a spiritually sensitive man who could hear God and responded to Him. It was Peter who first understood that Jesus was the Christ, the Son of the Living God. However, within an hour of that revelation, Peter rebuked Jesus for saying that He would die on the cross for our sins. Jesus saw that Peter was speaking by Satan's influence and rebuked Satan. That must have been a tough day for Peter, but he kept following the Lord. Peter allowed the Lord to be teacher and corrector.

On the night that Jesus was betrayed and tried, Peter tried to rescue the Lord by drawing a sword against the soldiers arresting Jesus. Jesus rebuked Peter and said those who live by the sword have to die by the sword. That must have stunned Peter. He still didn't understand that the cross was the mission that Jesus had to fulfill.

So, at the trial, Peter denied the Lord three times with cursing to a little servant girl. But Peter sorted through the confusion and stayed with the disciples. After the resurrection, Jesus told the ladies who came to His tomb to tell the disciples and Peter that He was alive. Jesus spoke to Peter and reassured him that the sin of denial was forgiven. Jesus was still going to use Peter to "Feed His Sheep" (*Luke 5:8-11; Matthew 16:1-23; 26:31-35, 69-75; Mark 16:7; John 21:15-17*).

In contrast, Judas was an ordinary man who was the son of Simon. Judas was called by Jesus and was a successful preacher and had a ministry of healing. He became the treasurer of Christ's ministry and then became a thief of the monies.

Judas was disappointed that Jesus was not directing the assets of the ministry to the poor and was concerned that Jesus didn't have the right political agenda. But all of this was because Judas wanted to use the monies selfishly, not for others. In spite of this, Jesus continued to love, bless, and entrust Judas even though He knew that Judas had become full of Satan's influence.

Judas betrayed Jesus with a kiss for thirty pieces of silver. Afterwards Judas knew that Jesus was innocent and returned the silver to the chief priest. Judas had remorse, and shame but he did not have repentance as Peter did. *Repentance is a gift that leads to faith (Acts 5:31, 11;18, 2 Timothy 2:25).* Judas went mad with guilt and shame. He hung a rope over a tree and committed suicide (*Mark 6:7-13; Luke 9:10; John 6:70; 12:4-6; Matthew 26:14-16; 47-50; John 13:2; 18:2-5; Matthew 26:24; 27:5; Acts 1:16-25*).

God wants to give us repentance that leads to faith and life. When we sow to the flesh it brings death. *Galatians 6:8* says, *"For he who sows to his flesh will of the flesh reap corruption"*. Sin always brings death. *Romans 6:23* says, *"The wages of sin is death"*.

But God wants to fill us with life. Life is a gift from God. *Romans 6:23* continues by saying that the *"gift of God is eternal life through Jesus Christ our Lord." Galatians 6:8* tells us, *"but he who sows to the Spirit will of the Spirit reap everlasting life."*

Sanity happens when we discern the choice and sow to the Spirit instead of to the flesh. Peter chose to sow to the Spirit and received sanity and life. Judas did not want the gift of repentance. He did it his way. In his pride, he hung on to his shame, his fear of rejection and hung himself. He was insane.

God has something better for us. He wants to restore us to sanity. He gives us sanity through the gift of repentance that brings faith. In repentance, like Peter, we turn to the Lord and trust His Word instead of our feelings. Things are not always the way they seem to be. So we choose to put our faith in God's Word, not what we see and feel.

Faith as a choice not a feeling

In each story, both could have been forgiven and restored. One chose to trust in the Lord's mercy and ability to restore Him, the other did not. One was restored to sanity; the other was not. God is no respecter of persons. He wants to help and heal all of us. He loves us all equally. God paid the same price for all of us. He gave His only Son as a sacrifice for our sins.

Whoever believes in Him will be saved (Hebrews 10:39). 1 John 5:13 says that, *"we can know that we are saved and on that God lives in us."* We can know that peace that passes all understanding by putting our trust in Him. It is available to all. The choice is ours.

All of us have faith. Every day we choose to put our faith in something that we don't understand, but we believe. I don't understand how cars work, but I believe if I put the key in the ignition that it will run and take me where I want to go.

We may not understand everything about God and how He works, but we can see the evidence of His existence in our lives and that if we will trust Him, he will keep His promises. If we choose to trust in

Him, He will restore us to sanity. If we don't we remain lost in our craziness.

We decide and He restores. We surrender to Him and recognize that *He is the power greater* that we need, and He comes to our help and aid. We can make that decision through simple prayer. Here is a prayer to help you:

Prayer

Dear Lord,

Thank You for loving me. It is obvious that I am driving myself insane by insisting on doing things "my way." I am sorry. I believe that Jesus is Your Only Son and died for my sins. I want Him to come into my life and restore me to sanity. Thank You for hearing my prayer and helping.

In Jesus' Name,

Amen.

Putting it to Work

Respond in writing and then discuss these things with your sponsor/ accountability partner.

1.   List some of the circumstances that have left you feeling crazy and insane.

_____

_____

_____

_____

_____

2.   What choice did you make to bring you into this process of recovery?

_____

_____

_____

_____

_____

3.   Describe the pattern of thinking that makes you feel insane and unsound in your mind.

_____

_____

_____

_____

_____

4.   What scriptures and thoughts can you dwell on that give you peace, sanity, and break the pattern of unsound thinking?

_____

_____

_____

_____

Restoring Broken People

Step 3 ~ We made a decision to turn our lives and our wills over to the care of God.

"And so, dear brothers, I plead with you to give your bodies to God. Let them be a living sacrifice, holy-the kind he can accept. When you think of what he has done for you, is this too much to ask?" (*Romans 12:1,* TLB).

We make our decisions and then our decisions turn around and make us.
~ F. W. Boreham

Decisions are the very things that make us who we are. All of us can remember some key decisions that shaped us in life. Perhaps it was a decision to give in to cynicism and hurt that led to bitterness and pride. Or maybe it was a decision to not take the next drink or hit of some chemical substance, and life started moving in a better direction. It may have been a moment of rebellion against authority that threw you into some very negative circumstances or perhaps it was a time of surrender to God that started your life on to an upward path. Perhaps it was giving in to temptation and you became a slave to your desires or a time when you decided it wasn't worth it and you stopped giving in that made life brighter.

Character is the sum total of the decisions that we make in life. If I decide to lie and continue over and over again, I become known as a liar. If I choose to forgive and to be gracious to people and do that over and over again, I become known as a kind hearted and loving individual. With each decision that we make, we are shaping our character, the person that we are.

In order to continue in recovery we must make two decisions and then practice them day-by-day.

Identify and say "no" to our character defects

Your capacity to say No determines your capacity to say
Yes to greater things. ~ E. Stanley Jones

Think about the things that you may be tempted to do that will keep you from receiving the best that God has for you. Ask yourself, "When I am feeling afraid I want to: Drink alcohol, get stoned, yell at people, put someone down to make myself feel big, run away and become antisocial, rebel against authority, take control of things or people that I cannot control, sleep excessively, quit, blame others for my mistakes, or _____ (fill in the blank). These are things that we have to say "No" to.

The problem with character defects is it is hard to say "No" when we come face to face with opportunity and we think no one is looking. So to say "No" we must do several things.

Flee the source of your temptation.

Several passages in the Bible teach us this truth. *1 Timothy 6:9-11* says, *"But those who desire to be rich fall into temptation and a snare, and into many foolish and harmful lusts which drown men in destruction and perdition. For the love of money is a root of all kinds of evil, for which some have strayed from the faith in their greediness, and pierced themselves through with many sorrows. But you, O man of God, flee these things" (see also 1 Corinthians 6:18; 10:14).*

Flee means to run away scared. We need to have a healthy fear of those things that tempt us to behave destructively. Make sure that you do not give yourself the opportunity.

God tells us to "make no provision for the flesh, to fulfill its lusts" (*Romans 13:14*).

Receive the Will of God through the Word of God.

Ephesians 6:17 says, *"the sword of the Spirit, which is the word of God".*
The Bible is God's Word and it is the sword of the Holy Spirit in our hands against the temptations of the enemy. When Jesus faced temptation, He successfully resisted because He understood the Will of God through the Word of God. He was able to quote the scriptures that showed Him the right decision. King David said *"he hid God's Word in his heart that he might not sin against God"* (*Psalms 119:11*).

Resist the devil and he will flee from you.

James 4:7 says, *"resist the devil and he will flee from you".*
There is a power that lives in the believer that is greater than all of the powers of darkness put together. He is the Holy Spirit. Satan is your adversary and resists the wonderful things that God wants to do for you and in you. He tries to put thoughts in our minds to get us to oppose the things that God wants us to know and to think. Why? Because as a man thinks, so is he. The battle is in our minds. But God has given to us the

weapons that we need to overcome the enemy.

2 Corinthians 10:3-5 says, *"For though we walk in the flesh, we do not war according to the flesh. For the weapons of our warfare are not carnal but mighty in God for pulling down strongholds, casting down arguments and every high thing that exalts itself against the knowledge of God, bringing every thought into captivity to the obedience of Christ"*.

Recognizing your enemy and resisting him gives you the edge. If Satan tempts you with your character flaw, then recognizing it is Satan's bait is half of the battle. Say out loud, "In Jesus Name, you spirits of temptation, accusations, unforgiveness, lust, greed, foolishness, be bound. In Jesus' Name be resisted." When we do, he sees that the Lord is in us and with us and he becomes the one filled with fear and flees!

Why? Because there is an authority and power in us that is greater than Satan and he knows it. The problem is that we often do not know it, or remember it. Just like the traffic policeman that can stop an 18-wheel truck, we can speak in the Name of Jesus and stop the activities of darkness. So, discern the spirits and then resist them in Jesus' Name. Not every thought is from God. We have to pull down the thoughts and imaginations that are not from God.

1 John 4:1-3 says, *"Beloved, do not believe every spirit, but test the spirits, whether they are of God; because many false prophets have gone out into the world. By this you know the Spirit of God: Every spirit that confesses that Jesus Christ has come in the flesh is of God, and every spirit that does not confess that Jesus Christ has come in the flesh is not of God. And this is the spirit of the Antichrist, which you have heard was coming, and is now already in the world."*

So test the spirits, the thoughts, and the imaginations and see if they are from God. Cast down those thoughts not from God and bind those spirits that throw those thoughts into your mind to oppress you. Start your day in prayer and stay in a prayer attitude all day long.

Matthew 26:41 says *"Watch and pray, lest you enter into temptation. The spirit indeed is willing, but the flesh is weak."* Prayer is simply conversation with God. The cool thing about prayer is that we can do it anywhere, anytime, and in any position. God hears us the moment we point our hearts towards Him. We are no match for the character defects that we battle, but God is. He will give us the power to say, "No."

1 Thessalonians 5:17-22 says, *"pray without ceasing, in everything give thanks; for this is the will of God in Christ Jesus for you. Do not quench the Spirit. Do not despise prophecies. Test all things; hold fast what is good. Abstain from every form of evil".*

Jesus said that we need to watch and pray to overcome the temptations of the enemy and then we are told that we have to do it every day, without ceasing. It is a continual process. We get the victory, then we have to stay in the victory over the enemy.

We are in a spiritual war. In war, if a battle is won, you still have to secure the area and then watch. Why; because until the enemy surrenders, they will come back to attack you again.

Our enemy will not surrender. He keeps attacking and the moment we think that he won't and the war is over, is the time that we will fall. The Bible says, *"Therefore let him who thinks he stands take heed lest he fall"(1 Corinthians 10:12).* We have to be careful because we get to flying high and can become arrogant. We feel like we don't need to be so careful. That is when the enemy can get the best of us.

Galatians 6:1-3 says, *"Brethren, if a man is overtaken in any trespass, you who are spiritual restore such a one in a spirit of gentleness, considering yourself lest you also be tempted. Bear one another's burdens, and so fulfill the law of Christ. For if anyone thinks himself to be something, when he is nothing, he deceives himself."*

Pursue the things God has for us

1 Timothy 6:11-12 says, *"Pursue righteousness, godliness, faith, love, patience, gentleness. Fight the good fight of faith, lay hold on eternal life, to which you were also called and have confessed the good confession in the presence of many witnesses".*

We say no so we can say yes to better and greater things from God. I remember seeing a documentary on TV about children who were presented with a choice. They were put in a room and left there for a period of time. On the table was a chocolate bar. They were told if they didn't eat the chocolate that when the researcher returned they would get a bag of chocolate to have for the rest of the day. Some of the kids just couldn't resist and gave in to the chocolate. Others resisted and received the reward. They tracked those children for some time and found that the ones who could resist became more successful in life than the others.

We are saying "no" so that we can say "yes." God has something better for us. It is a life of love, joy, peace, and confidence. It is a life that is filled with God's blessings, protection, and care.

In order to proceed in recovery, we have to make a daily decision to turn our lives and wills over to the care of God. It is a

Chapter Ten ~ Decision

decision that only you can make. *It is a decision that must be made every day. That is why Jesus said that we must* daily deny ourselves and pick up our cross. He said that the man who finds his life will lose it, but the one who loses his life for the Lord's sake, will find it.

Joel 3:14 says, *"Multitudes, multitudes, in the valley of decision! For the day of the Lord is near in the valley of decision".*

God wants us to make a decision. He will not force His love and blessings on us. We must choose that we want what He has for us. We must say "no" to say "yes."

God says *"How long will you go limping with two different opinions? If the Lord is God, follow him; but if Baal, then follow him"* (*1 Kings 18:21,* English Standard Version, ESV).

So we can choose for ourselves. We can choose life or death. We have to choose every day. Every day we have to put on the armor of God and choose to resist the enemy and to pursue God's will for our lives. Every day!

Prayer:

Lord,

Today I choose to place my life and will in Your care. I trust that Your way is the best way and will bring Your reward into my life.

In Jesus' Name,

Amen.

Putting it to Work

Respond to the following questions and discuss them with your sponsor/accountability partner.

1.   What decisions have you made that defined you as a person?

_____
_____
_____
_____
_____

2.   If you could do it again, what decisions would you make differently?

_____
_____
_____
_____
_____

3.   What have you had to say "no" to in order to be able to say "yes" to God's plans for you?

_____
_____
_____
_____
_____

4.   List some of the things that you believe God wants to do in your life.

_____
_____
_____
_____
_____

Step 3 ~ We made a decision to turn our lives and our wills over to the care of God.

"And so, dear brothers, I plead with you to give your bodies to God. Let them be a living sacrifice, holy-the kind he can accept. When you think of what he has done for you, is this too much to ask?" (*Romans 12:1*, TLB).

The **"Turns"** in our lives are powerful. They determine our direction and destination. A turn of the wheel in a car can mean life and death on a regular basis. A slight turn of the wheel on a ship can change the course by hundreds and even thousands of miles. So how we turn makes a difference in how our lives go and where we end up.

We can turn our lives towards God and away from God. When we turn towards Him He lovingly helps us and makes our lives the best they can be. When we turn away from Him, He lets us go, even though He doesn't want to. Without Him we find ourselves without the strength, wisdom, and power to be the people we want and need to be. Life becomes hollow and without joy.

God told Israel in *Numbers 32:15 "For if you turn away from following Him, He will once again leave them in the wilderness, and you will destroy all these people." Deuteronomy 4:30-31* tells us, *"When you are in distress, and all these things come upon you in the latter days, when you turn to the LORD your God and obey His voice (for the LORD your God is a merciful God), He will not forsake you nor destroy you, nor forget the covenant of your fathers which He swore to them"*.

Turning our lives and wills over to God?

> **TURN**
>
> **T** – Trust God completely and daily with every decision
> and for every provision.
> **U** – Understand God's will and ways through His Word
> and Spirit.
> **R** – Release your concerns and cares into His hands
> and let God handle it.
> **N** – Nourish your hearts with God's Word, Prayer, and
> sharing with others about God daily.

T – Trust God completely and daily with every decision and for every provision.

To trust God means that we abandon ourselves to Him and His will. Trust means that when things don't seem to be working out, we believe that God has our lives under control and that He has a plan for our good. Job said in his time of suffering, "*Though He slay me, yet will I trust Him*" (*Job 13:15*). That is trust at its ultimate.

Trust is seeking God. To trust God we have to seek Him for His will every day. We pray in the Lord's Prayer: "*Your kingdom come. Your will be done on earth as it is in heaven*" (*Matthew 6:10*).

Trust is a commitment. Lord I am trusting that you will open and close doors to direct me. It is not about having our way, but God having His way. When it doesn't go our way, we stand steady and trust that God is having His way.

Trust produces joy. When we trust God with all our hearts, we receive a joy and victory that keeps our hearts. *Psalms 5:11* says, "*But let all those rejoice who put their trust in You; Let them ever shout for joy, because You defend them.*" It is the joy of the Lord that is our strength.

Trust is believing that God can do anything and that all things are possible with God. Nothing is too big for Him.

> *It is impossible for trust to overdraw*
> *its account on the bank of heaven.*

U – Understand God's will and ways through His Word and Spirit.
Proverbs 20:24 says, "*A man's steps are of the LORD; How then can a man understand his own way?*"

We do not possess the knowledge necessary to understand all that our life is and means. Only God can see the totality of our lives. Only He can give us an understanding of our purpose and the plan that we were created to fulfill. Jesus said in *Matthew 13:14-15, "Hearing you will hear and shall not understand, And seeing you will see and not perceive; For the hearts of this people have grown dull."* In order to turn, we have to take God at His Word and live according to it. It is not just sitting in meetings or church and hearing the Word of God, but understanding and walking in God's Word that makes the difference in us. God's Word is a mirror to us to show us who and what we really are so we can see what to change and what to build on.

Chapter Eleven ~ Turn

"For if anyone is a hearer of the word and not a doer, he is like a man observing his natural face in a mirror; for he observes himself, goes away, and immediately forgets what kind of man he was" (*James 1:23-24*).

We don't always like what God is saying to us or even agree, but to turn we have to let God teach us and be willing to hear and see it God's way. The path to recovery is paved with understanding that comes from God's Word.

R – Release your concerns and cares into His hands and let God handle it. *"Let Go and Let God!!!!"*

This is the essence of faith. *Faith comes from hearing*, believing, standing on, and walking according to *God's Word (Romans 10:17)*. By faith we have to put our life and will into God's lap and let Him take over.

> *Some people ask the Lord to guide them;*
> *then they grab the steering wheel.*

In *Philippians 4:6-7* God tells us: *"Be anxious for nothing, but in everything by prayer and supplication, with thanksgiving, let your requests be made known to God; and the peace of God, which surpasses all understanding, will guard your hearts and minds through Christ Jesus."* The word "supplication" means to lay a situation and decision in the lap of someone else and leave it there. When we do this by faith in God, His peace fills our thoughts and feelings and His peace guards us from those thoughts and feelings that would cause us to turn away from Him and His plan for our lives.

> *Faith is not a pill you take, but a muscle you use.*

N – Nourish your hearts with God's Word, Prayer, and sharing with others about God daily.

> *Feed your faith and your doubts*
> *will starve to death.*

2 Timothy 3:5 says, *"having a form of godliness but denying its power. And from such people turn away!"* *2 Timothy 4:4* says *"and they will turn their ears away from the truth, and be turned aside to fables."* Who we hang out with will influence our thoughts and feelings. We need to choose our friends well.

Run with a skunk and you will smell like a skunk.

Hebrews 10:25 says, "Let us not give up meeting together, as some are in the habit of doing, but let us encourage one another-and all the more as you see the Day approaching" (New International Version (NIV).

I love eating a good meal prepared by a good cook. I can cook for myself, but it is not as fun as sharing a meal with others. Food is always better when it is shared with others.

In the same way, we need each other to stay focused on God, His will, and the power He has for our lives. We can't do it alone. We need to eat the food that will build up our spiritual muscles. We need to stay in God's Word and in touch with a sponsor and or a friend that holds us accountable in our recovery. Turning back to the old crowd is always a step towards relapse. Turning to the people that are working their recovery is always a step towards God and power.

Turn our lives and wills to the care of God.
To recover, we have to do it every day!

Prayer:

Lord,

You are so good and loving. I know that You always have my best in mind and You know what is best. Forgive me for not trusting You more. I turn my life and will over to You and Your care today.

In Jesus' Name,

Amen

Putting it to Work

Respond to these questions in writing and then discuss them with your sponsor/accountability partner.

1.   Name a few things that hinder you from trusting God. Describe an event where you had to trust God on a day-to-day basis with a decision.

_____
_____
_____
_____
_____

2.   What influence have your friends had on you and your choices in the past?

_____
_____
_____
_____
_____

3.   Give an example of how God has shown you His will from reading the Bible. How did that change you? Is there something that you need to release into God's hands in the present?

_____
_____
_____
_____
_____

4.   How do you think you need to exercise the muscle of your faith?

_____
_____
_____
_____
_____

Restoring Broken People

Step 3 ~ We made a decision to turn our lives and our wills over to the care of God.

"And so, dear brothers, I plead with you to give your bodies to God. Let them be a living sacrifice, holy-the kind he can accept. When you think of what he has done for you, is this too much to ask?? (Romans 12:1, TLB).

In Steps One and Two, we admitted that we were powerless to our addictions and compulsive behaviors and that we came to believe that there is a power greater than ourselves who can restore us to sanity. In Step Three, we begin the process of moving toward God and letting Him have His way in our lives.

What is life? It is a short number of days on this planet called earth. Every day we make a decision how we are going to use our days and what we will serve- self or others, evil or good, Satan or God?

God's Word says that: *"The days of our lives are seventy years; And if by reason of strength they are eighty years, Yet their boast is only labor and sorrow; For it is soon cut off, and we fly away" (Psalm 90:10).*

Our life is a loan from God. He gives us our life and days and all that we have. God allows us to use them however we want, but will call us to give an accounting for how we used our days when we leave this world.

The Bible says to us *"Who knows the power of Your (God's) anger? For as the fear of You (God), so is Your (God's) wrath. So teach us to number our days, That we may gain a heart of wisdom" (Psalm 90:11-12).*

The Bible says *"to give your bodies to God" (Romans 12:1-2).* The only thing that we really control is what we are going to do with our bodies. Our will controls our physical being, sight, speech, touch, smell, and taste. So we can decide what we will look at, what we will say, what we will touch, what we will smell, and what we put in our mouth.

What will we give our bodies to tonight, tomorrow, and each day after that? What we do with our body will determine how God rewards us in eternity.

God tells us, *"if anyone builds on this foundation with gold, silver, precious stones, wood, hay, straw, each one's work will become clear; for the Day will declare it, because it will be revealed by fire; and the fire will test each one's work, of what sort it is. If anyone's work which he has built on it endures, he will receive a reward. If anyone's work is burned, he will suffer loss; but he himself will be saved, yet so as through fire"* (1 Corinthians 3:12-15).

So what is our life? The word life refers to the inner person that you are. It is the real you. It is the time you have to live in a body on this earth before you go into eternity. It is your personality, thoughts, feelings, dreams, goals, intellect, talent, and memory. It is the spirit that God gave to you and will take back when your days are done on this earth. Our life is ours while we are here, but it is on loan and God will call us to answer for all of our life. Every thought, motive, and decision will be reviewed. So how do we give our LIFE over to the "care of God"?

LIFE

L - Looking to Jesus
I - Investing in God's Kingdom
F - Flowing with God and His people
E - Eternal rewards for giving yourself to God

Looking to Jesus – *Hebrews 12:2* says, *"looking unto Jesus, the author and finisher of our faith, who for the joy that was set before Him endured the cross, despising the shame, and has sat down at the right hand of the throne of God.*

God says that we receive real life by believing in Jesus Christ as our Lord and Savior.

John 3:14-15 says, *"And as Moses lifted up the serpent in the wilderness, even so must the Son of Man be lifted up, that whoever believes in Him should not perish but have eternal life."*

Jesus is the author and finisher of our faith. God became a man in Jesus Christ. That is what we celebrate at Christmas. He offered His sinless life as the sacrifice for our sins. He rose from the dead to prove that it is true and to present His sacrifice in Heaven on our behalf. That is what we celebrate at Easter.

When we come to believe, God accounts His righteous life to our account. He sees us in Christ. That means when God looks at a believer, He sees Jesus. Wow! That is great. Faith starts with Jesus making Himself known to us. He began our faith that led to life and He is the One who leads us through this life to the finish line.

Life is *looking unto Jesus*. When Israel was in the wilderness, they rebelled against God. Snakes entered their camp and the people were being bitten and dying. Moses prayed for the people and God told Him to put a bronze snake on a pole in the shape of a cross and that everyone who looked at the pole with the bronze snake would be healed. The snake is the symbol of our rebellion and sin being laid on Jesus on the cross. When we look to Jesus with faith, our sins are forgiven and we are healed. Life in Christ is looking unto Jesus and keeping our eyes on Him.

This verse is a reference to the Grecian gymnastic games. We still celebrate the Olympics today. We all understand that the winners, the medalists, are considered to be especially noble and blessed. It was amazing this year to see a Michael Phelps walk away with a record breaking and history making number of medals for swimming.[10] His name will long be remembered.

All those who participate in these events are trained to the "look". Athletes know that when they are competing that focus is everything. Many a races have been lost because a runner gave into the temptation to look to the side or behind them and in doing so broke their stride and gave up their place. This is the obvious reference for us. Look forward to the goal who is Jesus.

What we look at we become!

When girls get their eyes on certain starlets, soon they are trying to look like them, dress like them, and act like them. Let the guys get their eyes on some hero, great athlete, or star and soon they want to look like them. I remember when I was young. We were all saying that we wanted to be "individuals". We were the hippies and we weren't into the establishment or the status quo, except, we all had our heroes as well. People like the Beatles, Jimi Hendrix, Led Zepplin, etc. all became our stars and soon, we were all dressing like them, talking like them, and acting like them. What we look at, we become.

Life is good and fulfilling when we focus on Jesus Christ. He is our example and our goal. The more we spend time looking at Him in God's Word, in Prayer, and in Worship the more we become like Him. He is the author of who and what we are in faith. He is the finisher – the One who has already completed the faith life and totally embodies it.

Life is Looking Unto Jesus. Life is:

Investing in God's Kingdom –
John 12:25 says, *"He who loves his life will lose it, and he who hates his life in this world will keep it for eternal life".*

Where do we put our money, our time, our talent, and our opportunities? Every day we make the choice. They say that if a person begins saving money in his or her twenties, and is faithful, that by the time he or she reaches the age of 60, a million dollars is possible. Every day we are making investments. In the same way God asks us to make daily invest-ments in His Kingdom for the good of others. Just think what can be done by being faithful day-by-day.

Sometimes people want to know just how much God expects us to give. They will argue over percentages and over certain formulas. In *Romans 12:1,* God gives us the answer, *"I beseech you therefore, brethren, by the mercies of God, that you present your bodies a living sacrifice, holy, acceptable to God, which is your reasonable service".*

God asks us to give everything to Him. He wants it as a sacrifice. This refers to the whole burnt offerings that God told the Israelites to give. In this offering, the whole animal belonged to God. None of it was given to the priests. It was totally given to God.

It was a symbol of total dedication to the Lord. It showed that a person was laying his or her all down for God. It was a picture of Jesus Christ, giving His body and life as the sacrifice to God for us. Jesus held nothing back.

He said, *"For even the Son of Man did not come to be served, but to serve, and to give His life as a ransom for many" (Mark 10:45).*

When the Lord was battling against Satan, He declared His sacrificial life and said, *"Away with you, Satan! For it is written, 'You shall worship the Lord your God, and Him only you shall serve.'"* Jesus saw His sacrifice as not only His dying for God, but His living for God.

So how much does God want us to give? He wants us to give all of our self to Him. That means we yield all that we have and all that we are to Him and let Him have it. God wants our hearts. That means something different for each of us. For the rich young ruler it meant that

he had to sell all that he had and give it to the poor.

"Jesus said to him, "If you want to be perfect, go, sell what you have and give to the poor, and you will have treasure in heaven; and come, follow Me" (Matthew 19:21). Why? Because God knew that this young man worshipped his possessions. God knew that he was bound up with materialism and needed to be set free. Jesus came to set us free. God didn't need his money. Jesus could feed the poor without his money. Jesus fed the 5,000 with five loaves of bread and two fish. He told Peter where to find a fish with money in its mouth to pay all of their taxes. He didn't need the man's money. The man needed to be set free in his heart from his riches.

God doesn't want our things. He wants our hearts. The problem is not that we have things, but that things have us. God wants us to give our lives to His care. That means we have to invest our lives in Him. It means we have to become a living sacrifice given to God. Giving our lives to God brings fulfillment. Fulfillment comes by serving with our whole hearts the One who made us and gave Himself for us.

Fellowshipping with God and His People –

1 John 1:2-4 says *"the life was manifested, and we have seen, and bear witness, and declare to you that eternal life which was with the Father and was manifested to us--that which we have seen and heard we declare to you, that you also may have fellowship with us; and truly our fellowship is with the Father and with His Son Jesus Christ. And these things we write to you that your joy may be full."*

When we give our wills and lives to Jesus Christ, the result is that we have fellowship with God and with God's people. It is a wonderful triangle that results in a satisfying and joyful life.

John 12:26 says," If anyone serves Me, let him follow Me; and where I am, there My servant will be also. If anyone serves Me, him My Father will honor."

Giving your bodies as a living sacrifice means that we *willingly* serve Jesus Christ with our bodies. Jesus said that the greatest among you is the servant of all. On the night before Jesus was crucified, He served the disciples at what we call the Last Supper. He put on the robe of a servant and washed their feet.

Jesus was their Master. Jesus was their Servant. The Master was the servant. He did all He could to serve them with His life. He did not come to be served but to serve and bring salvation to all who believe. He asks us to follow His example and then says He will reward and honor us for doing it. Wow! We don't deserve it, but God offers it if we are willing to turn our lives over to God.

Have you turned your life and will over to Christ? Have you given your body to Him as a "living sacrifice?" He died for us and now He asks us to live for Him. Sounds like a good deal! He will reward you for living for Him.

Prayer:

Dear Lord Jesus,

Thank You for dying for me to pay for my sins and to set me free from myself and a self-centered life. I give my body to You as a living sacrifice. I want to live for You and Your glory.

Amen

Putting it to Work

Respond to these questions in writing and then discuss them with your sponsor/accountability partner.

1.   What things have you had your eyes on?

_____

_____

_____

_____

_____

2.   Is there an area of your life and will that you have not yet given to God? What is it?

_____

_____

_____

_____

_____

3.   In what ways do you think you can serve the Lord? Is there something He is asking you to do?

_____

_____

_____

_____

_____

4.   Do you have regular times of fellowship with God and with His people? Who and When?

_____

_____

_____

_____

_____

Step 3 ~ We made a decision to turn our lives and our wills over to the care of God.

"And so, dear brothers, I plead with you to give your bodies to God. Let them be a living sacrifice, holy-the kind he can accept. When you think of what he has done for you, is this too much to ask?" (*Romans 12:1,* TLB).

This step can be difficult because it is filled with the issue of trust. Many of us learned not to trust people and life at a very young age. Some of us were abused, neglected, abandoned, cheated on, lied to, and just plain humiliated. It left us feeling like we can't really trust anyone to care about us. So the saying goes, "You have to watch out for number one. No one else will."

But the problem is that we make a mess out of watching out for ourselves and find ourselves going crazy. It drives us to drink, to party, to sex, to control, to rage, to gamble, to drug, to overeat, and many other things.

So this step teaches us that we can resolve the trust issue by deciding to turn our lives and wills over to the care of God. Since in Step Two we came to believe that a power greater than ourselves could restore us to sanity, we now can make a decision to let God take care of us. Wow! Someone loves me and will take care of me. Someone will really watch out for me 24 hours a day and make the difference.

The Bible shows us how we can know that God cares.

God has accepted us just the way we are

Romans 5:1-2 says,*" Therefore, having been justified by faith, we have peace with God through our Lord Jesus Christ, through whom also we have access by faith into this grace in which we stand, and rejoice in hope of the glory of God"*.

We all have a problem. We stand as guilty sinners before a Holy God. If we want to become righteous in ourselves we have to keep God's laws perfectly for all of our life. That disqualifies all of us. The slightest thing cancels out all of the good. *Galatians 3:12* says, *"the man who does them shall live by them."* So it is a problem for us.

But God is not only **holy and just**, but He is **love**. In His love for us He declared us all guilty under the law. You say that doesn't sound like love. Here is how it works. He declared us guilty by the law so He could declare us righteous by faith. *Galatians 3:22* says, *"But the Scripture has confined all under sin, that the promise by faith in Jesus Christ might be given to those who believe."* You see God loves all of us and does not want to judge any of us.

In the novel, *The Shack,* by William P. Young, the Father asks Mack to choose one of his children to be judged forever. He is so torn up at the thought that he finally begs God to not judge any of them and to let him take their place. When God asked him, "Why?" he said that he loved all of them. He didn't want any of them to suffer.[11]

That is how God feels about all of us. He loves us all so much that He doesn't want any of us to perish and suffer. So, instead of judging us, He became a man to take our place in judgment so we could be declared righteous and set free. What love! That is why we can trust Him. All we have to do is believe to receive salvation and righteousness by faith, which is trusting God's Word.

God accounts **faith** for a **right standing** with Him. It is like a Judge saying to the person in front of them, "You are guilty of speeding and reckless driving, but trust me, I'll take care of the fine." Then you hear the defendant say, "Thank you Dad." God accepts us and makes us His children. We can trust Him to meet every single need that we have.

He always came through in the past and He will be there in the future

Romans 5:3-5 says, *"And not only that, but we also glory in tribulations, knowing that tribulation produces perseverance; and perseverance, character; and character, hope. Now hope does not disappoint, because the love of God has been poured out in our hearts by the Holy Spirit who was given to us".*

Sometimes we doubt when we are struggling. We are in a dark place and can't see how things are going to work out. We are tempted to not believe that there is a God of Love that we can turn our will and lives over to. But, then God always comes through. It may be in the midnight hour, but He makes a way when we trust. We can look back over our shoulder and see God's care. He is still the same. He has not changed.

Today I am in one of the greatest struggles of my life. It is so huge that I can't discuss it yet. It is a mountain of overwhelming proportions. In the natural I should be ready to give up. Why can I keep going? God has prepared me for this moment. Many past events of my life give me the confidence that God has everything under control and will make a way through this night season. He will calm the stormy seas.

I can look back and see how God brought me through the season of cancer. I can remember having nothing when we started in the ministry and how God miraculously supplied day by day! He was always there to make tragedy into triumph. He has taught me that I am not a victim, but a victor in Him and that through Him *I can do all things.*

We are called to be the head and not the tail and to be more than conquerors through Him who loved us. How can we know? We know through God's Word and through the experiences that prepare us. Look back on your life and you will see how God has prepared you for what you are experiencing. We know that God really cares for us because He has cared for us and He won't change. His care doesn't eliminate the evil of this world, but it does give us the strength and power to get through every horrible thing that the enemy throws our way.

Jesus died for us when we were still rebelling against Him and wanted nothing to do with Him

Romans 5:6-8 says, *"For when we were still without strength, in due time Christ died for the ungodly. For scarcely for a righteous man will one die; yet perhaps for a good man someone would even dare to die. But God demonstrates His own love toward us, in that while we were still sinners, Christ died for us".*

No greater expression of love could exist than that a person would die for another. Most of us would be willing to die for a friend, or an extremely good person. But Jesus loved us so much that he died for us when we were opposing Him and going our own way. What a wonderful God! He came to earth to show us that He cares for us.

1 Peter 5:6-7 tells us, *"humble yourselves under the mighty hand of God, that He may exalt you in due time, casting all your care upon Him, for He cares for you."*

CARE

C – Completely committed to your good
A – Allows only those things that can benefit you
R – Recognizes your hurts and weaknesses
E – Encourages you when you are discouraged

Chapter Thirteen ~ Care of God

It can be a scary thing to humble our self to someone else and put our self at someone else's mercy. We only want to do that if we feel that they really do care about us. God does care for us. He wants to bring blessing and help to us every day. But He will not force His blessings on us. He doesn't make us receive gifts from Him. We have to willingly yield to Him and let him bless us.

Since we know that He does care, we can yield to Him and trust Him. The word "care" is in a present, ongoing tense that means God cares now and will continue to care always for us. So we can give our cares to Him because He does care for us.

How Do We Cast our Cares on Him?

CAST
C – Claim God and His promises as your answer
A – Allow God to take control of your life and will
S – Stay away from anything that would distract you from God
T – Trust God completely to make things right

Casting means literally to give it to God or to throw it away on God. When we cast we say,

"Here God. You can have this. I can't handle it, but I know you can. I don't want anything to do with this. It is yours."

God knows how to take care of our children, our parents, our spouse, our jobs, our finances, and our life dreams. He has a plan, but just waits for the opportunity to show us what He has for us.

I heard of a little boy who had a broken toy and wanted his father to fix it. In his misguided care for his toy, he would not let go of it. He held it tightly to his chest. After a while he became angry with his father and asked, "Why won't you fix my toy?" Then the father said, "I will, but I can't until you let it go." Casting is letting it go so the Father can fix it.

It also means that we become willing to take direction and do what the Father tells us to do. God knows the things that will hurt and destroy us. He gives us instruction on what not to do and where not to go to protect us. We do what He tells us to do and trust Him for the results.

We needed help making the water in our pool clean and pure. We cast our need on the guys at the pool store. You know what they did?

They sold us the right chemicals and told us how to apply them. When we did, the mess was gone and the pool was beautiful. That is what it means to cast. We trust God with our lives and cares and allow Him to direct us as how to take care of them. He does and will. When we do, things get clear and beautiful.

Prayer:

Lord,

I give all of my cares to You. You know best what to do. You also have my will. I will listen to You and do whatever you tell me to do. I will trust You for the results.

In Jesus' Name,

Amen.

Putting it to Work

Respond to the following questions in writing and then discuss them with your sponsor.

1.   Do you have any cares that you need to cast on God? Make a list of them.

_____

_____

_____

_____

_____

2.   Do you struggle with believing that God cares about you? If so, write out why you feel that way.

_____

_____

_____

_____

_____

3.   Can you remember events that were overwhelming, but when you gave them to God, He took care of those needs? Describe them.

_____

_____

_____

_____

_____

4.   Why do you think you can trust God to take care of your life? Include a scripture and memorize it for future reference.

_____

_____

_____

_____

_____

Step 4 ~ We made a searching and fearless moral inventory of ourselves.

"Let us examine ourselves instead, and let us repent and turn again to the Lord" (*Lamentations 3:40*, TLB).

Searching is a universal human experience. Everyone spends those days of searching for something. Often I have searched for my car keys, only to discover that I was holding them in my hand the whole time! Boy, does that make me feel stupid. It has become a regular routine to search for my car in the parking lot after shopping or eating. I wonder who keeps moving it while I am in the store. Wow! Life is a search. Usually it ends up with us blaming someone else when really we are the one to blame or we blame ourselves when it was someone else who was wrong. It is hard to see it, but necessary in order to recover from our addictions and compulsive behaviors.

Step Four takes us into the stage of searching our own hearts. It is a lot easier to spend our days looking at the shortcomings, failures, strengths, and successes of others. They are easy to see. However, seeing our own shortcomings and or successes can be a terrifying task. It is so terrifying that often we spend our lives running from it. Fear is in control and with it comes anger, rage, hurt, bitterness, misunderstanding, addictions, compulsions, and all the things that destroy our lives. So, to move forward we have to face our fears and enemies. Someone said, *"I have seen the enemy and he is me."*

Seeing and owning our fears, our failures, our own moral corruption, our sins, and our offenses towards others is a major necessity for recovery. This is hard, but without this step we stay bound to fear and our addictions and compulsive behaviors. So how do we search ourselves?

Use others as a sounding board.

Have you ever been in a loud room talking really loudly to someone when all of a sudden everything got quiet and you were still speaking out? Everyone looks and you feel kind of foolish.

My dad has long suffered from a loss of hearing. When you walk in \o the living room of his home, the TV has often been so loud that you can hardly hear yourself think. It is deafening and impossible to carry on a conversation. For years the answer was that my mother had to let him know that the TV was too loud. Sometimes that irritated him, but it was necessary to function socially. Hearing aids and other devices have solved that problem and now Dad has a built in sounding board that lets him know where he is at with the volume.

Functions of sounding boards

1. Enhance the power and quality of the tone. 2. Reflect the sound toward the audience. 3. Deaden the sound. 4. A person or persons whose reactions serve as a measure of the effectiveness of the methods, ideas, etc., put forth. 5. A person or group that propagates ideas, opinions, etc.: He was more of a sounding board than a novelist. (From Random House Dictionary).[12] In the same way we need others to get an idea of what we are really like. We may know our intent, but they can tell us how we affect others. It is a way of bettering ourselves in life and relationships. It is a team approach. It also helps us to know when we have been wrong and don't realize it. *Proverbs 27:17* says, *"As iron sharpens iron, so a man sharpens the countenance of his friend."*

There are four situations in life that we all face: 1. You see it and no one else does. 2. You see it and everyone else does. 3. You see it and some others see it. 4. Everyone else sees it and you don't. We need each other. God doesn't call us to be islands and God doesn't have any Lone Rangers. Even the Lone Ranger had Tonto. Get in a group or find a counselor or join a church where there will be people that you can relate to that will magnify your strengths and help you quiet your weaknesses.

Ask God to help us search for the truth about our self

I remember taking a family vacation in Pennsylvania when our daughter was a teenager. We found a good deal on a resort in a travel guide with a coupon. The pictures were beautiful and the write up made it sound like heaven on earth. But when we arrived it was the most run down place we had ever seen. We tried to talk ourselves into staying there, but when my daughter sat on the bed and it fell apart, we looked at the torn wallpaper hanging off the walls, the dust under the furniture, the faded carpet and decided it was not the place for us. Moral to the story?

"Never judge a summer resort by the postcard."

Others are useful in helping us to know how we come off and where we have hurt others unaware, but they cannot know our hearts. It is possible to fool everyone else, but still be wrong in our hearts. It is possible to deceive ourselves and to honestly believe that we are right when we are wrong. That is where we need God. He is the only One who knows our hearts and can reveal them to us.

Sometimes we have a good heart but we are rough around the edges and come off hurtful. That is where others are helpful. Sometimes we are well groomed and refined and no one can fault us, but our hearts are wrong. We are doing what we do for all the wrong reasons. That is when we need God to help us.

This is why in the process of helping others; we are not to judge them. We don't know their heart. We can't know their heart even when we are very close to them. We don't. We can only say that we believe their behavior is having a certain affect. We can share our own experience and ask if it might match theirs. But only God knows our hearts. Only He can show us where we are wrong or right. *Psalms 44:21 says, "Would not God search this out? For He knows the secrets of the heart." Psalms 139:23 says, "Search me, O God, and know my heart; Try me, and know my anxieties;"*

Remember, we deceive ourselves about our bad and our good. Sometimes we have to recognize weaknesses we don't want to see. But sometimes we need to affirm strengths that we were not allowed to celebrate. We search for both the good and the bad. Only God can help us know that on the heart level.

So begin to pray daily for His help in the search. Ask God to speak to you from His Word about you, your good and your bad. I encourage you to own it so you can move forward in your recovery.

Prayer:

Lord,
Thank You for Your love and forgiveness. I am glad that Your mercy endures forever. I need the help of others and Your help to recognize my strengths and weaknesses, right and wrongs, good and bad. Help me to see myself the way that I really am so I can right my wrongs and enhance my strengths. Search me, Oh God, and know my heart. Amen

Putting it to Work

Respond to the following questions in writing and then discuss them with your sponsor/accountability partner.

1.   Do you have a sponsor/accountability partner? If so, tell how they are a benefit to you.

_____

_____

_____

_____

_____

2.   Make a list of some of your positive moral qualities. How do these qualities benefit others and you?

_____

_____

_____

_____

_____

3.   Make a list of your moral shortcomings. How have these shortfalls hurt others and you?

_____

_____

_____

_____

_____

4.   Take time to pray and ask God to show you anything that you need to see about your heart. What did He show you?

_____

_____

_____

_____

_____

Step 4 ~ *We made a searching and fearless moral inventory of ourselves.*

"Let us examine ourselves instead, and let us repent and turn again to the Lord" (*Lamentations 3:40,* TLB).

Do we want to be free? Then we have to face our fears head on. The truth is that we give ourselves over to compulsions and addictions because of fear. We fear pain, rejection, loss, sorrow, the future, memories, and death. It is interesting to note the things that people fear most often never come true. Most of the rest we have no control over. Only about one percent of our fears is well founded and can be changed. Fear robs us of energy, time, and growing forward in the wonderful things that God has prepared for us.

So we have to be fearless. Another word for "fearless" is "courageous". *Courage is not the absence of fear, but rather the choice to face our fears and trust God for the results.* The things we fear look very different when we see them in light of the greatness of God. Think of the immensity of the universe, the length of eternity, or even just how big this world and the history of mankind are. It makes the things that we fear look very small.

Nothing that we fear can compare to God. He says that He can do exceedingly, abundantly, above all that we ask or think. So, how can we be fearless, courageous? It happens when we put our lives in the hands of the Lord. He says that He wants to do more for us than we want Him to. He would not ask us to do anything that was not for our good. Examining ourselves, repenting, and turning to Him is His idea! It is for our good.

God spoke to Joshua when He was facing fear. Joshua was the new leader of a nation that had to possess the Promised Land from people who were described as giants. The task was frightening, but God told Joshua, *"Have I not commanded you? Be strong and of good courage; do not be afraid, nor be dismayed, for the Lord your God is with you wherever you go"* (*Joshua 1:9*).

When we do the things that God tells us to do, He goes with us. He will give us His wisdom, power, understanding, ability, counsel, and Presence to face whatever we have to face. We can do it because He is telling us to do it and because He is with us.

It can be really frightening to examine ourselves, but it is something that God tells us to do. Why? Because there are behaviors and patterns of thought that we have developed that are harming others and us. In order for us to experience freedom from our addictions and compulsions, we have to take a good look at ourselves. Don't be afraid. God puts His Presence on us in a special way and will help us. He is with us and for us. God is not trying to hurt us, but God is trying to help us.

Why we don't want to look at ourselves?

Pride –

Pride wants us to feel that there is nothing we need to change and that everyone else is messed up. That is "stinkin-thinkin" that gets us into trouble. Pride is "ego" and being "egocentric". Pride produces anger at anyone or anything that would try to get us to look at ourselves. Pride has to go in order to move forward. In *Galatians 2:20* the Apostle Paul tells us that once we are saved, we no longer live for ourselves, but for Christ who lives in us.

In order to move forward we have to die to our pride, ego, and let Christ take over. He wants to change and rearrange us every day. So, we have to crucify pride and say, "Lord, help me to see the good, the bad, and the ugly." We have to say Lord show me what you want me to see and have your way in me. Eat a little humble pie and let God show you what needs to change in you.

People – affect us in two ways.

First we fear what they will think of us if we change. We often want to live to please others. So we have to deal with the fear of the opinions of others. Certainly we need to be sensitive to people's feelings, but not out of fear. Love is sensitive, but fear is tormenting. It can be healthy to decide in a good way, that we don't care what others think of us. Instead we decide that we are more concerned with pleasing the Lord.

Secondly, we are affected because we spend our time examining others and looking at them instead of examining ourselves. This is a way to escape the process of self-examination. Obviously there is a time to examine others in order to help them, but first we must examine ourselves. Jesus said that we have to get the log out of our own eye before we take the spec out of our neighbor's eye.

Restoring Broken People

Procrastination –

Often we know that we need to examine ourselves, but we just don't want to take the time. After all, it is an effort to examine ourselves to see what things are good or what needs to change. It seems like there is always another day. However, it is important to see that God is saying, "Today is the day" and "Now is the acceptable time". He wants us to see where we are living for ourselves and doing things our own way. That is what has us messed up. He wants to help us move from being messed up to confessed-and-dressed up in Him. His plans for us are awesome, so we have to get rid of our ways and begin to walk in His ways. What are we waiting for? There is nothing more important than to let the Lord change us, rearrange us, and work in us and through us.

Sometimes we are just plain lazy. We just don't want to work. We would rather watch TV, play games, laugh with people, or even just sit like a bump on a log. Laziness is an American plague. There is a reason why the number one selling chair in America is called the "Lazy Boy." It is not "Work E Boy" or "Get Going Boy!"

Pretense –

Is defined as having wrong motives. Perhaps we are not really interested in recovering from our addictions, compulsions, pain, and situation. It might be that we are involved with the process of recovery for another reason. It could be that we feel forced by the courts, persons or a group of people, or by the opinion of others. It might be that we are just checking out the dating scene. Maybe we are just lonely and want to hang out with people. If we are not really interested in getting better, then we don't want to examine ourselves. So maybe we have to start with that thought. Why are we doing this? What is our real motive? If it is not to get better, then maybe we need to admit it to others and ourselves. Admitting it is the path to getting the right motive. Admit, repent or change our motive and turn to God to help us get our heart right. It will push us forward in the healing that God has for us.

Conclusion

Be courageous, fearless, and say to the Lord, "I am ready to start taking a good look at me. I will face the fear of seeing me the way I really am. No longer do I want to spend my days looking at others to avoid my own issues. It is time to look at me. There are good things that you will help me see, but there are unprofitable things that need to go and change. They are hindrances to my life with you and to my healing that you have for me. Lord, help me to examine myself, change, and turn to your ways for me."

Restoring Broken People

Putting it to Work

Respond to the following questions in writing and then discuss them with your sponsor/accountability partner.

1.   What are your top 5 fears?

_____
_____
_____
_____
_____

2.   Can you remember how you developed these fears? Describe those events.

_____
_____
_____
_____
_____

3.   Make a list of times that you have overcome those fears without using your addictions or compulsions.

_____
_____
_____
_____
_____

4.   What fears do you need to face today?

_____
_____
_____
_____

Chapter Fifteen ~ Fearless

Step 4 ~ *We made a searching and fearless moral inventory of ourselves.*

"Let us examine ourselves instead, and let us repent and turn again to the Lord" (*Lamentations 3:40*, TLB).

A lot of people want to argue about the word "MORAL" these days. Somehow they think for us to have morals means that we want to dictate to others how they live. It is not politically correct to be a person of "MORALS". Actually, most people misunderstand what the word means. So we need to define it.

Webster's Dictionary defines the word "MORAL" as:
1. Relating to principles of right and wrong; i.e. to morals or ethics; "moral philosophy".
2. Concerned with principles of right and wrong or conforming to standards of behavior and character based on those principles; "moral sense"; "a moral scrutiny"; "a moral lesson"; "a moral quandary"; "moral convictions"; "a moral life".
3. Adhering to ethical and moral principles; "it seems ethical and right"; "followed the only honorable course of action"; "had the moral courage to stand alone".
4. Arising from the sense of right and wrong; "a moral obligation".[13]

So basically it is the understanding of *right from wrong*. It is a standard of *right and wrong* or code of *right and wrong* that we live by. I have only found one instance of the word "moral" in the Bible, although the thought is found all throughout God's Word.

2 Chronicles 28:19 says, *"For the Lord brought Judah low because of Ahaz king of Israel, for he had encouraged moral decline in Judah and had been continually unfaithful to the Lord."*

In the King James Version it says Ahaz made Judah naked. Ahaz did not want to believe in God even though God offered to prove Himself to Ahaz by any means (*Isaiah 7:10-14*).

Ahaz blurred the lines of right and wrong and brought the practice of idol worship into Judah. It means that Ahaz had allowed Judah to break loose from the restraints of God's code of right and wrong. The result was that God lifted His blessings and Judah was brought low. They lost the clothing of God's glory and righteousness.

Chapter Sixteen ~ Moral

Another example of this thought is in the book of Proverbs. *"Righteousness exalts a nation, but sin is a reproach to any people"* (*Proverbs 14:34*). Having a moral compass is a source of blessing from God. A lack of it brings reproach. Now this does not mean that God doesn't want to forgive and restore. *Proverbs 21:21* says, *"He who follows righteousness and mercy finds life, righteousness and honor."*

God's *"ONE-TWO"* combination is *"righteousness"* and *"mercy"*. In other words we need to have a sense of right and wrong and strive to live right, but at the same time live under God's forgiveness and be forgiving to others. Even the best of our efforts fall short of God's code of righteousness and we need daily to be forgiven and to forgive those who hurt us.

So MORAL inventory means that we take a look at God's sense of ethics and take note of where we have succeeded and where we have fallen short. We look to see what has been right in our thoughts, attitudes, and actions and celebrate those things. We examine ourselves to see where God's image is shining through in our lives. It does shine through in all of us. It is His image and we give Him the glory, but we need to recognize and celebrate it. This is called *strengthening our strengths*.

MORAL inventory also means that we go through the painful process of seeing where we have fallen short of the glory of God. Where did we depart from His sense of ethics, His sense of right and wrong, and went our own way? Where did we break loose and throw off restraint? Why? We look at this because *Proverbs 29:18* says, "*Where there is no revelation, the people cast off restraint; but happy is he who keeps the law*". In the King James Version it says it this way, *"where there is no vision, the people perish"*.

In other words, getting a revelation and vision of God and His righteousness and then making it our daily goal to become more like Him, is the source to true happiness. If we want God's blessings on our lives to become truly fulfilled and whole people, we have to get a vision of what God has done in us, and what He wants to do in us. God's goal for us is that we be conformed to the image of Jesus Christ. None of us are there yet, but God wants us to grow daily to be more like Him.

1 Corinthians 15:49 says, *"And as we have borne the image of the man of dust, (this refers to Adam) we shall also bear the image of the heavenly Man" (this refers to Jesus Christ). 2 Corinthians 3:18* says,

"But we all, with unveiled face, beholding as in a mirror the glory of the Lord, are being transformed into the same image from glory to glory, just as by the Spirit of the Lord".

In simple terms what does it mean to be "MORAL"? It means to be like Jesus Christ. It means to have His values, to think like Him, and to act like Him. It means to get a vision and revelation of Him and to become more like Him. The more time we spend with Him looking at Him, the more we will be like Him.

So the point of MORAL inventory is to spend time with the Lord and to see where we are becoming like Him and where we are not. The transformation happens by looking at Jesus. We see Him in the Bible. He is the Word of God (*John 1:1*). The Bible is the Word of God. Jesus is the Word made flesh, the Bible is the Word made into a book. Study the Word. Spend time in prayer getting into a sense and awareness of His Presence. He will transform you into His image.

The Bible says, "*God is love*". So what does it mean to be "MORAL"? It means *to love God and to love others as we love ourselves* (*Mark 12:33*). So MORAL means, "*LOVE*". That means we need a picture of love. God gave us one in *1 Corinthians 13:4-8*:

"Love is patient and kind; love does not envy or boast; it is not arrogant or rude. It does not insist on its own way; it is not irritable or resentful; it does not rejoice at wrongdoing, but rejoices with the truth. Love bears all things, believes all things, hopes all things, endures all things. Love never ends" (ESV).

MORAL means that we see Jesus. Jesus is love. When we take inventory, this is our goal. We look at where we are loving and where we are not. Remember, this is not about being condemned, but being convicted. Jesus died for our shortcomings. We are already forgiven if we have believed on Him. This is about seeing Jesus better and getting a vision of what kind of person God wants us to be. Our forgiveness is already ours, now we are going to possess it and let God change us into His image.

Getting this vision will give us the power we need to be free and to stay free. Remember without a vision people perish, but when we have the vision and conform to Christ and His Image, we receive the power to be whole. So, we make a fearless and searching "MORAL" inventory of ourselves.

Putting to Work

Respond to the following questions in writing. Discuss them with your sponsor/accountability partners.

1.   How did Jesus show love to people? Name some instances from the Bible and how it makes you feel.

_____
_____
_____
_____
_____

2.   Have you ever had love shown to you that made a difference in your life? What happened?

_____
_____
_____
_____
_____

3.   In what ways do addictions and compulsions contradict the love of God?

_____
_____
_____
_____
_____

4.   What scriptures in the New Testament discuss the sense of right and wrong that God says we should have? Find some not used in this chapter.

_____
_____
_____
_____
_____

Step 4 ~ *We made a searching and fearless moral inventory of ourselves.*

"Let us examine ourselves instead, and let us repent and turn again to the Lord" (*Lamentations 3:40, TLB*).

As we come to the end of this volume we are brought to the work of making a searching and fearless moral inventory of ourselves. This is so important as we need to get a vision of Christ and how we compare to Him. This is not about how we compare to each other. He is the Vision and Revelation that we need to see. As we search our hearts in the Light of His Presence we will be convicted and encouraged. He wants to lift us up and encourage us. So, please do this in an awareness of His Presence, Forgiveness, and Love. He will help you.

The Prophet Isaiah had the experience of receiving a vision, being convicted and then receiving blessing from the Lord.

"In the year that King Uzziah died, I saw the Lord sitting on a very high throne. His long robe filled the Temple. Heavenly creatures of fire stood above him. Each creature had six wings: It used two wings to cover its face, two wings to cover its feet, and two wings for flying. Each creature was calling to the others: "Holy, holy, holy is the Lord All-Powerful. His glory fills the whole earth." Their calling caused the frame around the door to shake, as the Temple filled with smoke. I said, "Oh, no! I will be destroyed. I am not pure, and I live among people who are not pure, but I have seen the King, the Lord All-Powerful." 6 One of the heavenly creatures used a pair of tongs to take a hot coal from the altar. Then he flew to me with the hot coal in his hand. The creature touched my mouth with the hot coal and said, "Look, your guilt is taken away, because this hot coal has touched your lips. Your sin is taken away." Then I heard the Lord's voice, saying, "Whom can I send? Who will go for us?" So I said, "Here I am. Send me!" (*Isaiah 6:1-8*, New Century Version, NCV).

When Isaiah saw the Lord, He recognized His own impurity and shortcomings. He was convicted in God's Presence, but not condemned. The Lord touched Him with the hot coal, a symbol of God's love and purifying Presence and took away His sin. That is what God wants to do for you. So with faith, move into God's Presence and ask Him to let you see Jesus in the Bible and in Prayer. As you do, you will see you. Remorse, brokenness and a desire to change will fill you. So, be ready to let God do a work in you. Have a notebook in your hand each time you do this. We encourage that you write in a journal those things that you sense that God is teaching you about Him and yourself.

A NOTE. This is not the time to go to others and ask their forgiveness. This is a time for you to do a personal inventory of your heart and your life. God will do the work for you if you will allow Him to.

Restoring Broken People

Inventory of Character Flaws

These character flaws are stated in *Galatians 5:19-22*. Read through character flaws in column one placing an X next to the ones that you may have difficulty with. Read across and fill in the blanks as you answer the questions. This applies to Step 4.

Column 1	Column 2	Column 3
	Write a time when you exhibited these characteristics.	*Rate these from 1-10 with 10 being the most prominent and giving you the most difficulty.*
Pride [P]		
Lust [L]		
Anger [A]		
Greed [GR]		
Gluttony [GL]		
Envy [E]		
Sloth [S]		
Dishonest [D]		
Selfish [SEL]		
Self-Seeking Motives [SSM]		
Low Self-Esteem (Reverse Pride) [LSE]		
Inconsiderate [I]		
Jealousy [JE]		
Bad Gossip [BG]		
Judgmental [JU]		
Unforgiving [U]		
Controlling Others [CO]		
Other Character Flaws [OCF]		

Chapter Seventeen ~ Inventory

Restoring Broken People

Step 5 ~ We admitted to God, to ourselves, and to another human being the exact nature of our wrongs.

"Admit your faults to one another and pray for each other so that you may be healed. The earnest prayer of a righteous man has great power and wonderful results" (*James 5:16,* TLB).

We have come to another important step in our recovery. Step Five builds on the first four steps. Once we have admitted that we are powerless over our addictions and compulsive behaviors, that our lives have become unmanageable; once we have come to believe that a power greater than ourselves can restore us to sanity; after we make the decision to turn our lives over to the care of God; and we take the time to make a fearless moral inventory of ourselves; then we can work on step five. *We admit to God, to ourselves, and to another human being the exact nature of our wrongs.*

ADMIT

Acknowledge that we have wronged God and others.
Define the true nature of the harm.
Make our heart sorrow for the harm we caused.
Involve another to keep us honest.
Trust God for love, forgiveness, and acceptance.

How do we ADMIT?

Acknowledge that we have wronged God and others.
The basis of all relationship is trust and trust is built on honesty.
This takes 3 Steps:

1. First we have to be honest with ourselves.
1 John 1:8 says: "If we say that we have no sin, we are only fooling ourselves and refusing to accept the truth" (TLB).

It is easy to fool ourselves and to make ourselves believe that we are right when we really are wrong. It is unhealthy and destructive to deceive ourselves. It causes us to mistreat God, others, and ourselves.

Deceiving ourselves interrupts and even destroys our relationships with God and others.

2. Then we must be honest with God. Because God loves us and wants us healthy, He says that we have to confess our wrongs (sins) to Him to be restored to Him. This is tough love. He does it because He loves us and wants us well. *1 John 1:9-10* says, *"But if we confess our sins to him, he can be depended on to forgive us and to cleanse us from every wrong. And it is perfectly proper for God to do this for us because Christ died to wash away our sins. If we claim we have not sinned, we are lying and calling God a liar, for he says we have sinned"* (TLB).

3. Then we must be honest with another. This is so important because it is just too easy to forget about our admissions and commitments and fall back from the steps that we are taking forward. Being honest with another helps to seal the deal. It cements our commitments and attitude towards our self, God and others. We need this. It also allows for God to use a human voice to audibly acknowledge our confession and bless our honesty. Such support and confirmation strengthens us and helps us to grow.

Define the true nature of the harm. In order to admit we have to understand why it was really wrong.Is it just because someone said it was and we don't want to argue with them or is it truly wrong? Many in recovery programs will say what they think others want them to say, but don't really understand or believe it to be true. Sadly, these individuals are never successful in their recovery.

> *Many in recovery programs will say what they think others want them to say, but don't really understand or believe it to be true.*

What is wrong with those things that we did that harmed our selves, God, and others? Wrong is based on the law of love. *1 John 3:23 says, "And this is His commandment: that we should believe on the name of His Son Jesus Christ and love one another, just as He has commanded us"* (ESV).

Chapter Eighteen ~ Admitted to God

The Law of Love

God is love and made us in His image, which is love. *1 John 4:16* says, *"God is love, and the one who abides in love abides in God, and God abides in him"* (NASB). When we are selfish, uncaring, self-absorbed, and ignore the welfare and care of God, family, friends, and society we are not acting in love. Anything that is not done in love for God, others, and ourselves is sin. We are to love our neighbors as ourselves and to love God with all our heart, soul, mind, and strength.

Make our heart sorrow for the harm we caused. A woman who had done much wrong came to Jesus with very expensive ointments to wash His feet and apply the ointment to heal the many inflictions He would have suffered walking in the conditions of their times. In her love for Him, she knew that she had hurt Jesus and others deeply, so she was crying. In *Luke 7:37-38* says she stood at His feet behind Him weeping; and she began to wash His feet with her tears, and wiped them with the hair of her head; and she kissed His feet and anointed them with the fragrant oil.

She showed her sorrow over the wrongs she had done. This happens when we truly own the reality of the pain that we have created for God, others, and ourselves. Such tears are healthy and become the path to receiving forgiveness. Jesus said in *Luke 7:47, "Therefore I say to you, her sins, which are many, are forgiven, for she loved much. But he who is forgiven little, loves little"* (ESV).

The Bible says that godly sorrow produces change. When we truly feel the pain of our wrongs, it motivates us to change our ways. This is important to our recovery. **We need to feel the pain.** Let's face it: we use addictions and compulsions to avoid being honest with God and ourselves. We learn to use these things so we don't have to feel the consequence of our wrongs. Part of sobriety is coming back in touch with those feelings. The Bible says that godly sorrow leads to repentance or change. (*2 Corinthians 7:9-10*).

> *When we truly feel the pain of our wrongs, it motivates us to change our ways.*

Now, we have to be careful because God wants us to feel the pain to motivate us to change. But once we admit and address the issue, we need to receive God's peace and forgiveness. God does not want you to feel condemned, just convicted. There is a difference. In *Romans 8:1* we are told that there is no condemnation to those who are in Christ Jesus. So, God wants us to feel convicted and sorrow brings that. But once we admit it, He cleanses us and forgives us. *1 John 1:9* says, *"He casts our sin in to the depths of the sea never to be remembered again."* It is the devil that wants to keep you under condemnation. He is the accuser of the children of God (*Revelation 12:10-11*). The name "devil" and "Satan" means "accuser".

We overcome the accuser by the word of our testimony, the blood of the lamb, and by not loving our life more than God. What is our testimony? It is our story. I am messed up. I have addictions, compulsions, and I have sinned against God and others. But Jesus died to deliver and save me from my sins. In Jesus and by His death and resurrection, I am made whole. The word for salvation is "sotera[14]" and it means "wholeness". Jesus saves us; He makes us whole. He said to a woman who was miraculously healed of a disease of 13 years, *"Woman, your faith has made you whole* (sotera)." We are saved by faith in Jesus Christ and what He did for us on the cross.

So, sorrow leads us to repentance and repentance gives us faith in what Jesus did for us. Faith delivers us and makes us whole. When we ask the Lord to forgive us by faith, He does. He takes away our sin and heals us making us whole. He heals us *spiritually, emotionally, and physically (1 Thessalonians 5:23).* So we sorrow for a season that we might be made whole. Once we have repented, we need to stop beating up on ourselves. Your testimony is that you have been made whole in Jesus. Old things are passed away and behold all things become new.

Involve another to keep you honest. We need to feel forgiveness from our sponsor and recovery partner to bring healing to our heart. Owning our wrong and confessing it is the path to healing our mind, emotions, and spirit. It brings cleansing to our soul and our conscience. We need to know that God has forgiven us and it helps us to hear it from others that we can trust. *James 5:16* says that *when we do this and let others pray for us, that God will heal us.* That is a very powerful promise.

Not only do we need to feel forgiveness from others, but also we need those who will be honest with us. Perhaps we are not complete in our repentance. It is natural for us to say, "I was wrong, but it was because they said or did or..." This is incomplete repentance. True repentance recognizes our wrong. It is not about what others did. True repentance says, "My unforgiveness and bitterness was wrong". It says,

"My gossip and sarcasm was wrong." It says, "My addiction or compulsion was wrong." Why? Why do we have to recognize our wrong? We have to because we can't get better until we admit the true nature of our wrongs.

Trust God for love, forgiveness, and acceptance. God promised to forgive us and to cleanse us of all wrongs when we confess them to Him. Even if those we wronged will not forgive us, we can rest in and trust in God's forgiveness. The Bible says in *Ephesians 1:6-8, "Now all praise to God for his wonderful kindness to us and his favor that he has poured out upon us because we belong to his dearly loved Son. So overflowing is his kindness toward us that he took away all our sins through the blood of his Son, by whom we are saved; and he has showered down upon us the richness of his grace-for how well he understands us and knows what is best for us at all times"* (TLB).

Prayer:

Lord Jesus,

Thank you for Your patience and love for me. I admit that I have wronged You, others, and myself and want Your forgiveness. I am sorry and will change with Your help. Help me humble myself to others and use me as a source of healing them from the damage I caused. I pray that You will help them let go of the hurt so they can be free from the enemy and know You and Your joy. Help me to humbly show my sincere love for them.

In Jesus' Name,

Amen.

Putting it to Work
Please respond to these questions in writing. Then discuss your answers with your sponsor/accountability partner.

1.　　Can you remember some occasions of failure, character defects or times that you wronged someone that you need to admit? Please list them.

_____

_____

_____

_____

_____

2.　　Are you willing to talk to your sponsor /accountability partner about these incidences or defects of character? In some cases you may need to discuss these things with a pastor or a professional counselor. We encourage that you be discerning about this issue.

_____

_____

_____

_____

_____

3.　　Have you talked to God about these issues? How did it make you feel towards God, others and your self?

_____

_____

_____

_____

_____

4.　　Have you admitted these incidences and character defects to yourself? Have you been able to forgive yourself for these things?

_____

_____

_____

_____

_____

Step 5 ~ We admitted to God, to ourselves, and to another human being the exact nature of our wrongs.

"Admit your faults to one another and pray for each other so that you may be healed. The earnest prayer of a righteous man has great power and wonderful results" (James 5:16, TLB).

Most of us are freaked out at the idea of sharing our wrongs and their exact nature out loud. It makes us feel uneasy and scared. We fear what others may think. Even worse we fear we may be rejected, again. So why does it have to be "out loud?" Why can't we just "think it to ourselves? After all, God knows what we are thinking."

Well that is more of the "stinkin-thinkin" that gets us bound and keeps us bound up by the enemy through our addictions and compulsions.

Words create things. God spoke the universe into existence. God spoke and there was light. Jesus spoke and Lazarus came forth from the dead. The Apostles spoke and people were transformed from sinners to saints. We confess and we are saved (*Romans 10:9-13*). Why? It happens because words express the abundance of the heart.

"Brood of vipers! How can you, being evil, speak good things? For out of the abundance of the heart the mouth speaks" (Matt 12:34).

"A good man out of the good treasure of his heart brings forth good; and an evil man out of the evil treasure of his heart brings forth evil. For out of the abundance of the heart his mouth speaks" (Luke 6:45).

God knows that if we are really going to change and grow in Him, that it has to begin in our hearts. It cannot be some religious response to the culture around us. It cannot be some reaction to peer pressure or need to be accepted by people. It has to come from our hearts. Why? Those are the very things that connect us to the shame and guilt that gets us into our addictions. If it does not come from our hearts, then we just have an addiction to religion, but there is no real change. God has something better for us. He wants us to be set free and to live free in Him.

117

It is important for us to give voice to the things that we know we need to change. "We admit" is the path to repentance. Repentance is the path to true faith, and true faith leads to God's power and blessings on our lives.

Our words of "Admissions and Repentance" create life in others and us. When we confess, God creates in us a clean heart. When David confessed the exact natures of his wrongs to God, he said,

> *"Create in me a clean heart, O God,"*
> *(Psalm 51:10,* NASB).

Our words of "Admissions and Repentance" create life in others and us.

So we need to give voice to God and to another what the exact natures of our wrongs are and were. This is what brings real change. Repentance is the Bible word for "Change." God wants to change us, not just help us cope. He wants to transform us by the renewing of His Word.

> *"And do not be conformed to this world, but be transformed by the renewing of your mind, that you may prove what is that good and acceptable and perfect will of God"* (Romans 12:2).

God has the power to make us into New Creatures that are created after the image of Jesus Christ. He can make us into a person who bears fruit and does good works. That is God's desire for each of us. The first step is "Repentance". This word is brimming with meaning. There are words used in the Bible that are translated "repent" or some form of it. Each word gives us a different shade of meaning, but together, they give us the full thought.

Eight Bible Words for Repent

1.   Hebrew – Nachum[15] **– to sigh, breathe strongly, to be sorry –**
(Genesis 6:6; Exodus 13:17; Job 42:6; Jonah 3:10)
This means that repentance involves our emotions. It reflects the idea of being grieved. In the last chapter we discussed the importance being sorrowful for our wrongs. When real repentance takes place, we feel it. It moves us.

Some of us have allowed things to bottle up for so long that we know if we open the door that the floodgates of emotions will open. We may fear those emotions. Don't. It is the path to healing. When I first started this journey, I remember for one full year of attending church and other meetings that I wept through the meetings and continued to cry for some time afterwards. Why? There was a release of emotion that was working repentance in me. Let it happen. Don't be afraid. God will use it to make you a New Creature in Christ.

2.   **Hebrew – Shuwb**[16] **– to turn back –** *(1 Kings 8:47; Ezekiel 14:6)*

"Repent" means to "turn back". It is the idea of recognizing that we are headed the wrong direction and we do a 180 – and turn back to the right direction. In the process of repentance we have to draw a line in the sand and say, "No more. I am turning around." It means that we were walking away from God, but we have decided to turn around and walk toward Him.

3.   **Hebrew – Nochum**[17] **– regret –** *(Hosea 13:14)*

Repentance recognizes that we could have done things differently and better. It means that we wish in our hearts that we had the opportunity to do it over again, but this time right the wrongs. We can't get stuck in regrets because it can bury us in self–condemnation and destroy us. However, repentance does involve feeling regret, then allowing God to comfort us and to heal us of our regrets.

"In the multitude of my anxieties within me, Your comforts delight my soul" (Psalm 94:19). God wants us to feel regret so we can know true repentance, but He will comfort us and heal us in it. He will deliver you from all of your anxieties.

4.   **Hebrew – Nichum**[18] **– compassion –** *(Hosea 11:8)*

Repentance means that we take on a sympathy for those that we have harmed. One of the most difficult and painful things to do is to allow ourselves to sense and feel the pain and hurt that we have caused others. To think of their pain, hurt, and anguish that has come through our words, attitudes, behaviors, addictions, and compulsions is at times overwhelming. It is hard, but necessary to put ourselves into the shoes of our victims and feel their pain. This process helps us to understand the importance of changing.

When my daughter was in pre-school, she began to bite other children in the nursery. We tried to talk to her and explain why she could not do it. It was not until we were willing to give her some time out with it that she associated pain with her bites. In order for us to change, we have to allow our selves to sympathize with those that we have hurt. Feel their pain and recognize that we were the ones who caused it.

5.   **Greek – Metanoeo[19] – to change the mind for the better morally, to change the attitude toward sin** – *(Luke 13:3)*

Here we see "repentance" as the change of attitude or mind toward sin. This means that we make a decision to agree with God on the issues of "right and wrong." When we admit the exact natures of our wrongs, it means that we are willing to think and believe that God is right. It means that we change our attitude and mind wherever it disagrees with God and His Word. We make a decision that God is smarter and wiser than we are in all things, and especially on the issues of "right and wrong." Repentance means that we decide it is not about our opinions and feelings, but what God thinks about it. How does He say I should feel about it? It means that if I have felt and thought differently than God, I now understand that I was wrong and bringing harm to God and others.

6.   **Greek – Metamelomai[20] – to regret consequences of sin, not the cause** – *(Matthew 27:3; 2 Corinthians 7:8)*

Repentance means to "regret the consequences." Many times we will do nothing about our addictions and compulsions until we have been threatened with or delivered to "consequences." Perhaps someone reading this book is sitting in a jail cell because of some thing you did or someone you wronged. Perhaps someone is going through a divorce because of the wrongs you committed against your spouse. Perhaps someone has just lost their job and on and on and on and on. Addictions and compulsions give way to wrongs that bring consequences on us. We feel sad, unhappy, wishing we could turn the clock back. We begin to think, "I'll never do that again or do it that way." This is a part of "repentance." It is not complete repentance, but it is a beginning to it. It is a reaping of our sowing that makes us realize that we will reap what we sow.

"Be not deceived; God is not mocked: for whatsoever a man soweth, that shall he also reap. For he that soweth to his flesh shall of the flesh reap corruption; but he that soweth to the Spirit shall of the Spirit reap life everlasting. And let us not be weary in well doing: for in due season we shall reap, if we faint not" (King James Version, *Galatians 6:7-9*).

7.   Greek – Metanoia[21] **– a real change of mind and attitude toward sin and its cause, not merely the consequences of it –** (*Matthew 3:8,11; 9:13; Luke 24:47*)

Now we get down to the real life changing stuff about repentance. Here repentance means that we take a real good look at the reasons why the wrong was committed and change our mind and attitude towards the cause, not just the consequences. In other words, we take a good look at us. Who caused the sin? Some will say, "It was my environment." Some would say "It was my DNA." All which are factors, but the real cause of wrongdoing is a wrong doer. Somewhere we make choices that are wrong and it harms God, others, and us. Somewhere in our hearts we either didn't understand the consequence and wrongness because we were deceived, or we knew but out of our own desire did those things anyway.

Perhaps we did wrong out of fear and shame. Perhaps we did it out of revenge and bitterness. It may have been greed or lust; or possibly it was egotism and self-absorption. Whatever it was, we found ourselves doing something that caused harm.

Repentance is looking at the real root cause. What was in our heart and mind that was wrong? What kind of thinking did we buy into that caused us to bring such hurt? How did we talk ourselves into believing that a wrong thing was a right thing?

Identifying those root causes and allowing our selves to admit them opens the door to forgiveness, cleansing, and healing in our hearts and souls.

8.   Greek – Ametameletos[22] **– irrevocable –** (*Romans 11:29; 2 Corinthians 7:10*)

Repentance also means that we mean business. It means that we are serious about making a change in our thinking, attitude, and behavior and intend to stick to our guns. It does not mean that we will be perfect, but it does mean that we will have a goal of being different and wake up each day with awareness that we need God's help that day. It means that we are making a commitment to, *"Let go and let God."*

This is reflected in the idea of covenant. Covenant is best understood in "marriage." Marriage is not a contract for two reasons. First, a contract is something that you enter into with someone that you don't trust. Secondly a contract is something made with the thought that if it doesn't work out, you can break it.

Covenants don't work that way. Marriage is a covenant. We enter into it because we do trust that the other person loves us and will keep his or her word for the rest of our lives together. Marriage is not something we do thinking if it doesn't work out we can just throw it away. We make a life- long commitment and work our hardest to make it good for everyone.

Repentance means that we enter into covenant with God. We are saying to God that we are committing ourselves to Him, living for Him, and trusting Him, for the rest of our lives. In this commitment we are saying, "No turning back." Recovery involves repentance that opens the door to faith that releases God's promises on us.

Putting it to Work

Respond to these questions in writing and then discuss them with your sponsor/accountability partner.

1. Are you comfortable with sharing your wrongs or does it make you uncomfortable? Explain why.

_____

_____

_____

_____

_____

2. Can you think of when you have repented of a wrong that you committed? How did that work for you?

_____

_____

_____

_____

_____

3. Is there an example in your life of incomplete repentance verses complete repentance? Explain.

_____

_____

_____

_____

_____

4. From the list of eight words for "repent," talk about what kind of repentance you are experiencing? How does that compare to where you think you should be?

_____

_____

_____

_____

_____

Restoring Broken People

Step 5 ~ We admitted to God, to ourselves, and to another human being the exact nature of our wrongs.

"Admit your faults to one another and pray for each other so that you may be healed. The earnest prayer of a righteous man has great power and wonderful results" *(James 5:16,* TLB).

In *James 5:16,* above, we see that God's heart is to heal us, not hurt us. Hurt comes from the world, our selfish and self-centered nature, and the enemy who is an unseen personality that embodies evil. God is love and in His heart of love He wants to heal us.

In *Luke 4:18-19,* Jesus said that He was anointed for the purpose of healing the brokenhearted and to set at liberty the captive. His desire and heart for us is that we can be healed and set free.

What does it mean to be healed?

To be made whole or complete

God has a desire to bring the broken pieces of our lives together and make them into a beautiful work of art that fulfills us and brings glory to Him. He created us and made us for a good purpose. God does not make junk! He does all things well. He knows how He created us and what He made us to be. When we rebel and go our own way, our lives become broken. Sometimes we are broken from our own decisions and sometimes because someone else rebelled against God and we found our selves in brokenness.

Whatever the cause, God is love and wants to come alongside of us and heal us. In *Matthew 9:12* Jesus said, *"Those who are well have no need of a physician, but those who are sick. Go and learn what this means, 'I desire mercy and not sacrifice.' For I came not to call the righteous, but sinners"* (ESV).

Jesus was telling us that He is not into religion. Religious rites and exercises do not impress Him or obtain His favor. What He wants is "mercy." Mercy is another word for "forgiveness." This is what God desires. Why? It is because "forgiveness" is the key to us being made whole or complete. When we do not feel forgiven we become fragmented and broken people. This happens to all of us because we all fall short of being perfect *(Romans 3:23)*. When we do this, guilt and shame cause great pain and we try to find a way to get rid of it. We become divided, double-minded, and conflicted in an effort to cover our feelings of guilt and shame. This causes all kinds of emotional problems.

Then our enemy brings accusations and makes us feel worthless, hopeless, and broken. Our enemy is called Satan in the Bible. The word "Satan" means slanderer or accuser. He stirs up accusations against us to conflict us and condemn us (*Revelation 12:10*).

So Jesus came to be our "Physician." As our doctor Jesus says that the cure is "repentance." In the last chapter we discussed and defined it. Now we want to focus on the effect of it. Repentance is the pathway to our healing. Repentance bridges our hearts to forgiveness and healing. This is what God wants.

Forgiveness runs in two directions in us. *First* of all it has to do with us being and feeling forgiven for our wrongs. In order for us to be and feel forgiven, we have to admit to the exact nature of our wrongs. We have to own the truth about actions and attitudes. The truth is that we all fall short. We can't be and feel forgiven as long as we are blaming other things and people for our own short comings. But as soon as we admit them to God and another, God pours out a sense of His forgiveness on us and heals us.

> *We can't be and feel forgiven as long as we are blaming other things and people for our own shortcomings.*

Second, it is about forgiving those who have hurt us. Most of the time we do wrong because we have been wronged. They say that the most dangerous dog is a hurt dog. Hurting people hurt people. So in the same way that we need to feel forgiven, we need to forgive those who have hurt us.

Why do we have to forgive others? Jesus told us that when we don't forgive others, we allow the enemy to hold us captive and imprison us (*Matthew 18:32-35)*. Now please understand that God has sympathy for those who are victims of crimes and abuse. He loves us and totally dislikes any wrong that is or has been committed against us. God is not for abuse and crime.

However, God in His infinite knowledge and wisdom knows that we have all committed wrong to someone else. It may come in different forms, but God understands that it is all equally harmful and hurtful. So, He won't allow us to wash away our hurt by believing that we are good and right and others are bad and wrong. *We have all sinned and fall short of the glory of God (Romans 3:23,* ESV).

Mercy is about forgiving those who have sinned against us. It is about forgiving those who have trespassed against us. It is about forgiving those who are indebted to us.

Now this is important because when we harbor unforgiveness we become sick. Unforgiveness opens the door to bitterness, which becomes a root that grows in us under the surface. Bitterness means "bitten." It is like a snakebite that poisons us and makes us sick. When we nurse a grudge and hurt, it poisons us and allows death to run rampant through out our being.

"Strive for peace with everyone, and for the holiness without which no one will see the Lord. See to it that no one fails to obtain the grace of God; that no "root of bitterness" springs up and causes trouble, and by it many become defiled;" (Hebrews 12:14-15, ESV).

When someone gets a snakebite, we understand that they need anti-venom to get better. That is what forgiveness is. It is the anti-venom that counteracts the poison that is surging through us by the bite of being wronged. Someone will say, "When should I forgive a person who has hurt me?" The answer to that question is another question, "When do you want to be healed?"

In order for us to become "whole" or "complete," we have to feel forgiven and we have to give forgiveness. Jesus came to call us to repentance so we can be made whole. He is our doctor who has come to offer us the cure. We have to repent of our wrongs and that includes unforgiveness. It is wrong to ask for forgiveness when we are not willing to give it to someone who has hurt us. Forgiving others closes off the doorway of the enemy.

"Be angry and do not sin, do not let the sun go down on our anger, and do not give the devil an opportunity" (Ephesians 4:26-27, NASB).

When we hold on to anger and nurse a grudge, it becomes bitterness and gives the devil a place in our hearts where he can hold us captive. He then can use us to hurt others. As we focus on our hurt and nurse the grudge, our hurt increases. We become the hurting person who hurts other people. Forgiving those who hurt us changes all of that. So

God tells us to forgive before the end of the day. In other words, work through the emotion of anger quickly and forgive. Don't wait for an apology. Don't wait for a belief that the offender deserves our forgiveness based on their actions. Forgive them right away and let God deal with them. He will and we will be a much healthier and happier people.

When we are full of unforgiveness and bitterness, we increasingly hurt. So in order to feel better, we turn to our addictions and compulsive behaviors. This becomes the real cause. When we are made whole, we don't feel the need to dull the pain. God heals our heart when we forgive and the pain is lifted. It works! He is the Great Physician who calls us to repentance so He can make us well.

Healed means to be saved

In 1986 the doctors told me that I had a very deadly cancer. Left untreated this cancer would have killed me within two years. That would have been 1988. This is 2008 as I write this book. What happened? The Lord used the doctors to save my life. Through research the doctors had discovered a cure. It was hard and painful, but it worked and after a year of treatment and follow up, I was cancer free. After three years they declared me clinically cured. They said I had more chance of developing a totally different cancer than to recur with the one they treated. God used them to save me so I could do what I am doing now.

To heal means to save. It means to save from hurt, pain, disease, and death. Jesus came to heal us. That means that He came as our Physician to save us and to make us whole. This is God's desire for you. So from what does God save us?

First, He saves us from the power of selfishness and self-centeredness. He saves us from our "self". Selfishness is the opposite of love. When we repent and allow God to take control of our hearts, He saves us from the nature of selfishness. He takes over and makes us loving people, like Him.

Second, He saves us from bitterness and the pain and death that it produces. He totally takes the poison out of us. God says *that when we confess our sins that He not only forgives us, but He cleanses us from all unrighteousness (1 John 1:9).*

Third, He saves us from death. Death means to be separated. When a person dies, they are separated from this world, those that they loved, and all the things they owned and counted as valuable and familiar.

God is love and love is the glory of God. Because God is holy in His love, He cannot allow what is not of love to stand before Him. He cannot approve what is not of love. Our sin, our lack of love, separates us from God. In His love He does not want anyone to be separated from Him and creation for eternity. So, Jesus came to heal us from this deadly disease.

"For I have no pleasure in the death of one who dies," declares the Lord God. "Therefore, repent and live!" (*Ezekiel 18:32,* NASB).

Living without God, in bitterness and unforgiveness, is death. God does not want that for us. He wants us to turn to Him and let Him give us the cure. He wants us to live, live with Him and in Him. He wants us to have an abundant life.

Be Healed

So we can turn to Him and Be Healed. We do it by admitting to God and another the exact nature of our wrongs. Then we receive God's cure, which is "forgiveness". He will forgive us of all our wrongs and heal us from all of our bitterness. All we have to do is turn to Him and live.

Prayer:

Dear Lord Jesus,

Today I confess my wrongs. I am listing them before You and another. My bitterness, unforgiveness, and sins have hurt others and made me sick. Please heal those that I have hurt. I need Your healing. You are the One who heals the broken hearted. Come and heal my broken heart. Thank You for keeping your promise to heal us when we confess our sins. You are awesome!!!!!

In Jesus' Name,

Amen

Putting it to Work

Respond to these questions in writing and then discuss them with your sponsor/accountability partner.

1.   Can you recall a time that you received a healing in your life? How did that happen?

_____

_____

_____

_____

_____

2.   Do you believe that you can trust Jesus Christ to be your doctor and to receive His cure? Why?

_____

_____

_____

_____

_____

3.   Are you willing to do all that the Lord asks you to do to be cured of your disease? Why?

_____

_____

_____

_____

_____

4.   Are you holding a grudge against anyone? Are you ready to forgive them and to close off that door to the enemy?

_____

_____

_____

_____

_____

Step 5 ~ We admitted to God, to ourselves, and to another human being the exact nature of our wrongs.

"Admit your faults to one another and pray for each other so that you may be healed. The earnest prayer of a righteous man has great power and wonderful results" (*James 5:16*, TLB).

What is Prayer?

Prayer has been greatly misunderstood and communicated incorrectly. Over the years of history, religion has made prayer so mystical that most are afraid to even try it. It has been shrouded in ceremonies, rituals, and great fear to the point that most don't think that it is worth the effort. The ceremonial has been so emphasized that many do not believe that it has any power to make a difference in their lives. Nothing could be further from the truth. So what is prayer?

Simply put, *prayer is talking with God or* conversing with God, sharing with God, and spending time with God. It is a two way street. It means we share our heart with Him and it means that we listen to Him. Prayer relates us to God in friendship and connects us to Him spiritually.

God can hear us and does listen when we pray. God can talk and will speak when we want to listen. It may not be with an audible voice, though God has done that at times, but He uses a still small voice in our hearts to speak to us by the Holy Spirit. He uses the Bible, which is the Word of God, to speak to us. When we receive Jesus Christ as our God and Savior, He sends the Holy Spirit, who is God, to live in us. The Spirit leads us and speaks to us. We can hear God.

Jesus told us more about prayer than any other. He told us more about it because He knew more about it than anyone else. Though Jesus is God who became a man, He used prayer constantly and daily through out His life. Jesus depended on prayer to receive the direction and power that He needed from the Father as the Son of God. It was through prayer that He received power to overcome the works of the enemy and to set the captive free. If it worked for Him, it will work for us.

Restoring Broken People

In *Matthew 6:5-15*, Jesus gave us twelve keys to prayer.

1. Right Motives

"And when you pray, you shall not be like the hypocrites. For they love to pray standing in the synagogues and on the corners of the streets, that they may be seen by men. Assuredly, I say to you, they have their reward" (verse 5).

God knows what we are thinking and why we are praying. We can't trick God. He knows. He looks at the motives of our hearts. If we want to play games with God, He will let us, but He won't listen and answer our prayers. We have to examine our hearts and get our motives right to be friends with Him. If we will get our motives right, He will listen and answer.

2. Real Faith

"But you, when you pray, go into your room, and when you have shut your door, pray to your Father who is in the secret place; and your Father who sees in secret will reward you openly" (verse 6).

Sometimes we pray hoping that the right person will hear what we say and make something happen for us. That is not the prayer that God will hear and answer. God looks for faith and faith is exhibited by our leaning totally and exclusively on Him. God says that *Faith is the assurance of things hoped for, the conviction of things not seen. (Hebrews 11:1, ESV).* So real faith believes that God is real and really there to hear and to answer us. Real faith takes God at His Word and stands on it. So we are told by God to, *"ask in faith, with no doubting, for the one who doubts is like a wave of the sea that is driven and tossed by the wind. For that person must not suppose that he will receive anything from the Lord; he is a double-minded man, unstable in all his ways."* (*James 1:6-8*, ESV).

3. Refuse to be Religious

"And when you pray do not use vain repetitions as the heathen do. For they think that they will be heard for their many words. Therefore do not be like them. For your Father knows the things you have need of before you ask Him" (verses 7-8).

Jesus said that God is not interested in a religious show. Instead God wants a heartfelt friendship with us. He is more interested in our

132

hearts than our form or words. Jesus said that we do religious forms for people, not for God. He is not impressed. He wants to have a true friendship.

Have you ever felt like someone was acting like they were listening you, but they weren't? They were only acknowledging you out of obligation to not look bad in front of somebody else? That is what religious ceremonies foster. Don't misunderstand me. A person can connect in any environment if they are seeking God from their heart. But the trappings of religion do not cause us to reach God's heart. God is looking at our hearts. Are we seeking Him? Do we believe that He will hear us and help us? Or do we think it is about a ceremony that will somehow magically make something happen? Or do we just not really believe at all and put up with it to not look bad?

4.   Relate to God as your Father

"In this manner therefore pray: 'Our Father in heaven, Hallowed be your name'" (verse 9a).

God is our Father in two ways. He is our Father because He created us. Each one of us is uniquely created and made by God. I heard a speaker say that the DNA code for each of us is complicated that if it was hand typed on paper 8½ inches wide that the document would stretch from the earth to the moon and back. God has written a unique DNA code for each of us. No two of us are the same. God is our Creator Father who knows us better than we know our self. If we created something so wonderful, we would care about it and want to help it when it needed our help. So, God is our Father Creator. He knows us and cares about us.

God adopts us into His family when we receive Jesus Christ as our Lord and Savior. *Romans 8:15-16* says, *"For you did not receive the spirit of bondage again to fear, but you received the Spirit of adoption by whom we cry out, 'Abba Father.' The Spirit Himself bears witness with our spirit that we are children of God, and if children, then heirs--heirs of God and joint heirs with Christ."*

This means that God has chosen us to be members of His family. He loves us and wants to spend time with us. There is nothing more enjoyable for me than to spend time with my children and grandchildren. I will make any sacrifice necessary to be around them when they want to be. If that is true of me, think of how God feels about us. So, Jesus says to talk to God as our Father.

"Abba Father" is a term of endearment. It is like saying, "Dear Daddy." That is how God wants us to see him. That may be hard for some of us who were treated abusively or neglectfully by our fathers, but understand that God is the Father that all fathers should be. Prayer is successful when we treat Him that way.

5.   Recognize the Greatness of Our Source
"In Heaven" (verse 9b).

God's dominion is over Heaven and Earth. He rules everything. Sometimes we have a hard time recognizing that because we live in a world that is rebelling against God. Remember that the rebellion of this world is temporary and, in God's time, He will bring His rule of love over all creation. There is nothing too difficult for God. He can do anything. Jesus told us, *"All things are possible with God."* When you pray, recognize the greatness of God and His power. Pray expecting God to do something. He can and will.

6.   Reverence God's Character
"Hallowed be Your name" (verse 9c).

His Name. God has many names in the Bible. Each one of those names tells us something about who God is and what kind of a person He is. He is powerful; He is righteous; He is loving; He is faithful to keep His promises; He is all knowing; He is all wise; He is the Healer; He is Our Commander and Chief; He is our Savior. That is just the tip of the iceberg. When we pray, we need to approach Him with a respect for who and what He is. He is God who is holy, just, and loving.

7.   Refocus on the Big Picture
"Your kingdom come" (verse 10).

God is the King over all kings. He governs all things, all nations, all planets, all creatures seen and unseen. He is the supreme ruler. Even Satan and the demons have to obey the Lord. Though Satan has this world in rebellion against our Lord Jesus, Christ is still the King and will return to call everyone into account. Jesus promised to come again to the Earth to Rule and Reign over this world forever. When He does, there will be no more war or sickness. Death will cease to exist. It will be a wonderful time. We are to pray for that day to come and for the Lord to have dominion in our world today. As we pray it, God moves into action and God works in our world. God is on His throne and has everything under control.

8. Roll off your burdens on the Lord

"Give us this day our daily bread" (verse 11).

One of the difficulties of faith is that we want to feel secure. We think that security comes by having an abundance of things. We want enough money to last a lifetime, friends and families that will never have problems, or suffering to exist. We want a pain-free, problem-free existence that affords no stress at all. This sounds good. That is heaven for us. Here in this day Jesus tells us to look to God to take care of us, "One day at a time." This reminds us of the nation of Israel in the wilderness. Without food and defense, God showed up each day. He gave them just enough manna each morning and evening to last for the day. It spoiled over night so they had to daily depend on God and receive from Him.

That is how we have to approach prayer. We have to cast off the worry about tomorrow's problems and focus on the present needs. God will show us day-by-day, step-by-step, and item-by-item how He has planned to take care of us. Cast your cares on Him let Him take care of you.

9. Receive God's Mercy

"And forgive us our debts" (verse 12a).

We have said much about this in the previous chapter. Remember, in prayer we need to admit the exact nature of our wrongs and receive God's loving forgiveness.

10. Release hurts and offenses

"As we forgive our debtors" (verse 12b).

Again, much was said in the previous chapter. Let's remember that every time we pray we need to examine our hearts for any root of bitterness that may be taking hold. Daily we have to weed the gardens of our hearts to stay free from the bondage of the enemy. God says we need to *"take every thought and imagination that opposes God's will for us captive and cast it down" (2 Corinthians 10:3-5).*

11. Resist the enemy

"And do not lead us into temptation, but deliver us from the evil one" (verse 13).

Again, we are reminded that we are in a spiritual battle and war against principalities that are under the control of the "evil one." I did not add this thought. It is in the original text. We don't fight against people, but against spiritual wickedness in high places. The highest place of our being is our mind. That is where the enemy attacks us. He attacks us in our thoughts. That is the battleground. In prayer, we ask God to give us victory over the enemy. We allow God to identify any thought that is not from Him and to bind those thoughts.

God says that, *"greater is He that is in you than He that is in the world"* (*1 John 4:4*). God is referring to the Holy Spirit. The Holy Spirit is greater than all the demon spirits that seek to destroy us through temptations. God says, *"We are led by the Holy Spirit" (Romans 8:15)*. As we follow Him, He leads us into victory.

12. Reveal God's Glory in our Life

"For Yours is the kingdom and the power and the glory forever. Amen" (verse 13).

There has been a lot said about our "Purpose" in recent years. Rick Warren gave us a great book called, *The Purpose Driven Life*. In that book, Warren reminded us that our purpose in life is to bring glory to God. He is right. That is what Jesus is telling us to pray for. Prayer is successful when all that we ask and seek is for God's glory, not for our glory. It is about His will being done and His glory being revealed to us and through us. So prayer is powerful and successful when we humble ourselves to Him and ask that He work in us and through us to His glory. When we put our focus on our real purpose, it gives us a sense of calm and helps us understand that God is the One who is at work in us for "His Glory."

Chapter Twenty One ~ Prayer

Putting it to Work

Respond to these questions in writing and be ready to discuss your answer with your sponsor/accountability partner.

1.   Have you ever experienced answered prayer? Describe it please.

_____

_____

_____

_____

_____

2.   How often do you pray? Are you satisfied with this habit of prayer?

_____

_____

_____

_____

_____

3.   Describe best time you have ever had in prayer. Why was it special?

_____

_____

_____

_____

_____

4.   What special requests do you have at this time in your life? Please list them.

_____

_____

_____

_____

_____

Restoring Broken People

Steps 6 ~ We were entirely ready to have God remove all these defects of character.

"Humble yourselves in the presence of the Lord, and He will exalt you" (*James 4:10,* NASB).

Step Six is the step that separates the men from the boys and the women from the girls. "What does it mean to be ready?" The key to recovery is that we have to be both *ready* and *entirely ready*. We can only receive help when we are "ready" to receive that help.

READY – *"Voluntarily submit to every change God wants to make in my life."*

We formed our defects of character, our hang-ups, and our habits over periods of ten, twenty, or thirty years or more. In this principle we connect with God. Then together with God – we are deciding to go after those defects. All of them! But we don't do it all at once.

God says that this is a process, not an event. God spoke through the prophet Isaiah that holiness (which means to become like Christ) is a highway (*Isaiah 35:8*). It is journey to start and then walk every day. Holiness is God's perfect character of love, purity, goodness, and righteousness. We fall short, but with God's help we can begin to develop His holiness day by day. To start, we have to be ready.

When runners start a race, the starter often says, "Ready!" When a firing squad fires their arms together, the sergeant says, "Ready, Aim, Fire!" In this process we are putting to death the old us. It is a slow death, a "day-by-day" process. To get started, we have to be entirely ready. If we aren't ready to get real and serious about change, then it won't happen. It can't be hype, con, or manipulation. It has to be a heartfelt desire.

My grandson runs cross-country. As of now he is a freshman and runs against a field of other high school students ranging from freshmen through seniors. Out of several hundreds in his area, he ranks 34th. He is not first, but has a goal to become the best. He works day-by-day and week-by-week with his coach to improve his time and get a little closer to his goal. I believe that by the time he is a senior he will reach it.

That is how we have to approach this idea of character defects. In this step we are making the decision that we are entirely ready to take this journey and move toward our goal. It will be a lifetime process because there is always more work to do. So let's think about "Entirely Ready."

READY

Release control
Easy does it
Accept the change
Do replace your character defects
Yield to the growth

R – Release control

A man bumped into an old friend in a bar. He said, "I thought you gave up drinking. What's the matter, no self-control?" The friend replied, "Sure I've got plenty of self-control. I'm just too strong-willed to use it."

God is a gentleman and He does not force His will on us. He waits for us to be willing and to invite Him to help us. *Let go and let God.*

Willingness is the key that goes into the lock and opens the door that allows God to begin to remove your character defects.

Psalm 143:10 says, "Teach me to do Your will, For You are my God; Let Your good Spirit lead me on level ground" (NASB).

E – Easy does it

These steps are not quick fixes! You need to allow time for God to work in your life. This goes further than just not doing wrong. Remember the behavior is the symptom of the character defect. Sin is like a weed in a garden. It will keep growing back unless you pull it out by the root. So we have to allow God to go deep into the root of problem. Don't think that you have to do it all over night. Many don't feel ready because they think that means they have to be flawless and totally successful starting the next morning. Remember to take it easy. It is one day at a time. We just have to be ready to sincerely start. That's all.

A – Accept the change

The space between recognition and willingness can be filled with fear. Fear can trigger our old dependency on self-control and self-will. This principle will not work as long as we are operating in that state. We need to be willing to accept God's help through the transition.

"Therefore, preparing your minds for action, and being sober-minded, set your hope fully on the grace that will be brought to you at the revelation of Jesus Christ." (*1 Peter 1:13*, ESV).

"Humble yourselves before the Lord and He will lift you up" (*James 4:10*, ESV).

All we need is the willingness to let God lead us on our road to recovery.

D – Do replace your character defects

Every time God removes a hang-up, compulsion, obsession, and habit, He will replace it with something else that is good and healthy for you like recovery meetings, church activities and services, volunteering to help, and others.

"When the unclean spirit goes out of a man, he goes through dry places, seeking rest, and finds none. Then he says, 'I will return to my house from which I came.' And when he comes, he finds it empty, swept, and put in order. Then he goes and takes with him seven other spirits more wicked than himself, and they enter and dwell there; and the last state of that man is worse than the first. So shall it also be with this wicked generation." (*Matthew 12:43-45*).

Y – Yield to growth

Your old self-doubts and low self-image may tell you that you are not worthy of the growth and progress you are making in the program. Don't listen! Yield to growth. It is the Holy Spirit's work within you.

Sometimes pride rises up and we feel like no ones else should tell us what to do. We have to resist pride. Ego must be crucified so Christ can live His life in and through us (*Galatians 2:20*).

Sometimes we are comfortable with the old horrible, but predictable lifestyle. We fear starting to change because we are not sure what the future will look and feel like. Just remember that God loves you and wants the best for you. He will only lead you into those things will cause you to be the person He created you to be.

"The person who had been born into God's family does not make a practice of sinning, because now God's life is in him; so he can't keep on sinning, for this new life has been born in to him and controls him – he has been born again" (1 John 3:9, TLB).

This is about making our heart entirely ready for God to change us. It doesn't mean that everything changes right now, but that we are accepting in our heart our new life and lifestyle.

It has been said that a "man convinced against his will is of the same opinion still." We are the only one who can decide. So, get entirely ready to start. We'll be glad that we did.

Chapter Twenty Two ~ Ready

Putting it to Work

Respond to the following in writing and then discuss them with you sponsor or accountability partner.

1.   Do you believe that you are "Entirely Ready" to begin this journey of removing character defects? Please describe why you feel the way you do.

_____

_____

_____

_____

_____

2.   Describe what scares you about starting this process?

_____

_____

_____

_____

3.   What are some of the character defects that you believe God wants to remove from your life?

_____

_____

_____

_____

_____

4.   What are some positive replacements that God wants to put in your life?

_____

_____

_____

_____

_____

Restoring Broken People

Chapter Twenty Three ~ Have God Remove

Step 6 ~ We were entirely ready to have God remove all these defects of character.

"Humble yourselves in the presence of the Lord, and He will exalt you" (*James 4:10*, NASB).

The first time I went to a funeral it totally turned my world upside down. I was a teen and a lady that attended our church that I grew up in had passed away. She was talented. She used to play the cello in the services and I always looked forward to hearing her play. She was a member of the Philharmonic in Ft. Wayne, IN and really had a gift to create pictures in your mind with her musical artistry.

Now, all of that talent, gifting, sweet smile, and humility were lifeless to me. She didn't move or communicate. She was still like a stone. No longer did she live. No longer would she offer the world her person and giftings.

It moved me to tears. Sobbing began to erupt from the depths of my heart for someone that I had lost. Now if the truth be known, I had not attended the church for years and didn't plan to go back. As a teen I was caught in myself and living for me. There was not one thought of trying to make contact with this wonderful lady. So why was I feeling so much loss. I think probably because it made me feel my own mortality. This event drove home to me the reality that I too would die someday. That was really upsetting to me.

There is something built into all of us to resist the idea of dying. God tells us that it is because He created us in His image and He is eternal. So this death thing is really not natural nor was it intended. It came on us as a result of rebelling against God. When we choose to go our own way, cut off our source to eternal life, then we try to create our own life, but we are not capable of being eternal in and of ourselves. Many have tried. From cryogenics to the fountain of life, people have sought a way to make their own life without God.

That human tendency makes this step very difficult. This step requires that we lay down that life we sought to build for ourselves to accept the life that God has made for us. It means that we lay aside our "EGO" and move the big "I" off of the throne of our life. Then we allow Jesus Christ to have His rightful place to our heart. It means death to "I". So we wrestle with it.

So how do we get to that place of being willing to die to the Big "I?" What steps do we take to make ourselves decrease so the image of Christ can increase in us?

Let's consider two passages of scriptures that help us to understand a change of character.

In Galatians 2:20, we learn some powerful truths.
"I have been crucified with Christ. It is no longer I who live, but Christ who lives in me. And the life I now live in the flesh I live by faith in the Son of God, who loved me and gave himself for me." (ESV).

When Christ died, we died. Our sinful person was put to death. Remember that dead people are free from all debts. All of our sins were paid for by Christ's death on the Cross.

Christ now lives in us. This is the life that God promises. He said that He would live in us and no longer remember our sins against us. Wow!!!

We live by faith, not by what we see. Faith sees the unseen. It is the evidence that God is real and that His promises are true. Each time we take steps of faith, God proves to us that He is real.

Our faith is based on his love and power. We know that He loves us because He died for us. There is no greater love than that. We know He has the power because He rose from the dead. Nothing is too difficult for Him. He can do anything.

Three Steps to Overcoming Character Defects

1. Identify them.
Galatians 5:16-25 says, *"I say then: Walk in the Spirit, and you shall not fulfill the lust of the flesh. For the flesh lusts against the Spirit, and the Spirit against the flesh; and these are contrary to one another, so that you do not do the things that you wish. But if you are led by the Spirit, you are not under the law. Now the works of the flesh are evident, which are: adultery, fornication, uncleanness, lewdness, idolatry, sorcery, hatred, contentions, jealousies, outbursts of wrath, selfish ambitions, dissensions, heresies, envy, murders, drunkenness, revelries, and the like; of which I tell you beforehand, just as I also told you in time past, that those who practice such things will not inherit the kingdom of God."*

Chapter Twenty Three ~ Have God Remove

God lists 19 character defects that are common to us as humans. We all have defects that need to be removed and replaced. Just in case we don't think we see ourselves on this list, God gives the 20th one, "and the like." So if we don't feel that we specifically fit this list, God will show us where we need to change.

2. Let the Holy Spirit replace them.

"But the fruit of the Spirit is love, joy, peace, longsuffering, kindness, goodness, faithfulness, gentleness, self-control. Against such there is no law" (Galatians 5:22-23).

God's emphasis is on the doing, not on not doing. This works because when we focus on what the Lord wants us to be and do, we don't have time for the "not's" and the "don'ts." The key is to "walk in the Spirit." How do we change? We crucify the old person with all its' wretched tendencies. As we recognize those things we take them to the cross and put them to death. Then we walk in the new life that we have in Christ.

3. Crucify the passions and desires that lead to Character Defects.

"And those who are Christ's have crucified the flesh with its passions and desires. If we live in the Spirit, let us also walk in the Spirit" (Galatians 24-25).

Remember, you cannot crucify yourself. It is impossible. We have to ask God to help us to put those things to death. This requires that we begin to daily ask the Lord to reveal to us those pockets where the Big "I" is still motivating us. It means that we say to the Lord, *"Search me O God and see if there be any unclean way in me."* We need God to faithfully show us every little pocket of death that abides in our hearts. It takes God's Spirit and Word to help us to know what thoughts are from the Big "I." Then we have to ask God to forgive us for the very thought and feeling.

It has to begin in the heart. *"From the abundance of the heart the mouth speaks,"* Jesus said. "As a man thinks so is he," said the wise man. So in order to change our Character Defects we need the Lord to show us the very thought patterns and feelings that lead us to those Defects of Character.

To stop the destructive patterns of thought we have to replace them with patterns of thoughts from God's Word and the Holy Spirit.

Walking in the Spirit is where we get the victory. Walking is one day at a time. It is a journey.

Remember, **MISTAKES** are stepping-stones to learning how to avoid the pitfalls.

MISTAKES

Misinterpretation of facts and events
I is back in the Saddle of life
Sarcasm takes over for a defense
Thinking that stinks
Allowing wrong feelings to rule
Killing our God given opportunities
Enlisting others to support our wrong
Separating from our God Friends and God

Falling down doesn't make you a failure, but staying down will defeat you. Walking in the Spirit is One Day at a Time. Here are three things to do every day that will help you walk in the Spirit.

1. Read the Bible Every Day.
2. Pray every day.
3. Go to meetings, church, or talk to someone who is walking in the Spirit every day.

Dear Lord Jesus,

It is so amazing to know You and to feel Your love. Thank You for paying for all of my sins and shortcomings with Your blood. By Your grace I am saved. I am confessing my sins to You and trusting You to cleanse me of all unrighteousness. Help me to learn from my sins, shortcomings, and mistakes. It is my desire that I will be more like You every day.

In Jesus' Name,
Amen.

Chapter Twenty Three ~ Have God Remove

Putting it to Work

1.　　From the list in *Galatians 5:16-21* what are some of your character defects?

_____

_____

_____

_____

_____

2.　　From the list in *Galatians 5:22-23* what some things that God wants to develop in you to replace your defects?

_____

_____

_____

_____

_____

3.　　How often do you read the Bible? Describe your reading plan and how you study the Bible? If you don't have a plan, describe how you would like to begin to read the Bible.

_____

_____

_____

_____

_____

4.　　Who are some of the people that God has placed in your life who are "walking in the Spirit?" How does God use them to encourage you?

_____

_____

_____

_____

_____

Chapter 24 ~ Defects that Profit

Step 6 ~ We were entirely ready to have God remove all these defects of character.

"Humble yourselves in the presence of the Lord, and He will exalt you" (*James 4:10,* NASB).

So, there I am in the restaurant trying to decide what to get. I ended up asking for 10 chicken wings with celery and bleu cheese dressing. Yeah, they were good! No, they were great!!! I gobbled up those babies like they were going out of style.

But as I was eating those delectable delights, I realized that when I was younger, no one ate chicken wings. They were thought to be the junk part of the chicken. For years they were just thrown away or maybe fed to animals.

Then one day someone had the great idea of turning these defects in to a profit. So, they figured out that if you put a little something extra with them, they became a real treat. The result, they became rich and made thousands of others rich who followed their example. Now, we can find chicken wings in just about every restaurant in every town and city in America. What seemed like junk, something of no use, became a great source of blessing to those who saw the potential.

That is how God works. Our scriptures says that when we mix ourselves in with God, that He takes over and exalts us. When you mix things together the dominant always takes over and re-characterizes the thing. A sweet smelling home can become an odious habitat when someone begins to cook sauerkraut. Schewwww!!!!!! (I don't know how to spell that but you get the idea.) I remember sometimes coming home from school and from two houses down I could smell it. As a kid, it smelled like something dead to me. It took over the entire atmosphere. My mom was a wonderful housekeeper and our house always smelled clean. You know that Pine Sol smell. But when sauerkraut hit the pot, everything went south.

In the Old Testament of the Bible, God told Moses to offer their sacrifices and prayers with Frankincense and Myrrh. These two spices have a very powerful fragrance that when mixed together created a "sweet aroma." It was God's way of showing that when we offer ourselves to Him that we are to mix in His death, resurrection, and presence. The fragrance of His sacrifice, His resurrection, and His presence is the dominant that takes over the atmosphere. I am finding out that I need to get Rod Buzzard out of the way so the Lord can move and bless people. When the Lord's presence is felt and recognized, people don't even notice my defects or me.

When the children of Israel ended up in the wilderness at the Waters of Marah, they could not drink because the waters were bitter. That is the meaning of Marah. The bitter circumstance only revealed their defects. They were bitter. Here were two million plus people whining and complaining about the waters instead of trusting and believing.

Why should they be trusting God and Moses? They witnessed ten plagues that God used to prove Himself to them; a Passover Lamb that saved their firstborns from death; deliverance from the torturous hands of Pharaoh; and finally the Red Sea that opened for them to escape through and then collapsed on the armies of Pharaoh.

We see in this story that it is not our circumstances that make us bitter, but our bitter hearts make our circumstances bitter. Have you ever met someone who can make everything and everyone feel good no matter how bad things get? Bad times and things only serve to reveal what is inside of us. If we are sweet, full of God's presence, crucified in Christ, and walking in the power of His resurrection, then difficulty brings it to the surface. The opposite is also true; if we are full of un-forgiveness, resentment, retaliation, strife, hatred, murder, etc., then that is what surfaces.

God told Moses to throw a tree in the water at Marah. You know what happened? When they did, the waters turned sweet. Everyone settled down and they all had plenty to drink.

What does God want us to learn from this story? He wants us to know that He is greater than any circumstance and that if we will bring Him into the mix, He can turn the bitter thing into a sweet thing.

So how does this work? This verse tells us three things to do.

1.   Humble Yourself

The positive power of our defects is that they remind us to *be humble.* When our defects surface, (which is a daily and hourly occurrence for me), then we are mindful that we are weak, needy, and really nothing without the Lord. This is the safest place for us to walk. It is the passage that brings us into the move of God.

Chapter 24 ~ Defects that Profit

Our tendency is to want to brag on our accomplishments and focus on our talents. After all, that is how it works in the world. Except, in the world we see that is all temporary. It all fades away. Our life and accomplishments are temporary and usually give way to the revelation of our defects.

Think of the CEO's on Wall Street who have been worshipped by the world system until a chink is found in their armor. Then overnight they become a byword, a laughing stock, and some one to be abhorred. All of the sudden they are thrown away. Then the world moves on to some new guy or gal with his or her own defects that will be revealed some day.

Instead of promoting ourselves, God says, "Humble Yourself." Now that does not mean to efface ourselves, but it means to see ourselves for who and what we really are. We are the children and He is the Father. Jesus said that we couldn't enter the Kingdom of God unless we become as little children.

The Pharisees were a religious sect in the days of Christ that thought they were righteous because they knew God's law and kept it. They were "self-righteous" in their own eyes. But Jesus saw things the way they really were. He could see their hearts. He knew that under the veneer of religion they were just as lost as everyone else and maybe more so. Jesus said to them you have to become like "little children."

Underage means Under Grace

According to the teachings of the Pharisees and Jewish law, the children were not accountable to the law. The law could not condemn them or make them righteous. They were under God's grace because they were under age.

That is how God wants us to see ourselves. He wants us to understand that we are people with defects. We are under age. We cannot make ourselves righteous. But that is ok because He is the Father who loves us and will accept us under His Grace.

That is powerful. So while we are asking God to remove our defects, remember that they are the key. When we feel them clanging around in the closets of our hearts, we need to remember that we need God. Without Him we are nothing; just as chicken wings to be thrown out or fed to the animals. But with Him, all things are possible. Everything changes. With Christ all things are possible.

2.   Honor God's Presence

So if we don't promote ourselves, then whom should we promote? That leaves the One who truly deserves all the glory? The answer is God, the Creator, Savior, Restorer, and Provider. When Jesus taught us to pray He told us to finish by saying, "For Yours is the Kingdom, and the Power, and the Glory forever." The Psalmist said it this way,

"Give unto the LORD, O you mighty ones,
Give unto the LORD glory and strength.
Give unto the LORD the glory due to His name;
Worship the LORD in the beauty of holiness" (Psalm 29:1-2).

God is everywhere that we go. So when we say honor the Lord's presence, it means to practice recognizing God's presence in every situation. React in a way that brings a sense of His presence into the hearts of those who are around you. Make it your priority to promote and glorify Him in everything that happens.

When we allow ourselves to be aware of God's presence, it becomes easy to get humble. It is not so much a matter of seeing ourselves as worthless as it is seeing just how worthy He is. We pale in comparison to Him. The good that comes to us and through us is coming from Him. He is the source and we are but the recipients and distributors of His grace and goodness.

The Apostle Paul lived in a very religious world, but he found that it was healthier to emphasize the irreligious things in his life.

"And I know such a man--whether in the body or out of the body I do not know, God knows--how he was caught up into Paradise and heard inexpressible words, which a man is not permitted to speak. Of such a man I will boast; on my own behalf I will not boast, except in regard to my weaknesses. For if I do wish to boast, I will not be foolish; for I will be speaking the truth; but I refrain from this, so that no one will credit me with more than he sees in me or hears from me. Because of the surpassing greatness of the revelations, for this reason, to keep me from exalting myself, there was given me a thorn in the flesh, a messenger of

Chapter 24 ~ Defects that Profit

Satan to torment me—to keep me from exalting myself! Concerning this I implored the Lord three times that it might leave me. And He has said to me, 'My grace is sufficient for you, for power is perfected in weakness.' Therefore I am well content with weaknesses, with insults, with distresses, with persecutions, with difficulties, for Christ's sake; for when I am weak, then I am strong" (*2 Corinthians 12:2-10*, NASB).

So what we see is that it is all about Him, not us. We are made to glorify Him. We are created for His pleasure. He loves us and enjoys us. But, it is not about us. It is about Him. So as we humble ourselves in the presence of the Lord, He does the exalting.

3.   He will Exalt You

My grandkids are great. As a grandpa I live for the opportunity to do something to lift them up. Whether it is to pick up the little ones and make them laugh and feel good with a smile and giggle, or to brag on their athletic abilities and accomplishments, I love to lift them up. Nothing feels better than exalting them.

Now, here is the deal, if I feel that way and I am defective, just think how God must feel about us. He delights in lifting us up. He really does want to exalt us. He just doesn't want us to exalt ourselves. So here is how it works, our job is to exalt Him, and His job is to exalt us. He knows just how much we need and when we need it.

The problem is that sometimes we don't agree with just how much exaltation and just when it should happen. We get to feeling jealous, envious, or like we are a failure. To feel like God is playing favorites or doesn't care about us is to question His love and integrity. Just relax. If we keep our eye focused on our part, in due season, God will do His part.

Instead of letting those thoughts of doubt and unbelief take over, *resist the devil and he will flee from you* (*James 4:7*). The enemy wants to fill your head with "stinkin-thinkin". He wants you to believe that God is mean and doesn't care. That is what he told Eve in the garden and then convinced her that God needed someone to get things done better and quicker.

God will lift you up. He is the Healer of the Broken Hearted and the Restorer of those who need hope. He delights in you because He created you. He has a great plan for you. Just be patient and focus on honoring Him. He will do His part and in due season exalt you.

The Bible says that Jesus humbled Himself to the Father. The test was to the point of death. He took on the likeness of sinful flesh and took our sins on Him. He was literally the scapegoat for all of the wrong of the world for all of time. It was not fair, but it was in the plan of God. Because He humbled Himself the Father exalted Jesus. Listen to this.

"Let this mind be in you which was also in Christ Jesus, who, being in the form of God, did not consider it robbery to be equal with God, but made Himself of no reputation, taking the form of a bondservant, and coming in the likeness of men. And being found in appearance as a man, He humbled Himself and became obedient to the point of death, even the death of the cross. Therefore God also has highly exalted Him and given Him the name which is above every name, that at the name of Jesus every knee should bow, of those in heaven, and of those on earth, and of those under the earth, and that every tongue should confess that Jesus Christ is Lord, to the glory of God the Father" (Phil 2:5-11).

Chapter 24 ~ Defects that Profit

Putting it to Work

Respond to the following questions in writing and then be ready to discuss your answers with your sponsor/accountability partner.

1. When you hear the word "humble," what do you think of? Is it positive or negative to you?

    _____

    _____

    _____

    _____

    _____

2. Have you ever struggled with feelings of humiliation? Describe the events and the feelings.

    _____

    _____

    _____

    _____

    _____

3. Do your past experiences with humiliation affect your attitude now? In what way do they affect your attitude?

    _____

    _____

    _____

    _____

    _____

4. How do you believe that God wants to treat you as you are humble towards Him? Be specific.

    _____

    _____

    _____

    _____

    _____

Restoring Broken People

Step 6 ~ We were entirely ready to have God remove all these defects of character.

"Humble yourselves in the presence of the Lord, and He will exalt you" (*James 4:10,* NASB).

So my grandson is a pitcher. Boy, he loves to play baseball. He knows more about the game at the age of eight than I ever did. It seems to be ingrained in him. He is a ball player. He thinks baseball, eats baseball, and sleeps baseball. Only time will tell if he will be able to make a life of it, but for now he is a baseball player.

His cousin is a runner. He was a runner when he was just a little guy. All of his life he has enjoyed running. He is like the eighty-two year old lady who is running the New York Marathon this week who said that she wants to die running. That is what she is all about. So, in the same way, my grandson loves to run and has done so every day of his life. It is like breathing for him.

Now, his brother seems to be all about music and dancing. How does that happen? They are all my grandkids, but they are all different. The little guy hears music and responds to it with feet moving and hands flying.

My other grandson is just smart. I mean he is a five-year-old whiz kid. He grasps concepts and ideas so quickly that it is almost scary. He just seems to absorb it and with confidence can spit out the right answers. Give him an opportunity to see or hear a new concept and bam, he's got it.

Four grandkids, all are wonderful, but they are all different. They are all put together in a way that makes them who they are. It is like the watch that I wear. It is full of parts. It has springs, stems, hands, a face, batteries, a band etc. But no one part defines the watch. It is the sum of the whole that defines what my watch is. When you put it together it keeps time, so it is a watch. I know you are amazed at my intelligence right now. But please bear with me while I make a point.

Character is the sum total of our parts. It is not any one thing, but what we are when we put it all together. God has made all of us different, but there is one thing that He wants us all to be with the sum total of our lives. He wants us to be images of Him. He wants us to be mirror reflections of the One who created us and gave us our life. He says, "be

Holy as I am Holy". He has predestinated us to be conformed to the image of His Son, Jesus Christ. That is God's goal for us.

My grandsons are all different, a ball player, a runner, a dancer, and a brain. But they are all humans and they all have Christ in their hearts. When their tender lives on earth come to a close, I believe that they will be remembered as Christ lovers and followers.

What is character? It is the sum total of the parts. Character is not determined by an act or decision, but by the sum total of our actions and decisions. Here is the problem. The goal is to be like Christ, but the natural person that I am, wants to be something else. So there is a conflict. We are in a tug of war with two masters pulling at us to go in opposite directions. Since we grow up generally without the presence and direction of the Lord, we are filled with habits that are contrary to Him and His image.

> *Character is not determined by an act or decision, but by the sum total of our actions and decisions.*

So, how do we change? How do we get entirely ready for God to remove the defects of character? You know the other day I had to take my watch into the store for repair. It was still a watch. It looked like a watch. It had the face, hands, stem, band, and parts of a watch. But it wasn't acting like a watch. It no longer would keep time.

The problem was the battery had gone dead. Without that source of power it couldn't be what it was designed to be. So, what did I do? I didn't yell at it, hit it, threaten it, curse it or throw it away. I didn't make fun of it, put it down, or condemn it. I bought a new battery and it got better. It started acting like a watch again.

Wow! Seems logical doesn't it. Well that is what God does with us. He says that if we are to develop the character that He wants us to have, we have to be connected to the right power source. That power source is Him. That's right! Him!

We can always tell when we have spent time in His presence and when we have just been cruising along on momentum. There is a difference. Momentum can give us a false feeling of security. We think that we are rolling along all right until, ***wham***, we lose our energy. Then it happens. A test comes and we don't have any power. We can't seem to make it up the side of the mountain we are climbing. We are still His child and still wanting to be the person He wants us to be, but we don't have the power to act like it. Something happens and we don't reflect His image.

So what does God do? He doesn't yell at us. He doesn't hit us. He doesn't curse us. He doesn't throw us away. He doesn't put us down or condemn us. Instead He calls to us to come to Him for a new battery. You know sometimes all I need to get on my feet and do better is just hear someone say, "I love you. You are alright." Well, that is what the Lord does. He reminds us of His love and then refills us with His Spirit. Just like my watch, we start acting like His children again.

So are we *entirely ready* to let God find the broken and worn out parts in our watch and remove them? Remember, He is not interested in putting us down, but in lifting us up. We would all do well to read, study, and even memorize the following verses. They will help us think right for this step.

"There is therefore now no condemnation to those who are in Christ Jesus" (*Romans 8:1*).

"But if the Spirit of Him who raised Jesus from the dead dwells in you, He who raised Christ from the dead will also give life to your mortal bodies through His Spirit who dwells in you" (*Romans 8:11*).

"For you did not receive the spirit of bondage again to fear, but you received the Spirit of adoption by whom we cry out, "Abba, Father." The Spirit Himself bears witness with our spirit that we are children of God," (*Romans 8:15-16*).

"Likewise the Spirit also helps in our weaknesses. For we do not know what we should pray for as we ought, but the Spirit Himself makes intercession for us with groanings which cannot be uttered" (*Romans 8:26*).

"What then shall we say to these things? If God is for us, who can be against us? He who did not spare His own Son, but delivered Him up for us all, how shall He not with Him also freely give us all things? ...Yet in all these things we are more than conquerors through Him who loved us. For I am persuaded that neither death nor life, nor angels nor principalities nor powers, nor things present nor things to come, nor

height nor depth, nor any other created thing, shall be able to separate us from the love of God which is in Christ Jesus our Lord." (*Romans 8:31-32, 37-39*).

Prayer:

Dear Lord Jesus,

Thank You for declaring that You won't condemn us. Your mercy and grace are really incredible. I bring my broken parts to You. Please remove, repair, and recharge the pieces of my life. It is my desire that I can be a tool in Your hands. Remake me in the image of Your son, Jesus.

In His Name,

Amen.

Chapter Twenty Five ~ Character

Putting it to Work

Respond to the following questions in writing then be ready to review them with your sponsor/accountability partner.

1. When you look at the sum total of your life, how would you describe yourself? What are you?

    _____
    _____
    _____
    _____
    _____

2. When you are ready to leave this world, how do you want to be remembered?

    _____
    _____
    _____
    _____

3. Is there anything that is keeping you back from making a total commitment in letting God remove any defects in your character? What are they?

    _____
    _____
    _____
    _____
    _____

4. What do you most admire about Jesus Christ?

    _____
    _____
    _____
    _____

Restoring Broken People

Chapter Twenty Six ~ Humbly Asked Him

Step 7 ~ We humbly asked Him to remove all our shortcomings.

"But if we confess our sins to him, he can be depended on to forgive us and to cleanse us from every wrong. And it is perfectly proper for God to do this for us because Christ died to wash away our sins" (*1 John 1:9*, TLB).

Playing golf is fun for me. It is so inspiring to watch the pros like Jack Nicklaus, Tiger Woods, Ben Hogan, Bobby Jones, and Sam Snead play live or on their past archived clips. They all make it look so easy.

One thing that I have discovered is that they are all great because they are all humble. Maybe not in every way, but they all respect the authority and rules that govern golf. They humble themselves to the laws and powers that make a good swing and a good game.

When we are humble it means that we seek the power, authority, wisdom, and blessing of someone greater than us. So, we have to recognize that we are not number one and that there is someone or something greater than us and seek that someone.

When it comes to morality, we recognize that God is greater, better, and the best. The Bible says, *"All have sinned and fall short of the glory of God"* (*Romans 3:23*). God is greater in love, purity, holiness, goodness, and righteousness. He is the ultimate in morality. No one can compare to Him. However, He loves us and like any good teacher wants to help us to become the best that we can be. Since He is the Master of Love and Goodness, He knows how to develop His character in us.

The Key is that we "Humbly" ask. He has told us that if we will ask, we will receive, and that if we seek, we shall find.

Humbly means that we abandon our ideas and allow Him to begin to write a new set of guidelines into our hearts. That is how God removes all of our shortcomings. He points out those things that are not consistent with His loving and holy character and helps us to change those things.

The root word for blessing in the Hebrew language means, *"to bow or kneel*[23]*."* In order to be blessed, grow, and to increase, we have to become humble.

Now we are moving into the time of wrestling with God to completely change us. Character is the sum total of the decisions that we make in life. If I lie often or constantly, I am by character, a liar. If am kind to people often or constantly, I am by character a kind person. Character is developed over a lifetime. It becomes ingrained in us until it is an automatic response. In order to stay free of our addictions, we must look to God to truly remove all past wrongs and to help us to change our character and patterns of dealing with life, others, and ourselves.

Someone will say, "If God loves me, He will take me just the way that I am." That is true. God in His unconditional love receives us just the way that we are. He has provided the means for us to be declared holy, righteous, pure, loving, and good through His Son Jesus Christ. We are accepted in the Beloved who is Jesus Christ. It is by His grace and not by our works or personal character.

But this is not about gaining God's love and approval. It is about becoming healthier, developed, and living life more abundantly. God desires that we have a life that is more abundant. He wants us to be fruitful and that our seed would multiply.

In order for this to happen, He has to begin to change us. He has something better for us. In this step we "Humbly ask Him" to remove all of our shortcomings.

Each decision we make is a seed that is sown. When we sow seeds that are selfish, self-serving, and based on fear, shame, and blame, we reap the same. When we make decisions that are based on faith in God and love for others, then confidence and expectancy for God to help us springs up. This leads to many good fruits that multiply seed back to us.

"Do not be deceived, God is not mocked; for whatever a man sows, that he will also reap. For he who sows to his flesh will of the flesh reap corruption, but he who sows to the Spirit will of the Spirit reap everlasting life" (Galatians 6:7-8).

"Now He who supplies seed to the sower, and bread for food will supply and multiply your seed for sowing and increase the harvest of your righteousness" (2 Corinthians 9:10, NASB).

One thing that we learn quickly in this process is that we are either going forward or we are going backwards. There is no such thing as neutral or being on hold. The minute we stop walking in the ways that

God has for us, we move towards the old person with all of its' "stinkin-thinkin."

Three things we must do and understand in order to have a change of character.

1. Confess our need for His blessing

Jacob was one of the patriarchs. His name meant "schemer and supplanter." He was always lying his way through life. But one day God met with Jacob and wrestled with him. Into the night they wrestled. They continued until God broke his hip. Jacob realized that God was his answer and told God that he wouldn't let go until God blessed him.

This is how we truly begin to change. It is when we recognize that we need God's blessing in order to move forward, to grow, and to succeed. When we, like Jacob, realize that we need God, then things begin to change.

The Lord asked him his name. He said, "Jacob." Then God said that he would no longer be called "Jacob", the schemer and liar. His new name was "Israel", the prince of God; the one who rules with God. Jacob had to humble himself to God and confess; only then God changed him.

God does the same for us. When we confess who and what we are, God says, "I am going to change you and make you what I created you to be." He calls us "saints" and "priests" and those who rule and reign in the heavenlies with Christ Jesus. God can and will change us, when we humbly confess who we are.

2. Aim for Love

Recognizing sin is important. Sin by definition means to miss the mark. What is the mark? According to this verse it is the "glory" of God. What is God's glory? Love is His glory because God is love. Anything that falls short of Him, His love, His goodness, and His character is sin. Wow, when I look at it that way, I realize that I am lost in a sinful state without God.

Sin is disobeying God. Sin can be defined not only by what we do, but also by what we don't do. We can do what is socially acceptable, but if it is against God's will for us, it is sin. The Bible says that whatever is not of faith, is sin. That means whatever we do out of our ways and ideas are sin. Faith means we listen to what God says, believe that He is right and true, and that we trust Him for the results. We do it His way for His purposes and set aside our own agenda.

It is an attitude. I can go to work just to make money or I can go to work to glorify God by being a good and loving person on the job. When I go with a God attitude, people see and sense the Lord in me. God gets the glory and uses me to give Him glory.

In order to change, we have to really understand that when we sin, we are sinning against the God who created us and the Savior who died for us. All sin is against God.

3. Depend on God
Let go and let God.

We have to let God do the work of removing our sins, wrongs, and shortcomings. He made that possible by becoming a man and dying on the cross for our sins. There is a hymn that says, "What can wash away my sins? Nothing but the blood of Jesus." His blood bought our forgiveness and now continually cleanses us whenever we confess.

After a shower, I have a spray that cleanses the shower and prevents mildew. I confess, which means to agree with, that the shower is polluted with things that will grow into bigger problems. The same is true of our hearts. We can apply the cleanser that removes the contaminates from our hearts (God's Word in confession.) The result is like the shower that is once again fresh and clean; so are our hearts.

Daily we need to go to God and ask Him to show us where we are polluted in our actions, attitudes, and thoughts and then confess those things to God. We depend on God to cleanse those things out of us by the blood of Jesus. He said that He would be faithful and just to cleanse by the blood of Jesus if we would take the time to confess.

We cannot save ourselves. Only the Lord can remove our sins. Let Him do it. Then we ask Him to change our soul, desires, goals, and to help us personally to become like Him. We make pleasing Him our number one priority. We depend on Him to remove all defects of character by humbly asking Him to do so. Then we humbly walk in His presence.

Chapter Twenty Six ~ Humbly Asked Him

Putting it to Work

Respond to the following in writing and then be ready to discuss your answers with your sponsor/accountability partner.

1.   What do you think about "humbly asking" God to remove all of your defects of character?

_____

_____

_____

_____

_____

2.   Is there anything holding you back from taking this step? Please explain.

_____

_____

_____

_____

_____

3.   When you think about changing your character and lifestyle, how does it make you feel?

_____

_____

_____

_____

_____

4.   Is there any one thing that is holding you back from "humbly asking God" to remove all of your defects of character? Please describe what it is?

_____

_____

_____

_____

_____

Restoring Broken People

Chapter Twenty Seven ~ Remove All

Step 7~We humbly asked Him to remove all our shortcomings.

"But if we confess our sins to him, he can be depended on to forgive us and to cleanse us from every wrong. And it is perfectly proper for God to do this for us because Christ died to wash away our sins" (*1 John 1:9*, TLB).

So what does that mean, "remove all?" How does that work? Do we become perfect and incapable of ever falling short again? What happens? If we believe that we can achieve a place where we are incapable of wrong, we are setting ourselves up for certain failure. The Bible says that we need to take heed when we think that we stand, lest we fall. *After God removes all, we will still be tempted, but He will make the way of escape in each and every event of temptation.* (*1 Corinthians 10:13*). So, how does God do that for us?

It is always important to define words so there is a common understanding of what the sender says, and what the receiver hears.

Shortcomings can be likened to sin. Sin means "to miss the mark" like an archer missing the bull's eye on his target. When we do our best, we still miss the mark. So even our best is never perfect. All of us fall short of the glory of God, which is the love of God in Jesus Christ. We want God to make up the difference day by day and to help us to become more like Jesus. He daily removes our shortcomings by the blood of Jesus and teaches us to be more like Him.

Sin also means, "to transgress the law." This is a deliberate crossing over the line. It is rebellion against God or authorities. In this sense we know what we are doing is wrong and will hurt others and us, but we do it anyhow. *God is faithful to remove these shortcomings by forgiving us and cleansing us from every wrong* (*1 John 1:9*). When we confess our wrong, God removes our shortcomings.

Shortcomings also mean that we have "character defects." The way that we grow up creates patterns of thinking in us. Some patterns seem good and right, but are sick and wrong. In AA, they call the wrong patterns, "stinkin-thinkin." That is a good way of looking at it. Everyone has some kind of "stinkin-thinkin" that needs to be discerned and dealt with. The

Bible says, *"The heart is deceitful above all things, and desperately wicked" (Jeremiah 17:9).*

Our human nature is to lie to ourselves. We need to make sure we understand the truth. *Jesus said that if we know the truth, the truth will make us free (John 8:32)* The truth has the power to correct our "stinkin-thinkin" and to give us a sound mind. We ask God to show us those patterns of wrong thinking and to give us new patterns of thinking that will result in His removing our shortcomings.

REMOVE

Let's define the word "Remove".
Webster's Dictionary[24] gives us four definitions.

1.   To Transfer -
   a: to change the location, position, station, or residence of <*remove* soldiers to the front>

Psalms 103:12 says, *"As far as the east is from the west, So far has He removed our transgressions from us."*

   b: to transfer (a legal proceeding) from one court to another.

When we confess, agree with God about our shortcomings, He takes our offenses out of the court of our hearts and of Satan's. He places them in His court and Jesus is our defense attorney.

1 John 2:1 says, *"My little children, I am writing these things to you so that you may not sin. But if anyone does sin, we have an advocate with the Father, Jesus Christ the righteous"* (ESV).

A judge could actually declare a guilty person innocent within the Roman court system at the time of Jesus. This could be done as an act of mercy because of the circumstances or just because the King asked for it to be done. We call this a pardon.

Similarly, in the United States when a President leaves office for good, one of his last acts is to make a list of those he wants to pardon. Often those pardoned are very guilty of some terrible things, but as a favor, the President graciously allow them to go free and clear their records of all wrong doing. They are restored to full status of citizenship and allowed to function in society as though they never had committed a crime. They don't earn it or deserve it. They just have an advocate who intercedes on their behalf. Their part is to receive grace from the most powerful man on earth.

So God removes our sins by transferring our case into His court and then appoints Jesus as our Advocate who says, "They belong to me. I already paid for their sins." Then by grace, God says, "Pardoned and restored to full citizenship." That is "Amazing Grace."

2. To move by lifting, pushing aside, or taking away or off <*remove* your hat>

Hebrews 9:28 says, *"So Christ was offered once to bear the sins of many."* When we confess, refuse to deceive ourselves, our shortcomings are lifted off of us and placed on Jesus. He paid for our sins by His death on the cross.

In the Old Testament they would lay the sins of the people on a goat called the "scapegoat." The sins of the nation for the whole year were laid on that scapegoat and then the goat was led into a place in the wilderness where it could never find its way back to the camp. God was letting Israel know that He had laid their sins on that goat and that they could never return back on them to be used against them again.

God says in the Bible that Jesus is our Scapegoat. What does that mean? It means that God has legally laid the guilt of our sin on Jesus Christ, the only Righteous One. He has taken all of our sin, past, present, and future and laid it on Him. Jesus Christ has taken those sins away so that they can never be used against us again. We are free of the guilt and penalty of our sin in God's heart. He won't use it against us again.

I remember a time of failure as a youth. The guilt was so horrible that even though I asked for forgiveness, I still felt bad. I felt as though God and others were seeing me according to the wrong that I had done. I was full of shame and didn't feel worthy to be around people or to be in God's presence. I remember saying to God, "God please forgive me." Then I felt God say in my heart, "For what?" I said, "You know, my sin and failure." Then I felt the Lord say to me, "I don't remember that." Then I got the idea; He had forgiven me in Christ and had removed my sin. He was not going to keep putting me down and making me feel guilty. It was over. My sin was laid on the Scapegoat and taken into the wilderness never to find its way back to me.

That is what God wants to do for each one of us. Our sins are laid on Christ. Once we confess, He forgives and cleanses us of all our unrighteousness. How many times? His mercies endure forever.

3. To dismiss from office –

Romans 6:17-18 says, *"But thanks be to God that though you were slaves of sin, you became obedient from the heart to that form of teaching to which you were committed, And having been freed from sin, you became slaves of righteousness"* (NASB).

God moves us out of the office of serving selfishness, stupidity, and carelessness to the office of serving others, God, and goodness. Our new office is to serve these things instead of self, sin, Satan, and our addiction. This happens when we change our thinking patterns.

When Israel lived in Egypt, they were slaves. But when the Red Sea opened, they were set free. They were no longer physically slaves. They entered the wilderness as free men. But there was a problem. They were free men in position, but not in their minds. They still thought like slaves. They didn't have the mentally of those who were free with a right to fight for what belonged to them. Their slave mentality kept them subservient to those old ways. They perpetuated the abuses of the past in their own minds. They complained, murmured, and continued to live like they were in Egypt.

It was so bad that God had to wait for all of them to die off before He could take Israel into the Promised Land. It was their children who grew up viewing themselves as free that God used to take the land. They had the thinking of free men. They understood their rights in God and could fight for them to win the Promised Land.

In order for us to be free, we have to begin thinking like free men. We have to say to the old masters of addictions, "I am no longer your slave. I will not let you control my thinking. Jesus paid the price and set me free and whom the Son sets free is free indeed. I will not let you control me any longer. You no longer own me."

God's promises are true, but we need to claim them. We are in a spiritual battle and have to fight for the blessings that God has promised us. So we stand in the Lord and the power of His might to cast down all imaginations of still being the slave of our addictions. We cast down those imaginations and begin to think the way that God wants us to. We begin to say, "I am not a slave to my addiction *but I am a conqueror through Him who loved me"* (*2 Corinthians 10:1-3; Philippians 4:8; Romans 8:37*).

4. To get rid of: <u>ELIMINATE</u> <*remove* a tumor surgically>

Hebrews 4:12-13 says, *"For the word of God is living and powerful, and sharper than any two-edged sword, piercing even to the division of soul and spirit, and of joints and marrow, and is a discerner of the thoughts and intents of the heart. And there is no creature hidden from His sight, but all things are naked and open to the eyes of Him to whom we must give account."*

God, by the Holy Spirit uses the Word of God to show us the diseased places in our hearts (thinking and attitudes) and then removes them. So we can be healed. God tells us in the Bible to *no longer be conformed to this world but to be transformed by the renewing of our minds (Romans 12:1-2).*

That means that as we faithfully study, memorize and think on God's Word, it causes us to change our thinking patterns to the way that God thinks. So, as a man thinks, so is he. It makes us more like God everyday. God is not controlled by anything, including addictions. His way of thinking will give us power daily over the shortcomings of our addictions. As we are filled with His love, His love controls us and sets us free from our fear and shame (*2 Corinthians 5:14; 1 John 4:18*).

So, every day, first thing, we need to get into His Word and let it fill our hearts and minds so we will think the way that God thinks. By this change of thinking, God removes our shortcomings, day by day. When we don't do this, the old slave mentality will come back on us and we will fall sooner or later.

Romans 8:11 says, *"But if the Spirit of Him who raised Jesus from the dead dwells in you, He who raised Christ from the dead will also give life to your mortal bodies through His Spirit who dwells in you."*

Mortal means those things that are "liable to die", things that will kill you.

Romans 8:13 says, *"For if you live according to the flesh you will die; but if by the Spirit you put to death the deeds of the body, you will live."*

The Key – Choice

God is a gentleman. He shows us what needs to change, but He gives us a choice. The Holy Spirit uses the Bible to point out things that are deadly in us so we can change our thinking and then change our lifestyle. God wants to heal us and give us an abundant life. So, like a good doctor, He will surgically remove anything that is not good for us by showing us the diseased thinking.

Through this we have a choice to go in a way that brings death or a way that brings life. God removes our shortcomings by showing us our wrong patterns of thinking, then giving us a good pattern of thinking. It then becomes our choice to whether or not we will think that way through out our day. Our choice is the key. God says that we are to choose life. God provides the opportunity for freedom, but we choose to walk in it.

Prayer:

Dear Jesus,

Thank You for making me free. Thank You for wrestling with me that I might learn to lean on You. I choose today to be Your servant. In Your power I am free to live for You and to glorify You. Thank you for making it possible by Your death on the cross. Let Your Holy Spirit fill me and use me for Your glory.

In Jesus' Name,

Amen.

Putting It to Work

Please answer the following questions and then discuss your answers with you sponsor/accountability partner.

1.   What are your thoughts on "remove all" as it relates to our sin? How does that work?

_____

_____

_____

_____

_____

2.   Describe a shortcoming that has been removed in your life? How did this happen for you?

_____

_____

_____

_____

_____

3.   What shortcoming do you currently have that you feel you need to ask God to help you remove from your thinking and lifestyle?

_____

_____

_____

_____

_____

4.   In what ways can you now handle your shortcomings differently than in the past?

_____

_____

_____

_____

_____

Restoring Broken People

Step 7~We humbly asked Him to remove all our shortcomings.

"But if we confess our sins to him, he can be depended on to forgive us and to cleanse us from every wrong. And it is perfectly proper for God to do this for us because Christ died to wash away our sins" (*1 John 1:9*, TLB).

In *Psalms 19:12-13,* David asked God to help him with his secret faults and to keep him from his presumptuous sins. In doing so he said that he would be kept from the great transgression. When reading that it caught my attention and I wanted to know what it meant. Here is what I found out.

Secret Faults – are those areas of our nature that are grey areas to us. They are our blind side. Others may see them, but we don't. We may go a lifetime with some of those things and never quite catch it. It is the part of us that falls short of the glory of God and won't be fixed until we get to heaven. God says that when we see Jesus, we shall be like Him. None of us can claim to be like Him in this life. But, we make it our goal and target to be more like Him every day.

Presumptuous Sins – are those willful sins that we commit in direct opposition to God. They are acts of defiance and rebellion. Pharaoh in Egypt saw God's power demonstrated in the 10 plagues that came from the hand of Moses. Moses gave Pharaoh the Word of God to let go of God's people, Israel. But Pharaoh was presumptuous and obstinate. He defied God. We can do the same thing in our lives.

Great Transgressions – are those sins of habit. They are those things that we do habitually that are wrong, hurtful, and offensive to God, others, and ourselves. But we do them anyway. We are aware that they are sin, but we harden our hearts and do it in spite of God's goodness. His desire is to help us and set us free. Like a physician with a patient, God wants to heal us and give us freedom over those habits that keep us bound.

How does God heal us of the great transgression? How does He set us free so we can truly have the shortcomings of our addictions removed? It begins with our receiving His forgiveness. This happens when we are ready and willing to confess our shortcomings and to acknowledge that we need God's help to overcome them. *Jesus taught us that the Holy Spirit convicts us of our sin (John 16:8).* That means that if you are reading this book and working on your addictions, that God's Spirit has made you aware of your shortcomings and your need to get help to change your habits and life style. God believes in you and thinks that you are special. He has a better plan for your life that includes freedom and abundance.

The key is forgiveness. Confession means to agree with the Holy Spirit that our shortcomings are sin and that we need to be forgiven. That agreement with God releases His power on us that gives us the means for our victory over our habits. What is that power?

The Blood of Jesus – that has the power to cleanse us from all of our unrighteousness. *Sin gives us a sense of unrighteousness that lives in our conscience and creates a continual pain (Psalm 32:3-4).* It is disturbing and causes us to want to find a way to remove it. The human way, without God, is to lie to ourselves and decide that it isn't really wrong. Or we know it is wrong and live with the pain. To deal with the pain we cover it over with an addiction that anesthetizes our aches. But, when we confess, the blood of Jesus cleanses away that sense of unrighteousness and replaces it with a sense of being right with God. The pain goes and we have peace with God.

The Love of Jesus – that makes us aware of how much God does love and accept us. Shame is the fear of being rejected, but God's total acceptance of us removes that fear. It creates in us a sense of being loved unconditionally. *We know that He loves us because the Holy Spirit sheds a sense of God's love into our hearts continually (Romans 8:14-17).* This sense replaces our addictions. We are free and can live without them. We know that God in His love has forgiven us for all our wrongs and shortcomings. We are accepted in the Beloved, who is Jesus Christ. Since we are in Him, God sees us in His Righteousness and accepts us. We are in! We belong! We don't have to be afraid

> *We have peace in God and our pain is removed. We no longer need our addictions.*

of being ridiculed, embarrassed, rejected, or left out. We have peace in God and our pain is removed. We no longer need our addictions.

The Forgiveness from Jesus – that makes us know that our shortcomings will never be used against us again.

Forgive – Means to send off, let go of, or to reverse.

Just like the scapegoat, God has sent off our sins and no longer holds them against us. Let's see what that means to us. Again according to Webster's Dictionary[25] "forgive" means:

1. a: To give up resentment of or claim to requital for. *<forgive* **an insult>**

Luke 23:34 says [on the cross], *"Then Jesus said, Father, forgive them, for they do not know what they do. And they divided His garments and cast lots."*

All sin is against God. God created every person. That means that when we sin against another human being, we are sinning against God's creation. But, God wants us to know that He is not like some unforgiving, abusive person who never let's go of a wrong. He has forgiven us once and for all.

Jesus declared our forgiveness on the cross. It is already a done deal. All we have to do is claim it and receive it. We do that by humbling ourselves to Him, admitting we need forgiveness, turning from our sin, and then thanking Him for what He has already paid for by His death.

He has given up His right to claim requital from us for our offenses against Him. We have insulted Him and rejected His goodness. We have gone our own ways. We have abused Him and mocked Him in our words and actions, but He has given up resentment against us. He has forgiven us.

b: To grant relief from payment of *<forgive* **a debt>**

Ephesians 1:7 says that, *"In Him we have redemption through (the shedding of) His blood, the forgiveness of sins, according to the riches of His grace."*

Jesus paid our debt of sin. He has forgiven us. We could work a lifetime and never be able to pay for our sins. The only way we could pay for our own sins is to die and then be separated from God and others forever. So God did for us what we cannot do for ourselves. He died in our place and paid the price. He redeemed us. He went to the bank and paid our account in full as a favor. He did this out of love for us.

181

2. To cease to feel resentment against (an offender: <u>PARDON</u> *<forgive* one's enemies>

Matthew 6:14-15 says, *"For if you forgive men their trespasses, your heavenly Father will also forgive you. But if you do not forgive men their trespasses, neither will your Father forgive your trespasses."*

This shows us how important forgiveness is to God. To be free from our addictions, we have to forgive others in the same way that God has forgiven us. Unforgiveness is a shortcoming. It is a sin that we have to let God remove from us. To forgive is a decision, not a feeling. If we wait to feel it, we will never do it. Our thoughts control our feelings. The Bible says *that as a man thinks in his heart, so is he.* So to forgive means that we make a decision to think differently and not hold offenses against another. It is a decision.

When we confess our shortcomings, God forgives us. God made his decision to forgive us based on His love for us. He simply said in His heart, "I love them and will forgive them. All they have to do is come in faith and receive my forgiveness that I have provided through My Son." What love!

He wants us to forgive others as well. Why? Because, we can't sense His forgiveness when we are in a state of unforgiveness towards others in our hearts. He wants us to do for others what He has done for us. We didn't deserve His forgiveness; likewise He wants us to forgive those who don't deserve our forgiveness.

The Lord's Prayer

"The world is full of so-called prayer warriors who are prayer-ignorant. They're full of formulas, programs and advice, peddling techniques for getting what you want from God. Don't fall for that nonsense. This is your Father you are dealing with, and he knows better than you, what you need. With a God like this loving you, you can pray very simply. Like this: Our Father in heaven: Reveal who you are. Set the world right; Do what's best - as above, so below. Keep us alive with three square meals. Keep us forgiven with you and forgiving others. Keep us safe from ourselves and the Devil. You're in charge! You can do anything you want! You're ablaze in beauty! Yes. Yes. Yes. (Matt 6:7-13, The Message).

Putting It to Work

Please answer the following questions and then discuss your answers with you sponsor/accountability partner.

1.   Have you experienced the peace of God that comes from confessing your shortcomings and feeling God's forgiveness? How did that look for you?

_____

_____

_____

_____

_____

2.   Have you experienced presumptuous sins? What did they look like?

_____

_____

_____

_____

_____

3.   What is the great transgression in your life?

_____

_____

_____

_____

_____

4.   Have you experienced the freedom that comes from forgiving others' of their offenses against you? How did that look in your life?

_____

_____

_____

_____

_____

Restoring Broken People

Step 7 ~ We humbly asked Him to remove all our shortcomings.

"But if we confess our sins to him, he can be depended on to forgive us and to cleanse us from every wrong. And it is perfectly proper for God to do this for us because Christ died to wash away our sins" (*1 John 1:9,* TLB).

In order to be set free from our addictions and to stay free we have to recognize our shortcomings. This is very difficult because we deal with blind spots, pride, and the desire to blame others. As long as we live, we remain the slaves of those things that keep us bound. So how do we see our shortcomings so we can be and stay free? We have to recognize seven things:

1.   We recognize our Shortcomings
Shortcomings are universal to mankind. *The Bible says that all have sinned and come short of the glory of God (Romans 3:23).* Jesus Christ is the glory of God and we all fall short of His love, goodness, justice, and holiness. He is the only Righteous One. *Our righteousness is like filthy rags compared to Jesus (Isaiah 64:6).*

2.   We see our Pride
In our pride we try to make ourselves righteous. We justify, defend, and excuse our actions. We say that our character defects and shortcomings aren't our fault. *There is always an excuse. We are rebelling against God.*

3.   We Humble ourselves
When we humble ourselves we acknowledge our shortcomings. We admit that we are flawed and have made a mess of our lives. We humbly ask God to help us.

4.   We acknowledge our true Source of help
Then God does two things for us:

- *a.* God forgives us and removes the eternal consequence of our shortcomings. *Romans 6:23* says, *"The wages of sin is death but the gift of God is eternal life through Jesus Christ our Lord."*
- b. God daily helps us by giving us strength for the day to overcome our weaknesses by:
- • Leading us by His Word (The Bible)

- Speaking to us by the still small voice of the Holy Spirit within us
- Providing medical and professional help
- Giving us fellowship and encouragement with others who have won and continue to fight the battles of addictions
- *2 Corinthians 12:9 says, "And He said to me, 'My grace is sufficient for you, for My strength is made perfect in weakness.' Therefore most gladly I will rather boast in my infirmities, that the power of Christ may rest upon me."*

5.   We stay aware of God's Grace

This means "undeserved favors." Thankfully God does not give us what we deserve: condemnation and punishment. He helps us to overcome our shortcomings day by day. They are still there, but God gives us the wisdom, strength, programs, people, and everything that we need to overcome the temptation to give in to our shortcomings.

This means that God positions us in a right standing with Himself, The Holy One, not by works, but by grace through faith. (*Ephesians 2:8-9*). This means that we can come to God with boldness whenever we need help. *Hebrews 4:16* tells us He will not reject us when we come to Him with faith in Jesus Christ. What an awesome promise and comfort! He is really there waiting for us to come to Him. He always has the right and best answer. All we have to do is trust Him to take care of us. He will! *2 Corinthians 1:20* says, *"For all the promises of God find their Yes in him. That is why it is through him that we utter our Amen to God for his glory"* (ESV).

6.   We lean on our True Strength

In the garden of Gethsemane Jesus asked the disciples to pray with Him for an hour. He said, "Pray that you enter not into temptation." He was letting the disciples, and us, know that we have to pray in order to have the strength to resist temptation. We can't do this on our own. That strength comes from the Lord. So we have to get close to God and allow Him to pour His strength into us to overcome. Our weakness keeps us on our knees, humbly seeking His help to overcome.

7.   We daily Press towards the goal

"Not that I have already attained, or am already perfected; but I press on, that I may lay hold of that for which Christ Jesus has also laid hold of me. Brethren, I do not count myself to have apprehended; but one thing I do, forgetting those things which are behind and reaching

forward to those things which are ahead, I press toward the goal for the prize of the upward call of God in Christ Jesus" (*Philippians 3:12-14*).

Perfected means, *"to be complete, lacking nothing for the task"*. It comes from the original word that was used by sailors to say that a ship was ready to go to sea and face a voyage. It means that we are fully equipped and ready to face any circumstance and to succeed. God daily gives us what we need to face the battle for that day. We receive it by humbling ourselves to God and seeking His help. It is one day at a time. *2 Corinthians 3:17-18* says, *"Now the Lord is the Spirit, and where the Spirit of the Lord is, there is freedom. And we all, with unveiled face, beholding the glory of the Lord, are being transformed into the same image from one degree of glory to another. For this comes from the Lord who is the Spirit"* (ESV).

Paul was a great Christian leader, but he had to take it one day at a time. He had not yet arrived and knew that each day he had to get close to God and allow God to give Him the plan and the means for that day. In doing that God used Paul and made Him more like Christ. Our freedom from our shortcomings comes from daily guidance with God.

Prayer:

Dear God,

Forgive me for my pride and arrogance. All too often I think I can do life without You. It is so wrong. Today I humble myself to You. You are my only hope and help. It is by grace that I am saved and I don't deserve anything that I have or will receive from You. It is my desire that I press in to my future in You. Help me to do You will in Your strength and power. To You be all the glory for any good that is accomplished.

In Jesus' Name,

Amen.

Putting It to Work

Please answer the following questions and then discuss them with your sponsor/accountability partner.

1.   Of the seven things to do to acknowledge your shortcomings, which of these seems most difficult and why?

_____

_____

_____

_____

_____

2.   How have you justified or defended your wrong actions in the past?

_____

_____

_____

_____

_____

3.   What are hindrances that keep you from leaning on God's strength?

_____

_____

_____

_____

_____

4.   List some things that you have received from God in your daily devotions or prayer?

_____

_____

_____

_____

_____

Chapter Thirty ~ We Made

Step 8 ~ We made a list of all persons we had harmed and became willing to make amends to them all.

"And just as you want people to treat you, treat them in the same way" (*Luke 6:31*, NASB).

When building a structure you spend many months and even years talking, planning, preparing, discussing, and developing before you actually build. Consultants are consulted. Architects, engineers and contractors are hired. Municipal and state agencies are petitioned for permits to build. The future facility is carefully examined for both strengths and weaknesses. Answers for all potential weaknesses are sought out. But at some point in order to build a building you have to decide to start.

We have done that in the first seven steps, but now it is time to start putting it to work. It is time to move forward into victories that God has prepared for us. We have the plan for the finished product in Jesus. He is our vision. Being like Him is the goal. Look at these passages from the Bible that show us that vision.

"I have been crucified with Christ; it is no longer I who live, but Christ lives in me; and the life which I now live in the flesh I live by faith in the Son of God, who loved me and gave Himself for me" (*Galatians 2:20*).

"But the fruit of the Spirit is love, joy, peace, longsuffering, kindness, goodness, faithfulness, gentleness, self-control. Against such there is no law" (*Galatians 5:22-23*).

"to put off your old self, which belongs to your former manner of life and is corrupt through deceitful desires, and to be renewed in the spirit of your minds, and to put on the new self, created after the likeness of God in true righteousness and holiness" (*Ephesians 4:22-24*, ESV).

"Therefore be imitators of God, as beloved children. And walk in love, as Christ loved us and gave himself up for us, a fragrant offering and sacrifice to God" (*Ephesians 5:1-2*, ESV)

God is the master architect and engineer who is also the builder. He has the plan for what we were made to be. *"For we are his workmanship, created in Christ Jesus for good works, which God prepared beforehand, that we should walk in them"* (*Ephesians 2:10*, ESV).

He has planned that we will grow daily and become more like Jesus Christ. So how do we get started in the process? How do we experience the change from our former self to being more like Jesus everyday? Jesus came to earth to make amends with us. He desired that we have a right relationship with Him. He now wants us to work on our relationships with others. In doing so we reflect His love for people and His desire to be friends with all people. So we make amends to show the love of God to others and to clear the slates of any offenses that we have committed. This is God's work in us, for us, and for others. It is God making us more like Jesus.

Becoming More Like Jesus – *James 1:1-8*
God has given us some definite keys to use in order for us to become more like Christ. These steps are modeled in the lives of God's people. God put their examples in the Bible as a pattern for us to follow on the road to victory. What do we do to become more Christ-like?

1. We adopt the attitude of a Bondservant – (verse 1)
"James, a bondservant of God and of the Lord Jesus Christ, by:"
- Making a decision that we are going to serve Him in all things. A Bondservant is a slave who volunteers out of love. One of the titles for Jesus is the Lord. Lord means the Master, the One in charge with all authority. Jesus is Lord, but He is also loving. In His love, He won't force anyone to be His servant; he wants willing servants.
- Making a contract with God to serve Him and His purposes.
- Staying faithful in our commitments to God and people.

We can see the spirit of a bondservant in the life of the woman named Ruth in scripture. Ruth is in a country called Moab. She is married to the son of an Israelite woman who moved there with her husband to find food during a time of famine. In time Naomi's husband and two sons died leaving Ruth a widower. According to tradition, Ruth and her sister-in-law stayed with Naomi rather than returning to their native land. One day Naomi decided to move back to her home in Israel. Naomi told the sisters that she was releasing them to return to their native land and need not follow her to Israel. They said, "No", and that they wanted to stay with her. After Naomi insisted, Ruth's sister-in-law returned to her homeland. But Ruth had another attitude. It was the

190

attitude of a bondservant.

"And she [Naomi] said, "Look, your sister-in-law has gone back to her people and to her gods; return after your sister-in-law." But Ruth said: "Do not urge me to leave you, Or to return from following you; For where you go, I will go; And where you lodge, I will lodge; Your people shall be my people, And your God, my God. Where you die, I will die, and there will I be buried. May the LORD do so to me and more also if anything but death parts me from you" (Ruth 1:15-17, ESV).

When the Lord is your Master, He takes care of you and honors you for serving Him. When Ruth arrived in Israel she met the well off relative of Naomi, a man named Boaz. Even though Boaz was older, Ruth honored him and soon was married to Boaz. In time they had a son named Obed, who had a son named Jesse, who had a son named David, who eventually became the King of Israel.

Because Ruth possessed the heart of a love servant, God rewarded her to become the great grandmother of the King David and eventually of Jesus Christ. This royal lineage was a great blessing!

Wow! That is how it works. When we just stay faithful to God, He rewards us and blesses us by causing us to fulfill our created purpose.

2. We identify with the Body of Christ – (verse 1b)

"To the twelve tribes, which are scattered abroad: Greetings."

James wrote this scripture as a letter to the Jewish Christians who were scattered geographically due to persecution. They were displaced, distressed, and disoriented. James didn't allow distance and difficulty to disconnect him from the people of God. He remained connected and cared about them enough to write encouragement and instruction as found in this letter.

We need to identify with everyone who follows Jesus Christ as his or her Lord and Savior. It doesn't matter what the denomination is. All who know and love the Lord make up the Body of Christ.

The Body of Christ is His (Jesus') Body and we are a part of something big. It is the fastest growing concern on earth. The Bible still remains the number one best seller in the world.

Let's rejoice in the success of other's efforts and pray for our brothers and sisters everywhere. Discovering that, "It is not all about me," is one of the keys to growing in love. Love is always focused on others and God. The Lord said that when we *"seek first His Kingdom and its righteousness, then all these things will be added unto you"* (Matt. 6:33). We need to connect with a local church to faithfully attend and serve. It is in this atmosphere that God supplies us with His power, presence, and perfects us through teaching and relationships.

3. We decide to believe God in every circumstance – (verse 2)
"My brethren, count it all joy when you fall into various trials."

Christians are tried in many ways. We decide that circumstances do not dictate our decision to be joyful or depressed. We stand on our faith in God's love and promises. *We say that God has a plan and that He will use the circumstance for our good (Romans 8:28)*. We praise God in all things. We thank Him in all things knowing that it is His will for us to be thankful. We thank Him knowing that our praise and thanksgiving releases His power in our lives and brings answers to our prayers. God *"gave us the garment of praise instead of the spirit of despair"* (Isaiah 61:3). We make a decision to put it on. Faith is first, and then feelings follow. God says, *"Let it be an opportunity for joy"* (*James 1:2*).

4. We recognize that God does bless us through trials – (verse 3)
"...knowing that the testing of your faith produces patience."

The testing of faith makes us patient people. People who are always getting their way tend to become spoiled brats. Testing makes us sensitive to the feelings of others. Sometimes we bully our way through life. Testing or trials humble us and remind us that we need to seek God. They remind us that we are not in control; God is.

King Nebuchadnezzar thought that He was responsible for the glory of his vast empire. He claimed to be the almighty and was full of pride and arrogance. God warned him to give the glory to God, but he would not. So God sent the prophet to tell him that he would become insane for seven years - which he did. He began to wander the fields like a beast with wild hair and uncut finger and toenails. He ate grass like a cow and behaved like a lunatic. It was terrible - but it humbled him. Then he knew that God was God, and he was not. So, the Lord restored his sanity and his kingdom. God never wastes our hurts. He always uses them for our good to help us learn, develop, and ultimately to bring glory to God.

5. We don't bail out in the process – (verse 4)

"But let patience have its perfect work, that you may be perfect and complete, lacking nothing."

God is not in a hurry. We learn patience by waiting on God. He is on time. It is our schedule that is messed up. *Psalm 46:10 says, "Be still and know that I am God"* (NIV). God told Isaiah, *"They that wait upon the Lord will renew their strength. They shall mount up with wings as eagles. They shall run and not be weary. They shall walk and not faint" (Isaiah 40:31)*. Patience is not a gift; it is learned through suffering and then seeing God work a miracle of deliverance. Too often we bail just before the day of our deliverance. We stand in our faith. We trust God. He is bigger than the storm that we are in. He can calm the angry waves and see us through. We need to keep our eyes on Him and He will carry us through our storm in the night.

6. We take our burdens to God in prayer – (verse 5)

"If any of you lacks wisdom, let him ask of God, who gives to all liberally and without reproach, and it will be given to him"

God hears and answers every prayer that we pray. *God wants us to leave our anxieties with Him and He reminds us He will take care of our every need (Philippians 4:6; Philippians 4:19)*. God is delighted to hear from us and to help us. *Jesus even lives to make intercession for us as our High Priest (Hebrews 7:25)*. God calls us to come to a throne of grace to receive help in the time of need. God calls us to get closer to Him through our trials. The Bible says, *"Cast all your anxiety on Him because He cares for you"* (1 Peter 5:7, NIV).

7. We trust God's bigness and brilliance – (verses 6-8)

"But let him ask in faith, with no doubting, for he who doubts is like a wave of the sea driven and tossed by the wind. For let not that man suppose that he will receive anything from the Lord; he is a double-minded man, unstable in all his ways."

When we walk in faith we leave the battle with God. We let Him choose and fight our battles. We follow His lead and trust Him to bring a good outcome. He has never lost a battle yet. Faith released brings a peace that passes all understanding. Faith released frees God to take charge and make the impossible happen. Instead of telling God how big our problem is, tell our problem how big our God is.

Prayer:

Oh Awesome God,

It is so good to know You as my Lord, my Savior, and my Friend. Thank You for all the good things that You have allowed in my life. Thank You for helping me in the hard times. Help me to know each day the steps that I should take. I often lack wisdom, but You said You would provide it if I would ask. So, I trust You to know how to use the good things that You have given to me. Help me to be slow to speak, slow to anger, and quick to listen. Thank You for hearing my prayer and keeping Your Word to me.

In Jesus' Name,

Amen.

Chapter Thirty ~ We Made

Putting it to Work

Please answer the following questions and then discuss them with your sponsor/accountability partner.

1.   According to this chapter, what must take place in our hearts before we are ready to make amends to the people who have hurt us?

_____

_____

_____

_____

_____

2.   How do you think you can put the thoughts of this chapter to work in your life?

_____

_____

_____

_____

_____

3.   Which of the steps/keys in this chapter do you find the most challenging and why?

_____

_____

_____

_____

_____

4.   How can your sponsor be of support to you in this journey?

_____

_____

_____

_____

_____

Restoring Broken People

Step 8 ~ We made a list of all persons we had harmed and became willing to make amends to them all.

"And just as you want people to treat you, treat them in the same way" (*Luke 6:31*, NASB).

How It Works

Taken from Alcoholics Anonymous *Big Book*:

> *"We have a list of all persons we have harmed and to whom we are willing to make amends. We made it when we took inventory. We subjected ourselves to a drastic self-appraisal. Now we go out to our fellows and repair the damage done in the past. We attempt to sweep away the debris, which has accumulated out of our effort to live on self-will and run the show ourselves. If we haven't the will to do this, we ask until it comes. Remember it was agreed at the beginning we would go to any lengths for victory over alcohol."* [26]

All Persons? Who are they? We already worked on this in our inventory, but it is time to review and commit. People are not mind readers and many of them are suffering from the effects of our behaviors while under the influence of our compulsions and impulses. So let's think about it.

1.	Family	6.	Co-Addicts
2.	Friends	7.	Society
3.	Employer	8.	Church
4.	Co-Workers	9.	Yourself
5.	Neighbors	10.	God

What the Bible says about this.

There are many references in the Bible that emphasize that our priorities need to be about others. Put others first and God will take care of you. Let's look at some of those scriptures.

"But I discipline my body and keep it under control, lest, after preaching to others I myself should be disqualified" (*1 Corinthians 9:27*, ESV).

This discipline and subjection of putting others first is a painful process. Our selfish person doesn't want to do this. It is not pleasant, it is time consuming, and it is stressful. This process causes us to relive bad memories and to face our shame. It takes discipline, but just as Paul did, we have to discipline ourselves in order to make amends. If we don't submit to this discipline, we will allow the nails of guilt and shame to remain in our minds. This creates more pain and future temptation to go back to our addictions.

"For in eating, each one goes ahead with his own meal. One goes hungry and another gets drunk" (*1 Corinthians 11:21*, ESV).

Our addictions drive us to act selfishly and without regard for others. Many times we do damage that we cannot remember. But are reminded by those we have hurt. Part of walking free is that we communicate to others our sorrow for hurting them and try to find a way to right the relationship.

"Nevertheless, in church I would rather speak five words with my mind in order to instruct others, than ten thousand words in a tongue." (*1 Corinthians 14:19*, ESV).

It is not about us. It is about others. The point of this verse is that we don't do what we do in church to draw attention to ourselves and build up ourselves. We are to do what we do in church to build up others; those who are in the audience.

Making amends is like that. We are going to give them the opportunity to heal. We do it in an effort to allow them to put away the hurts and bitterness that are holding them captive.

Making amends makes us more sensitive to others in the future. God has many more opportunities planned for us. He wants us to show the love of Christ to others and behave in a way that lifts them. He does not want us to be selfish and rude, but rather caring and loving.

"For I do not mean that others should be eased and you burdened" (*2 Corinthians 8:13*, ESV).

Chapter Thirty One ~ All Persons

This is not a formula for self-deprecation. That is not how God works. When we lovingly put others first, God rewards us. It is an act of faith on our part. We no longer promote ourselves, but let God take care of that. Instead we promote others and let God promote us. He will. He is watching and He cares.

"Nor did we seek glory from people, whether from you or from others, though we could have made demands as apostles of Christ" (*1 Thessalonians 2:6*, ESV).

When we are walking in love, we don't worry about being recognized. Sometimes we think that making amends is about the other person forgiving us and making ourselves feel better. Look out! *That is a trap!* Many times our efforts for amends will be met with disdain, anger, and bitterness. Remember, those are their issues. All you can do is offer an apology and do your best to demonstrate sincerity. The rest is up to God and that person. We cannot demand that they respond in the way that we think that they should. Love does not do that. We make amends and then put it in God's hands.

"The things that you have heard from me in the presence of many witnesses, entrust these to faithful men who will be able to teach others also " (*2 Timothy 2:2*, NASB).

As we make amends we are setting an example for others to follow. Our example speaks much louder than our words. We need to set a good pattern so the ones that we influence will learn what decisions and actions will truly help and bless them. God lets us experience circumstances and situations so we can teach and comfort others from the lessons that we have learned in life (*2 Corinthians 1:3-5*).

"But others save with fear, pulling them out of the fire, hating even the garment defiled by the flesh" (*Jude 1:23*).

We are to love others with a pure heart, fervently in the way that God loves us. He demonstrated that love on the cross. We show God's love forever and the way of salvation by willingly humbling ourselves and sacrificing our pride to show them the love of Christ. Even when they don't receive our amends, they remember and a seed of God's Word is planted that will some day bear fruit (*Isaiah 55:11*).

"Know therefore that the LORD your God is God, the faithful God who keeps covenant and steadfast love with those who love him and keep his commandments, to a thousand generations" (*Deuteronomy 7:9*, ESV).

This work is painful, but necessary. We are breaking generational curses that will bring God's blessings on future generations. Unborn children, grandchildren, great grandchildren, and on and on will be blessed by our brave honesty. Though there is pain involved, the gain is for future generations as well as yourself. Our pain brings gain for future generations.

"Grace be with all who love our Lord Jesus Christ with love incorruptible" (*Ephesians 6:24*, ESV).

God wants us to love Him. He created us and has a good plan for us. How does our bad behavior toward others make the Lord feel? Our offenses grieve the Holy Spirit according to *Ephesians 4:30*. It is necessary that we place the Lord at the top of our list of amends. Ultimately all sin is against God. David told the Lord, *"Against You, You only, have I sinned"* (*Psalm 51:4*). He knew that He had to make amends with God in order to move forward in his life. Why? It was not for God, it was for his own health. He couldn't say he loved God until he had made things right *with* God. When David acknowledged his sin, God forgave him and restored him to the plan David was created for. God does the same for us as we make amends with others and God.

So here is our work. We humble ourselves and begin telling those that we hurt of our sorrow and ask forgiveness. We start with God, because He has already promised to forgive us and because He is the most important One (*1 John 1:9*). Remember to not make amends when you know that it will only cause further hurt. Let a sponsor help you with this. In this step, God will set you free from guilt and shame and give you confidence and courage.

Chapter Thirty One ~ All Persons

Prayer:

Dear Lord,

It is not easy to face some of things that I have done in the past. Yet I know that it is important. Help me to remember those that I have hurt. Where possible, show me how to make amends with them. It is my desire to mend the broken fences and heal the wounds that I created. Thank You for mercy and grace.

In Jesus' Name,

Amen.

Putting it to Work

Please answer the following questions and then discuss them with your sponsor/accountability partner.

1.   Have you reviewed your list of persons to whom you need to make amends? How do you feel about this?

_____

_____

_____

_____

_____

2.   Recall a situation in your past when another person made an apology or amends to you. How did that make you feel? What was the outcome?

_____

_____

_____

_____

_____

3.   What is the cornerstone / motivation for making amends? Discuss the conflict between this motivation and your addiction.

_____

_____

_____

_____

_____

4.   How did your feelings about others change when you attempted to make amends in the past?

_____

_____

_____

_____

_____

Step 8 ~ We made a list of all persons we had harmed and became willing to make amends to them all.

"And just as you want people to treat you, treat them in the same way" (*Luke 6:31*, NASB).

I was angry for ten years with a group of people that I felt had done me wrong. The result was that Satan destroyed me and used me to hurt many of them. It was sad. My addiction to self and selfishness was destroying the very ones and things that I loved dearly and that I had sacrificed to create. This is such an important step. It deals with our heart and the heart of our addictions. Healing happens when we truly forgive and make amends.

Jesus emphasized forgiveness and said that we cannot know and experience God's forgiveness until we are first willing to forgive those who have hurt us. This is a double-edged sword. It is a constant flow of humbling ourselves and recognizing that we have and continue to hurt others. We need to confess our wrongs to them and ask for their forgiveness. Then it is necessary for us to let go of the offenses and hurts that others have and do place on us, forgiving them in the same way that the Father in Heaven forgives us.

So, who do we need to apologize to? We start by making a laundry list of all those that we have hurt and have yet to make it right. In the process of our addictions, we hurt many. It could be family members, friends, co-workers, perfect strangers, and those that we encouraged to be addicted along with us. We start by cleaning up the past so we can begin to daily walk in love and humility with others. Then we need to make a list of those that have hurt us and let it go by forgiving them. It is not necessary to tell them unless it will help them. Sometimes to tell people they hurt us is a backhanded way of getting revenge and retaliation. In these cases it only serves to puff us up and to hurt them. We have to be discerning of our motive and the impact of our actions.

So what does it mean to make **"AMENDS?"**

A -	Allow God to deal with you and those who have hurt you.
M -	Make healing your goal as you discern your motivation.
E -	Empathize with the pain of others.
N -	Never act out of the offense again.
D -	Decide to treat offenders as you want to be treated.
S -	Submit to God's plan and purposes for your life.

Let's look at this in a little more detail.

A - **Allow** God to deal with you and those who have hurt you.

Pride constantly plagues us and is our nature. It is the "I" syndrome that thinks we have to play God in the circumstances of our lives. It is really insecurity. We are afraid that if we don't handle things, it won't get done, or we are afraid that if we don't handle things, we will be put down and rejected by someone else. To make amends, we have to let God be God.

It means that we allow God to show us what is right and what is wrong in our thinking and actions. We humble ourselves by admitting we are wrong and needing God's help and forgiveness. Then we do the same when we are wronged. We allow God to deal with that person and choose not to walk in the unforgiveness, pride, and revenge that come so naturally to us.

M - **Make** healing your goal as you discern your motivation.

In making AMENDS, we have to be careful with our motives. It is too easy to get defensive and make it all about justifying our actions. The old "Sorry I hurt you, but if you hadn't done this then I would have never hurt you" is false humility and pride. It is not amends, but just a continuation of the hurt.

In making AMENDS, we have to make healing the other person, ourselves, and the relationship with them our goal. We have to sincerely be sorry for the hurt that we caused them and for the damage that we created in the relationship. It is a desire to repair the damage and to move forward to a better relationship with that person.

It is important to remember that we are not trying to control the outcome. We cannot control their response to our attempt to make amends, only our desire to bring healing. Sometimes people are so hurt that they don't want to forgive and rebuild the relationship. We have to know that when that happens, God is pleased with our trying and will heal our hearts for being faithful to make the effort. God receives our amends and faithfully forgives us. We can count on His love!

E - **Empathize** with the pain of others.

Healing happens in us when we truly feel the pain of those that we have hurt. This is hard and especially when there have been years of neglect and abuse due to our addictions. It is extremely difficult to allow ourselves to catch up with all the pain of others that we caused. We spent years escaping that pain with our addictions that now we have to face. It can be painful for us. We will be tempted to not try or to give up and go back. Don't do it. The pain is that of the surgeon's knife cutting deep, but the surgeon knows how to cut so it will bring healing.

Allow the people you hurt to express their hurt to you. Let them get their anger and frustration out. Don't defend yourself. Listen and learn. The memory of their pain will give you fuel to daily conquer your addiction in the future.

N - **Never** act out of the offense again.

One of the tricks of the enemy is to keep us in bondage and under the mistakes of our past. He tries to heap condemnation on us. Remember that once we have confessed our wrongs, in God's courts the books are wiped clean. It is done and it is settled. So, stand in His grace. When the enemy tries to pile on the mistakes of the past, stand against it. Tell the enemy that he is a liar and that the Lord has already forgiven it. It is done. He is like a bill collector trying to collect on a debt that has already been settled. *"Resist the devil, and he will flee from you"* (ESV, *James 4:7*). *"Put on the whole armor of God, that you may be able to stand against the schemes of the devil. For we do not wrestle against flesh and blood, but against the rulers, against the authorities, against the cosmic powers over this present darkness, against spiritual forces of evil in the heavenly places"* (*Ephesians 6:11-12*, ESV).

D - **Decide** to treat offenders as you want to be treated.

As a child my mom used to say to me, "Remember the golden rule – *Do unto others as you would have others do unto you.*" This was good advice. She got it from Jesus. He taught us to love our neighbor as ourselves. Love is not a feeling. It is an action word. It involves the attitude that we have towards others and the way that we treat them. Love is the rule of God for us as believers. Jesus said that all of God's law is summed up in two of the commands: *"You shall love the Lord your God with all your heart and with all your soul and with all your strength and with all your mind, and your neighbor as yourself"* (*Luke 10:27*, ESV).

So who is our neighbor? Jesus answered that question in the parable of the man who was beaten by thieves on the road. The priest was too busy with religion to help him; the Levite was too occupied with his duties to help him; but the Samaritan stopped and helped him. The Samaritans were the enemies of the Jews (God's chosen people), but he stopped and helped. He helped his enemy. In this Jesus gave us a paradigm shift. He said we need to think outside of the social and religious boxes of this world. God puts us where we are to help those in need that are in front of us. Jesus taught us to "love our enemies".

Making amends means that we have a change of heart and attitude that motivates us to treat others the way we want to be treated by them, especially the ones who have and continue to hurt us. We sow seeds of love and kindness into them and trust that God will heal and bless them. This takes faith. This is the kind of faith that destroys the works of the devil. It allows God to use us to bring His love and power into their lives. As we do this, His love and power fills us as well. It fills us up to overflowing so that in our abundance we are able to give to others.

S - Submit to God's plan and purposes for your life.

Submission allows the Holy Spirit to guide our lives. God places His power on us to accomplish His plan and purposes. Life is no longer about us getting our way and having power over others. That is witchcraft and God does not bless witchcraft. It is about God blessing us so we can be the persons that He created us to be. He has a plan for our lives, but He will not force His plan on us. His plan is the best plan we can imagine. We have to willingly accept His plan and yield to Him. When we do, He pours out His Holy Spirit on our hearts to give to us hope, peace, love, joy, and wisdom (*Romans 5:1-5; Galatians 5:21-22*). His power is there to not just help us, but to help others. There is great peace in knowing that we are in God's will and that whatever happens,

Chapter 32 ~ Amends

God is using it for the good of His plans and purposes.

Prayer:

Dear God,

As I review this list, I know that I have hurt many in the same way that I have been hurt. Your forgiveness is so wonderful. Now help me to make my crooked ways straight and to humbly amend my broken relationships with others. As I seek forgiveness, help me to forgive those who have despitefully used me. Help me to let it go and to be free of all unforgiveness and bitterness.

In Jesus' Name,

Amen.

Putting it to Work

Please write out your answers to the following and then discuss them with your sponsor/accountability partner.

1.   How would you define the word "AMENDS?"

_____
_____
_____
_____
_____

2.   Have you ever attempted to make amends with anyone? Give some detail.

_____
_____
_____
_____
_____

3.   How did that work for you?

_____
_____
_____
_____
_____

4.   Describe the steps you use to discern your motivation.

_____
_____
_____
_____
_____

Chapter 32 ~ Amends

Inventory

Harm to Others by Breaking the Law of Love

Answer the following questions of yourself after reading the Law of Love in *1 Corinthians 13:4-7*.
This is completed for Steps 8 and 9. Complete columns 1-4 for Step 8, and Column 5 for Step 9.

Column 1	Column 2	Column 3	Column 4	Column 5
Whom have I harmed?	*How did I hurt them? How did I break the law of love? How could I have reacted in love?*	*Did I cause the person I harmed to have negative thoughts and feelings toward me or others leading to bitterness?*	*Was I only thinking of my own well-being, stretching the truth, and having my own way?*	*I can make amends by making a plan of how and when.*

Restoring Broken People

Step 8 ~ We made a list of all persons we had harmed and became willing to make amends to them all.

"And just as you want people to treat you, treat them in the same way" (*Luke 6:31,* NASB).

Anger is one of the big issues of life. Anger rises from the fires of the fear of loss and self-preservation. Anger is not evil or bad in itself. As a matter of fact the Bible tells us to be angry, but not let it turn to sin.

"Be angry and do not sin; do not let the sun go down on your anger, and give no opportunity to the devil" (*Ephesians 4:26-27,* NASB).

When it takes control of us and causes us to act out with destructive behavior, we end up hurting others and/or ourselves. It gives the devil a foothold in our heart.

The problem with anger is that when we don't know how to control it and we allow it to control us. It turns to vengeance and we are never fair in our revenge. That is why God says that vengeance belongs to Him in *Romans 12:19*. He is the only fair and just One.

Unforgiveness and Bitterness

Anger turns into: unforgiveness, resentment, retaliation, bitterness, depression, cynicism, pride, hatred, and violence. It is the result of denying that we have a need, an addiction, a fear, or a sense of weakness. Instead we rise to fight and allow anger to set a fire ablaze within us that burns without boundaries and control. It consumes everything that it touches, especially those things and persons that we love the most.

James, the half brother of Jesus, wrote a letter to Jewish Christians who had lost families, homes, businesses, friends, and all the comforts of life from persecution. They were set up for anger, bitterness, depression, and fear. God spoke to them some truths to help them stay straight in those circumstances, which apply to us today. These are the truths that will help us to not allow anger to control us and destroy us.

Overcoming Anger

Read through *James 1:9-25* and apply the following thoughts with scriptures that directly apply to the statements. To overcome anger's destructive side we:

1. Decide to believe that trials are opportunities (verses 1-8)
Facts:
- Nothing can touch us unless it goes through our Father's hands first.
- God loves us and has promised that He will cause that all things will work for the good to those who love Him.
- We ask God to give us His wisdom to know what He is doing and how to handle each unexpected turn in the road.
- We stay committed to trusting God because to waver makes us unstable. *James 6-8* tell us, *"But let him ask in faith, with no doubting, for he who doubts is like a wave of the sea that is driven and tossed by the wind. For that person must not suppose that a double-minded man, unstable in all his ways, will receive anything from the Lord."*
- With the Lords help we can make decisions and act on them in life from what we know as true, not by what we feel. Feelings are controlled by our thoughts. When we see a thought that is not in line with what God has said is true, we reject it. We change our thinking and that inevitably changes our emotions.
- God says that He will provide for our every need and that He will use all things for our good and His glory (*Philippians 4:19; Romans 8:28*).
- What the devil intends for our harm, God intends for our good. (*Genesis 50:20*).

2. Deal with Desires by filtering them through the Holy Spirit
How? By asking ourselves, "Does this align with scripture? Is there anything in this desire that would be displeasing to God?" Is my desire more important than my love for God?" God is your source. *James 9-11* says, *"Let the lowly brother boast in his exaltation, and the rich in his humiliation, because like the flower of the grass he will pass away. For the sun rises with its scorching heat and withers the grass; its flower falls, and its beauty perishes. So also will the rich man fade away in the*

midst of his pursuits.

3. Dedicate ourselves to God's Plans (verse 12)
Through seeking His will for our life in His Word daily and through prayer, God will:
- Bless you for serving Him.
- Give you a crown of life for resisting desire and loving God with all of your heart, soul, mind, and might.

4. Don't blame God for our weakness and sin, and openly admit it to Him (verses 13-16)
- God doesn't tempt you to sin. He is holy and just.
- Temptation is the product of our own appetites and desires.
- *"I acknowledged my sin to you, and I did not cover my iniquity; I said, 'I will confess my transgressions to the LORD,' and you forgave the iniquity of my sin"* (Psalm 32:5, ESV)

5. Delight ourselves in God as our good Father by talking with Him regularly (verses 17-18)
- God is the source of all good and perfect gifts.
- He never changes. He is the same now as when He helped the saints of old.
- He doesn't have insincere motives. He is not a hypocrite.

6. Develop a listening ear and heart for others (verses 19-20)
- People trust you when you listen.
- You gain understanding that quenches your anger.
- You have time to find a soft answer in response.
- Most mistakes are made when we speak too quickly out of emotion, instead of knowledge and wisdom.
- We make it our goal to represent God to others and bring glory to Him in our day-to-day relationships.

7. Delete the viruses in our hard drive and registry files (verse 21)
Our lives are like personal computers.

We all need to do a regular house cleaning. Dirt just gathers. We need to keep the channels clean for God to accomplish His purpose and plan for our lives.

In the Old Testament, Isaac had to re-dig the wells of his father, Abraham, because the Philistines had filled them in. They resented that God was working in Abraham and resisted God's work by filling in these wells. They again resisted God's work this time in Isaac, when he re-dug the wells (*Genesis 26:15-21*). The Philistines are a type of the flesh (our natural and carnal person without Christ). Our flesh continually resists the work that the Holy Spirit is doing in our hearts.

The flesh rises up with anger that leads to unforgiveness, resentment, retaliation, hatred, violence, and destruction. Satan uses these things to try to destroy God's good work in us. Satan wants to steal, kill, and destroy us. Satan injects into our thinking "viruses" to make us crash. Satan stirs our flesh to stop God's work in us. But Jesus came to give us abundant life.

We experience that abundant life by keeping our wells clean; our hard drive free of viruses. Our computers have programs that discern the presence of a virus and delete them before they can get control of our computer's thinking process. That is what we have to do to experience the abundant life. We have to become discerning. We do that by allowing the Holy Spirit to do a full cleaning out of all dirt and viruses in our thought life. We allow Him to change our habits of thinking and begin to think in the mind of Christ. That is why we have to decide to make amends with all people that we have harmed.

Once the well is free of dirt, the waters that flow are clean. When new dirt appears, we can spot it quickly and easily. Then deal with it before it deals with us. This allows us to walk in the Spirit and to walk in Faith. "*For who has known the mind of the Lord so as to instruct him? But we have the mind of Christ*" (*1 Corinthians 2:16*). We can put on the mind of Christ.

8. Do the will of God, not just talk about it (verses 22-25)

- God's Word isn't just for academic study.
- God's Word is for application.
- Forming the habit of doing God's will causes us to become sensitive to moving outside of His will through carnal desire and impulse.
- The more we walk in God's will, the easier it is to know when we are not in His will.

214

- The Holy Spirit lives in us to show us God's will.
- As we stay conscious of His presence in us, we are affirmed in doing God's will and checked when we don't.
- God's Word is to instruct us for obedience and thus blessings.

Prayer:

Dear Lord,

Help me to apply the truths in this chapter. There are so many. Give me understanding and let me know just where and how these words are for me. Let me grow in You. Help me to be more like You day by day. Help me to know Your will and how to do it.

In Jesus' Name,

Amen.

Putting it to Work

Please answer the following in writing then discuss your answers with your sponsor/accountability partner.

1.   What are the triggers in your thought life that release anger?

_____
_____
_____
_____
_____

2.   Where did those triggers come from? (What life experiences allowed you to develop those patterns of reactions?)

_____
_____
_____
_____
_____

3.   What can you do differently that will help you develop a new way of dealing with life and the surprises that it presents?

_____
_____
_____
_____
_____

4.   Why is it important to confess your sins regularly and not hide them?

_____
_____
_____
_____
_____

Step 9 We made direct amends to such people whenever possible, except when to do so would injure them or others.

"So if you are standing before the altar in the Temple, offering a sacrifice to God, and suddenly remember that a friend has something against you, leave your sacrifice there beside the altar and go and apologize and be reconciled to him, and then come and offer your sacrifice to God" (Matt 5:23-24, TLB).

Sometimes we can make things right indirectly. Such as when we forget to pay back a friend the ten dollars that we borrowed, and after seeing that friend's wife, give it to her. That works as long as she remembers to give it to him, or at least tells him that she received it. On second thought, that doesn't work either does it?

Direct is important. It means that we don't just tell someone to tell someone, to let someone who might know our friend to know that maybe he or she should suggest to our friend that we have had a change of heart. That sounds silly, but isn't it what we would like to do if we could get away with it? It is difficult to face someone that we have hurt, humbly admitting that we are sorry for the pain that we caused that person and that we want to make things right. But hard as it may be, it is important for our growth and sobriety that we do it. Without it, we wallow in a pool of guilt and shame that creates the kind of pain that we like to cover with our addictions. So...it is time to put it to work.

God is DIRECT with us. He meets us one-on-one to reconcile us to Himself so we can have a personal relationship that is based on love and forgiveness. Listen to how God relates to us.

"Come now, and let us reason together, Says the Lord: Though your sins are like scarlet, they shall be as white as snow; though they are red like crimson, they shall become like wool" (Isaiah 1:18-19, ESV).

"Come to me, all you who labor and are heavy laden, and I will give you rest. Take my yoke upon you, and learn from me, for I am gentle and lowly in heart, and you will find rest for your souls. For my yoke is easy, and my burden is light" (Matthew 11:28-30, ESV).

"Now all these things are from God, who reconciled us to Himself through Christ and gave us the ministry of reconciliation" (2 Corinthians 5:18, NASB).

217

"Behold, I stand at the door and knock. If anyone hears my voice and opens the door, I will come in to him and eat with him, and he with me" (Revelation 3:20, ESV).

God is awesome. He cares enough about you and me that He directly touches us and makes Himself real to us. He let's us know individually that we are important to Him and that we can come to Him as a good father and receive the nurturing that we need. He invites us to reason out our differences and to come into a peaceful relationship with Him. He does this by personally knocking on the door of our hearts by His Spirit who seeks an opportunity to reconcile us to Himself. He sends messengers who confirm the work of the Holy Spirit in our hearts and encourage us to respond to God. So what does it mean to be "DIRECT"?

Direct means we:

D - Deal personally with each one that we need to reconcile to ourselves.

I - Invite him/her to meet, discuss the past, and lay a new foundation for the future.

R - Repent of our wrongs done and humbly ask forgiveness.

E - Empathize with the pain of the one we wronged.

C - Correct our wrongs when possible.

T - Trust God for the results knowing that there is no guarantee of a positive reaction from the one wronged.

D - **Deal** personally with each one that we need to reconcile ourselves to.

This is not a time for mass group meetings. It is time to acknowledge the pain we caused individuals to suffer and to make amends. That means it will cost us time and expense to make things right. There is no easy way out for reconciliation.

Chapter Thirty- Four ~ Direct

When God wanted to reconcile the world to Himself, He could not find an easy way out. If there had been one, He would have used it. He couldn't find a law that He could write that would save us (*Galatians 3:11*). The only way that God could reconcile us to Himself was to become a man and to die for our sins, personally. It cost Him dearly. He suffered rejection and pain. He was humiliated and socially outcast. It was not easy, but reconciliation never is, is it? In the same way we have to be ready to deal with each one and to pay whatever price it may take to be reconciled to that person if he/she is willing.

I - **Invite** him/her to meet, discuss the past, and to lay a new foundation for the future.

God calls us to a meeting. In the verse above, *Isaiah* reminds us that God says, *"Come now and let us reason together."* In the same way we need to purposely call and invite those that we have hurt to meet with us in a way that is convenient and comfortable. We need to remember to meet people where they are. That is how God reconciles us to Himself. He comes and meets us where we are. He humbled Himself to draw us near to Him.

R - **Repent** of our wrongs committed and humbly ask forgiveness.

When we do meet those that we have hurt and wronged, it is time to be remorseful and ready to demonstrate both a change of heart and attitude towards the person and your actions. It is important to say the words, "I was wrong. I hurt you. I am sorry." To repent means to have a change of mind and direction. So it is time to let the individual know that you are changing. To reconcile there must be renewed trust and that trust has to be earned, it is not a gift that we can demand.

E - **Empathize** with the pain of the one we wronged.

This cannot be emphasized enough. That is why we are repeating this step again even though we dealt with it in the last chapter. Making amends can only happen when we allow ourselves to truly feel the pain that we caused the other person. It is important to allow him or her to express that pain to us, no matter how uncomfortable it may make us. It is not time to argue, make excuses, or to defend ourselves. It is time to humbly hear and feel what was felt when we hurt them. The only response can be to cry with him/her and to be truly sorry for bringing that hurt on that person.

God empathizes with our pain, even though He is not responsible for it. It is part of His love For us. He is called the *"Father of mercies and the God of all comfort"* (*2 Corinthians 1:3*, ESV). That word "mercies" means compassion. He feels our pain and then comforts us or helps us with our situation.

> *The only response can be to cry with him/her and to be truly sorry for bringing that hurt on that person.*

So we empathize with the pain out of love, but also out of remorse because we are the ones who caused the pain to begin with.

C -   Correct our wrongs when possible.

It is one thing to say that we are sorry, but it is another thing to correct our mistakes. Some mistakes can never be corrected. We all know that there are some things that happen that cannot be changed and nothing can turn the circumstance around. Some suffer as adults from the pain of abuse endured as a child. Some never received much needed love and nurturing from an addicted parent. You cannot go back and redo it. We understand that those circumstances exist and that it is necessary to ask for forgiveness and hope in building a positive and hopeful future that will bring healing.

But, when it is possible to right a wrong, we need to bring all of our resources to bear on that situation. Whatever the cost, amends will mean that we make it right whenever possible. It is necessary in order to be sincere in our love and repentance.

T -   Trust God for the results knowing that there is no guarantee of a positive reaction from the one wronged.

Part of the craziness of addiction is the desire to want to control the results. Lack of control makes us fearful and desirous of our addictions to calm the fear. This mental state pushes us deeper and deeper into our insanity and cycle of destructive behavior. How do we get out of this state of mind? How do we stop worrying about the future and the results? How do we stop fretting about how people think of us and talk about us?

Faith is the only way. We have to believe that there is someone who is greater than us who can take control of the results and who will in the end turn all things for the good. We hear the saying, *"Let go and let God."* Listen to how God says it to us in the Bible:

"Trust in the Lord, and do good; dwell in the land, and feed on His faithfulness. Delight yourself also in the Lord, and He shall give you the desires of your heart. Commit your way to the Lord. Trust also in Him, and He shall bring it to pass. He shall bring forth your righteousness as the light, and your justice as the noonday" (*Psalm 37:3-6*).

Dear Lord,

Please give me the courage I need to face my past, the wisdom I need to know just how and when to make amends, and peace of mind in the process. It is right for me to face those that I have hurt. Help me to be humble and sincere even though he/she may not receive or believe my apology. It is good for me to close the door to the past. Help me to remember that when I feel afraid and want to give up. Into Your hands I commit myself in this process. Thank You for being there, always.

In Jesus' Name,

Amen.

Putting it to Work

Please answer the following questions in writing and then discuss them with your sponsor/accountability partner.

1.   Describe how God has modeled the importance of making amends to you personally.

_____

_____

_____

_____

_____

2.   What is your biggest fear in making amends with the people that you have hurt?

_____

_____

_____

_____

_____

3.   What is the goal and hoped for outcome of making amends?

_____

_____

_____

_____

_____

4.   How does the prospect of making amends make you feel?

_____

_____

_____

_____

_____

Step 9   We made direct amends to such people whenever possible, except when to do so would injure them or others.

"So if you are standing before the altar in the Temple, offering a sacrifice to God, and suddenly remember that a friend has something against you, leave your sacrifice there beside the altar and go and apologize and be reconciled to him, and then come and offer your sacrifice to God" (Matt 5:23-24, TLB).

People are the object of our amends. That makes this something very special and important because each person was directly created by God and is made in His image. When we hurt a person, we hurt God because they are His creation and image. That is why all sin is against God. God says that we cannot love Him and hate people at the same time. It is impossible. He calls us to love one another (place value on and treat one another according to that value).

In the Old Testament, God dwelt among Israel, the nation of His chosen people, in the Tabernacle and later the Temple. The Tabernacle and Temple had to be built according to the pattern that God gave to Moses. He told Moses to build the Tabernacle in three sections: The Outer Court, the Holy Place, and the Holy of Holies. The Outer Court was what everyone saw from the outside, which was plain and ordinary. It just looked like a big black tent pitched in the Sinai desert. Then when you entered the Holy Place it changed. It was decorated in red, gold, blue, and white and looked heavenly. Its purpose was to draw the worshipper into a sense of what Heaven is like. Then in the Holy of Holies there was even greater beauty. It was the place where God dwelt as a fire. In that place, the high priest fellowshipped with God and made confession for the nation of Israel. This Tabernacle is a picture of us as people.

People are made in three sections. That is how God created us. We have a body, a soul, and a spirit. The body is the tent that we live in. It houses our soul and spirit. It is the part of us that others see and relate to. They know us by the appearance of our body. However, the body is not the real us. It is only the expression of us like a musical instrument to a musician. Our bodies appear ordinary to others and as we get older, they become even more ordinary and plain looking.

Restoring Broken People

Our soul lives in the body. It is comprised of five things. It is our will, our memory, our emotions, our intelligence, and our imagination. This is a very sensitive part of our being. In the same way that our body can suffer hurt, pain, and weariness, so also can our soul be weary, hurt and suffer. It is especially sensitive to the hurts, disappointments, rejections, and offenses that are put on us by those that we love and trust. So, it can suffer greatly. It can become so full of fear and mistrust that it loses its' desire to trust in God. Since we are made in God's image, our imaginations can play tricks on our soul and make us believe that God is bad, mean, abusive, and hurtful like the people that we love and once trusted.

Our spirit is that part of us that comes directly from God. He puts an individual spirit in all of us that is our life. It is what separates us from the animal kingdom. Our spirit has five parts as well. Our spirit has worship, reverence, faith, hope, and God-consciousness. But guilt, shame, and the fear of being rejected darken our spirit causing it to disconnect from God. When it does, we die spiritually.

Making amends is important because it is about people; people, who are confused, darkened in their soul and spirit, without hope, full of shame, guilt, hurt, and spiritual darkness. People are important to God. We are not just numbers to God; we are people that He personally loves and wants to help.

"So it is not the will of my Father who is in heaven that one of these little ones should perish" (*Matthew 18:14,* ESV).

He wants to come into them and be the light, the glory, and the fire that burns in love within them. He wants to give back to each one the spiritual life that was lost through our sin, guilt, and shame. He wants each one of us to be the Temple of the Holy Spirit, just like the Tabernacle and the Temple in Israel.

So making amends is important because it is about people. It is about healing hurts and restoring hope. It is about giving people a witness that God is real and that He cares about them. It is showing them that He cares enough to change you and make you into a better person. He cares enough about them that He wants them to see that He is not an abusive, painful, and hurtful character that we portrayed Him to be. It is about PEOPLE; People who need the Lord.

Chapter Thirty- Five ~ People

What are PEOPLE?

P -	Personal creations of God full of purpose and ability.
E -	Eternal beings made in the image of God.
O -	Open to hurt, pain, misunderstanding, and mistrust.
P -	Powerful instruments God uses to touch others.
L -	Less than God, but greater than angels by creation.
E -	Energy embodied in clay made to manifest God's love.

P -   Personal creations of God full of purpose and ability.

Each person is God's personal creation. The same God who created all the stars and calls them by name, knows us personally and cares about us. He cares so much that he numbers the hairs on our head. We daily make that easier for Him. He wants us to care for others the way that He cares for us.

E -   **Eternal** beings made in the image of God.

Each person is made in God's image. We are marred from sin, but if we look closely enough, we can still see the remnants of His glory on the soul of every human being. Imagine the pain we caused a person. Now imagine that person is the Lord. They were made in His image so it means that when we hurt someone, we are hurting the image of God.

O -   **Open** to hurt, pain, misunderstanding, and mistrust.

People are like a fine piece of China, valuable, but fragile. People are especially fragile in their formative years and very impressionable. Behavioral researchers tell us that 80 percent of everything that we will ever know is learned by the age of five. That means what is happening to us in those years is leaving a big impression in us. As we grow up, we remain impressionable and subject to hurt, misunderstanding, and mistrust. It is important to attempt to repair the damage whenever possible. *"Jesus came to heal the brokenhearted and to proclaim liberty to the captives and recovery of sight to the blind and to set at liberty those who are oppressed" (Luke 4:18)*. He wants to heal people. Our repentance and making amends is a tool that He uses to accomplish His purpose in people.

P -   **Powerful** instruments that God uses to touch others.

Each of us is an instrument that God wants to use. We are those that God has gifted and called to be His witnesses of His love, death, and resurrection to others. He wants us to be witnesses to those that we have hurt and wants to use them to be His witnesses to others. This is powerful. Our making amends makes us the instruments of God and releases others to know the Lord and be used of Him. *Acts 1:8* says *"you shall receive power when the Holy Spirit comes upon you and you will be my witnesses...."*

L -   **Less** than God, but greater than angels by creation.

This is amazing. *Psalm 8:5* says that, *"Yet you [God] have made him [man] a little lower than the heavenly beings and crowned him with glory and honor"* (ESV). He goes on to say that *we were made to have dominion over the works of God's hands.* God has made each person to have a place of greatness in Him. We are raised up in Christ to be restored to this place that we were created to occupy. *Ephesians 2:5-6* says that, *"even when we were dead in trespasses, {He} made us alive together with Christ - by grace you have been saved - and raised us up with him in the heavenly places in Christ Jesus"* (ESV). How powerful is that? That is God's vision for people. He wants us to make amends to demonstrate His love and to help Him restore people to that place He created them to occupy by His side in heavenly places! What a privilege!

E -   **Energy** embodied in clay made to manifest God's love.

The word "spirit" means breath or wind. It refers to the energy that God puts in each of us that grants life. It is the light or candle of God that searches our hearts. We are energy embodied in clay. God made us in His image when He gave us a spirit. He made us both spirit-beings who are connected with heaven through our spirit man and earth-beings through our natural or fleshly person. This is awesome to think about. We have the ability to be both in heaven and on earth at the same time. In Christ we exist in two realms, heaven and earth.

That is why we are to pray that God's will be done in earth as it is in heaven. God wants us to see what is happening in heaven or in the heavenly realm and to make that happen on earth or in the natural realm. He wants us to see the love and glory of God that is in heaven and then to show it to others that are here on earth. That is why we need to spend time with God in prayer and in His Word. That time enables us to get our spiritual eyes and ears in tune so we can see God in His glory, power, and love. Then we are to use our earthly bodies to share with others what we have seen of the Lord. Making amends makes us God's agents of His love and power to those who are in darkness; in part from the hurt we caused them in the past.

Putting it to Work

Please answer the following questions in writing and then discuss them with your sponsor/accountability partner.

1.   How often do you pray and study the Bible?

_____
_____
_____
_____
_____

2.   What kind of affect has it had on you? Give some specific examples.

_____
_____
_____
_____
_____

3.   How do you think that praying and studying the Bible will help you to make amends?

_____
_____
_____
_____
_____

4.   How do you think you should see those that you have hurt? Does that differ from how God sees them?

_____
_____
_____
_____
_____

Step 9 We made direct amends to such people whenever possible, except when to do so would injure them or others.

"So if you are standing before the altar in the Temple, offering a sacrifice to God, and suddenly remember that a friend has something against you, leave your sacrifice there beside the altar and go and apologize and be reconciled to him, and then come and offer your sacrifice to God" (Matt 5:23-24, TLB).

Possible is a word that creates boundaries. We make amends when possible. It is hard to accept limitations in life. We used to play baseball in the backyard when we were kids. Our backyard was used so much by our friends that it had permanent grooves cut in the shape of baselines. Between that and the dog running the fence-line by the alley, my poor parents didn't have much of a chance at keeping a picture perfect back yard, but we were having fun.

The neighbor on the other hand insisted on having a nice back yard. He kept the yard filled with roses and peonies and many other beautiful plants and flowers. He was so obsessed with it that he created a boundary. The rule was if we hit a ball in to his back yard, we were not allowed to get it unless he was there to help us. Through the summer he was gone more than he was there, so it often became impossible to keep playing ball because we would hit many of the balls into his yard. It just was not possible to continue.

Now of course we could have gone ahead and gotten the balls and hoped that he wouldn't notice. As a matter of fact, I remember a couple of occasions when we did just that. "He'll never notice. It will be ok. We can get away with it." But...he was like God. He could see all, know all, and tell all. Man did we get in trouble from my parents.

We make amends when possible. That means that there are times when it is just not possible to make the amends we desire to make. When are some of those times?

When the other person is not interested in meeting.

This may be hard to accept because, with best intentions, we may want to right our wrongs and have the opportunity to heal our relationships. It is painful to find out that some people have become so hurt and bitter that they are just not ready to receive an effort for reconciliation. It is in these times we need to just accept it. Perhaps they will be ready tomorrow, next year, or a long way down the road.

Love is something that can be given, but not forced on another. Even though we may know that it may be for their best and the best of others, we cannot force the issue. We have to imitate God in not being forceful. He reaches out continually to all of mankind to reconcile us to Himself. He says, "All you have to do is believe and receive. I will forgive you and we can have a restored relationship." Why does God say we have to believe to receive a restored relationship? It is because believing reflects trust in God and a personal desire to receive the reconciliation that He offers. Just as mankind refuses God's offer, our offended one might as well. God loves us and in His love He does not force Himself on us. We too must not force ourselves on our offended ones.

When the offended people will not listen to us.

So, maybe they will meet, but they have made up their minds before the meeting: it is a waste of time. They don't believe in us and they don't believe that we have changed or that we are sincere. Possibly they have been conned by us so many times that they believe this is just one more, and that we are setting them up for another world of hurt. They put up walls of protection around their hearts so they cannot feel any more pain. They don't want to be made a fool again and look stupid in front of people. They won't listen. Sometimes they want to listen, but someone else in their life feels threatened by our reaching out to them. They fear losing the relationship they have with that person if they receive amends from us.

What do we do when they won't listen? *We do our best and let God do the rest.* It may seem like bouncing bee bees off a glass, but we make the effort anyhow. We cannot control their responses, only our heart and our attitude. When we are rejected, we identify with Jesus' rejection. We can remember and recognize what it must have felt like for Him*, who was God that became a man, left His glory in Heaven, and came to His own (people) and His own received Him not (John 1:10).* It is a time to identify with the sufferings of Christ. We are doing our best to follow the Lord and to correct the wrongs of our past. We want to make amends, but it is not always possible. The rejection hurts.

Chapter Thirty- Six ~ Possible

Peter told us that, *"if we do well and suffer and take it patiently that it is commendable before God. He said that it allows us to follow the example of Christ in His sufferings"* (*1 Peter 2:20-22*). The big difference is that Jesus never did any wrong, but we on the other hand, have given people plenty of reasons to not trust us.

We remember that *trust is not a gift bestowed freely. It is earned.* People may not listen today, but perhaps if we say we are sincerely sorry and state our desire to right the relationship, the person will quietly watch and, in time, learn to trust again. We plant the seed and then stay faithful. We commit it to the Lord and let Him do the rest. He said that, *"my word be that goes out from my mouth; it shall not return to me empty, but it shall accomplish that which I purpose, and shall succeed in the thing for which I sent it"* (*Isaiah 55:11*, ESV).

When they refuse to reconcile.

There are those times that we run into people who will go so far as to meet, listen, and believe, but refuse to reconcile. They just are not interested in being a part of our life ever again. They never will be interested. They have decided to move on and have no desire to be reconciled. We see this happen often in marriages. Many times the hurts of dysfunctional relationship pile up so that one of the partners just loses their ability to believe that with God all things are possible. They don't want to and just refuse to try. This could be a child, a friend, or anyone else as well.

What do we do? *Let go and let God.* It is time to say to the Lord, "I did everything that I knew to reconcile and they won't let it happen. Now, God I trust you to bless me and *to give me a hope and future."* (*Jeremiah 29:11*). It is not possible to make others do what they don't want to do. Some will never change. We have to accept and go on. God is pleased that we made the effort and He will bless us.

When they have become inaccessible.

This happens through many ways. Death, serious sickness, mental disorders that render a person without senses, distance, and geographical barriers can create a situation that makes it impossible to make amends.

So what can we do in these circumstances? Here are some suggestions:

a.　　We may visit the person's grave and tell them we are sorry. He/She is not there, but it gives us expression in God's presence. Or we could write a letter and read it aloud to God, asking God to let our loved one know. God is big enough to make the person aware in eternity. Actually, the moment a person enters into heaven, he/she already knows and forgiveness is given. But it is good for our soul to make the confession. *It brings forgiveness and cleansing to our spirit. It sets us free from the enemy's snare of pride and bitterness.* (*1 John 1:9; 2 Corinthians 2:11*).

b.　　We may visit a counselor or trusted friend and ask that individual to listen to our amends as a proxy (stand in the place of another) for that person. As we confess to one another and pray for one another, God says that we will experience healing in our lives and hearts. (*James 5:16*).

c.　　We may go to someone else who has suffered similar pain by another and ask him/her to listen to our amends and ask his/her forgiveness. Why make amends when we can't talk to the person we have harmed? We do it for our own healing sake. We do it because sharing with another who was hurt in a similar fashion and listening to his/her pain, will help us to gain insight and healing in our hearts.

Prayer:

Dear Lord Jesus,

With You all things are possible. Yet, there are some things that You have set off limits for me. Even in this process of making amends, it won't be possible to reach out to all that I have hurt. Help me to know where those lines are. Help me to know how to make amends indirectly with those that I can't face directly. Let Your will be done.

In Jesus' Name,

Amen.

Putting it to Work

Answer the following questions in writing and then discuss them with your sponsor/accountability partner.

1.   Do you need to make amends with people that cannot or will not make amends with you? Please describe.

_____
_____
_____
_____
_____

2.   Have you dealt with this in the past? Describe how you handled it?

_____
_____
_____
_____
_____

3.   Describe what sharing in Christ's sufferings means to you.

_____
_____
_____
_____
_____

4.   Do you need to make amends with someone that is not available to you physically or emotionally? How do you think you want to handle it?

_____
_____
_____
_____
_____

Restoring Broken People

Step 9   We made direct amends to such people whenever possible, except when to do so would injure them or others.

"So if you are standing before the altar in the Temple, offering a sacrifice to God, and suddenly remember that a friend has something against you, leave your sacrifice there beside the altar and go and apologize and be reconciled to him, and then come and offer your sacrifice to God" (Matt 5:23-24, TLB*).*

Exceptions to the rules; it happens in everything. "I" before "e" except after "c" was the rule that we learned in grammar school as children. There are exceptions to rules. When I was a teen, this country was drafting soldiers to fight in the war. The rule was that everyone was eligible if they were physically fit and mentally sound, except if they were in college or married. I know a lot of guys who went to college or got married to avoid going in the military in those days. Life became dictated by the exceptions.

Exceptions create the rules that we live by in making amends. In this step we see that we make amends, except when to do so would cause injury to our offended one or to others. The exception to the rule of making amends is "if we cause injury to others by implicating them in our wrong doings or by giving out information that only harms the hearer or others whether they are guilty or innocent." It is very important that we take our time on this step and consult with our sponsor/accountability partner about our strategy for making amends. There are those times that we will need to simply ask for God's forgiveness and leave the situation in God's hands. In this instance talking it over with our sponsor/accountability partner or writing a letter that we never mail will have to suffice. In this case making amends causes injury to others, not to us. This is not a cop out for not making amends, but a serious warning. Through routing around in the past, we can uncover and promote facts that will become damaging to other people. Be wise in your actions. Don't proceed out of impulse or haphazardly. The good and needs of others are more important than our feeling the satisfaction of gaining someone's approval.

"Respect" means that we allow others to make their own confession of wrongs in their own way and at their own time. This is not

a license to be some ruthless reporter who is intent on getting the next scoop no matter what the cost to people and society. Love does cover a multitude of sins. This is not an excuse to "tell all" and "let the chips fall where they will." Such recklessness is only a reflection of pride and selfishness that governed our addictions to begin with. Listen to what God says in His Word to us.

"Hatred stirs up strife,
But love covers all offenses"
(*Proverbs 10:12,* ESV).

"Whoever who covers an offense seeks love,
But he who repeats a matter separates close friends"
(*Proverbs 17:9,* ESV).

In *Genesis 9,* God tells us the story of Noah's drunkenness. It seems that when he left the ark Noah planted a vineyard and after the harvest, made wine. At some point in time, Noah began to enjoy that wine and used it to excess. The indication is that he became drunk and in his drunkenness became naked in his tent. In the original language the implication is that Noah was being sexually inappropriate in his behavior. He was being lewd and lascivious. When his son, Ham, discovered his father's condition and behavior, he decided to broadcast it to what was literally the whole world, the camp of their family. (*Genesis 9:21-22*).

It was a spirit of exposure and rebellion. It was pride. It was an occasion of putting someone down to elevate self. It was not done to help anyone. It was just plain injurious to everyone in their family and in the world. It was strife, stirring up anger in the rest of the family, and separating them. It was Ham telling God that He had made a mistake in making Noah the King of the world and that God should let Ham have the job.

God weighed in on this topic and when Noah became sober God gave Noah a prophecy. The prophecy was a curse on Canaan, the descendent of Ham that occupied the land of "Canaan" or what we today call Palestine (Modern-day Palestinians are not the Canaanites referred to here). God was so gracious that He used Noah's fall and weakness as an occasion to reveal Himself to the world and to show His plan. He told them that Canaan would become a servant to his brothers, Shem and Japheth. That is another Bible study, but it demonstrates God's desire that we be both gracious and discreet.

Shem and Japheth acted differently than Ham. When they heard of their father's nakedness, they found a large cover and walked backward, into the tent, refusing to look on their father's nakedness and sin. Instead they covered him and gave him the opportunity to sober up. They let God deal with their father's weakness and maintained his dignity. God honored their act of respect and love. Their love covered the multitude of sins. Did Noah need to make confession and amends? Yes, but it was not for Ham, Shem, or Japheth to force the situation. That time of reconciliation needed to come from Noah as the result of his sense of personal remorse and repentance.

So, just like Shem and Japheth, we make amends in a way that protects others from injury. We are discreet, gracious, and focused on our personal wrongs, not revealing or pointing out the wrongs of others.

Measuring the Results

In the Bible, God gives us the ruler that we can use to measure the source and results of our actions. It is important that we weigh these before we act out. Listen to what God says:

"Who is wise and understanding among you? Let him show by good conduct that his works are done in the meekness of wisdom. But if you have bitter envy and self-seeking in your hearts, do not boast and lie against the truth. This wisdom does not descend from above, but is earthly, sensual, and demonic. For where envy and self-seeking exist, confusion and every evil thing are there. But the wisdom that is from above is first pure, then peaceable, gentle, willing to yield, full of mercy and good fruits, without partiality and without hypocrisy. Now the fruit of righteousness is sown in peace by those who make peace" (*James 3:13-18*).

Dear Lord Jesus,

Thank You for being the Prince of Peace. Help me to minister Your peace to all that I speak to. Let the wisdom that is from above be my portion today.

In Jesus' Name, Amen.

Putting it to Work

Answer the following questions in writing and then discuss them with your sponsor/accountability partner.

1.   Have you ever been tempted to use false humility and to shamelessly expose others in the guise of humbling yourself or been the brunt of this situation? Explain when and how.

_____
_____
_____
_____

2.   What is the measurement of Godly wisdom that helps us discern our motivation and actions?

_____
_____
_____
_____

3.   In the following verse there are two heart conditions/motivations that are connected and lead to two very different outcomes. *"Hatred stirs up strife, But love covers all sins"* (*Proverbs 10:12*). Describe the importance of how keeping your heart condition pure can lead you to make good choices and act accordingly in the future.

_____
_____
_____
_____

4.   Can this become a learned behavior, which can bring you peace of mind? Explain.

_____
_____
_____
_____

Step 10 - We continued to take personal inventory and when we were wrong, promptly admitted it.

"So be careful. If you are thinking, 'Oh, I would never behave like that'- let this be a warning to you. For you too may fall into sin" (*1 Corinthians 10:12*, TLB).

My mom used to read the story of the tortoise and the hare to me at bedtime. *We all remember the slow tortoise that just plugged along in the race. It was steadily plodding along while the hare, fast on its feet, was off like a flash, but constantly distracted. So often distracted that, while it was enjoying some fun and pleasures, the hare lost the race to the steadily plodding tortoise.*

She used to always say that this story tells us that if we will stick with something, we can accomplish our goals. It also tells us that we can get distracted; easily side-tracked and miss out on all that we were to achieve. Good advice from my momma!

This is especially true of addictive personalities. The drive for pleasure and to escape the pain and boredom of life can catch up with us at any point. There is no such thing as arriving at a place where we are above the temptation to turn back. We still have to guard ourselves against our worst enemy, us. The danger comes when we think that we have completed the course and that we don't need to work at it anymore. This will never be the case for the addictive personality. Jesus taught us that the demon leaves and looks for another home. When it doesn't find one, it comes back and finds its old home clean and empty. It then moves back in with seven other demons. He was teaching us the need to continually be filled with God and to grow in Christ.

Continuing is similar to "abiding." *Jesus said that if we abide in Him and His words abide in us that we will bear fruit (John 15:3-6).* God wants us to be fruitful. He wants to give to us an abundant life that is productive and profitable; to others and us. The key is continuing in the Lord. By continuing in Him and His Word, He causes us to be fruitful; then to bear more fruit and as we continue on, much fruit. *John 15:7* says, *"If you abide in me, and my words abide in you, ask whatever you wish, and it will be done for you."* (ESV). God honors faith and faith is connected to faithfulness. As we continue in God through the words of Jesus, He sees our faithfulness and honors our prayers.

So what does "CONTINUED" mean? It means we are:

C -	Conscious of self-deception and pride.
O -	Open to correction from God and others.
N -	Never allowing an opportunity for relapse.
T -	Talking to others daily that share our goals.
I -	Investing time daily in prayer and Bible study.
N -	Navigating life with the leading of the Holy Spirit.
U -	Understanding that God has new lessons and challenges for us.
E -	Existing to share God's love with others.
D -	Dealing with our issues daily.

C - Conscious of self-deception and pride.

God tells us in *1 Corinthians 10:12, "to be careful ... for you too may fall ..."* It is dangerous to feel and believe that we are above sin. "Sin" means "missing the mark." It is both the acts we commit and our very nature. We can sin without doing anything. Sometimes it is merely our attitude. I used to hear people testify that they had never sinned. But I could see their sin and observe it in their attitude. God tells us that all have sinned and fall short of His glory (*Romans 3:23*), which is His love and pure holiness. No matter how much we pray, read the Bible, go to meetings, and church, we still have to deal with the nature of sin that is in our being. The Apostle Paul said that *we carry it around like a dead man chained to us (Romans 7:23-24).* God says that *if we believe we have no nature of sin, that we are deceiving ourselves* but if *we will acknowledge daily our nature of sin, that the blood of Jesus cleanses us* and we walk in an awareness of God's presence in our lives (*1 John 1:8-9*).

O - Open to correction from God and others.

Attitude determines our altitude. ~ Zig Zigler

I didn't write that, but have always appreciated this saying. Our circumstances and created abilities cannot determine our boundaries. It is our attitude that determines them. When our attitude is one that we believe we have arrived at and have nothing to learn from others, look out; we are in trouble. To continue means that we are forever the student and know that we have something to learn each day. We believe that God orders our steps and puts people in our lives that we might learn from them. We are aware that others see us in a way that we don't see ourselves and we are not only open to their correction, but ask them if they see anything going on in our attitudes or actions that could potentially cause hurt and harm. Jesus said, *"Blessed are the poor in spirit for theirs is the kingdom of heaven"* (*Matthew 5:3,* ESV). *"Blessed are the meek, for they shall inherit the earth"* (*Matthew 5:5,* ESV). If we want a great inheritance in God, we need to be humble and meek, not just once, but continually. Love is not proud, but it is humble. It does not seek its own, but it comes under the control of the Holy Spirit and does the will of God.

N -   Never allowing an opportunity for relapse.

God tells us to *"crucify the flesh"* (*Galatians 5:24*). "Flesh" is the Bible term for our nature of sin. It has to be put to death. That is why the Apostle Paul said that he *"died daily"* (*1 Corinthians 15:31*). Jesus said that we have to *"daily pick up the cross and follow after Him"* (*Luke 9:23*).

To continue means that we know those places that we go that trigger our addictions. Whether our addiction is worry or crack, there is a place that we go that triggers that addiction in us. What is that place? Where is that place? What pattern of thinking gets us moving in our addictions? What attitude moves us back to addictions? We identify those places and decide to not allow an occasion for the flesh (our nature of sin).

T -   Talking to others daily that share our goals.

Fellowship is a powerful key. God said of us that it is not good that we should dwell alone. He created us to need each other. We are not to be co-dependent, existing for the other person and aiding them in their addictions. But we are to be inter-dependent. We receive encouragement and insight from one another on a daily basis.

God tells us that we are to carry concern for each other "daily" and, in turn, find concerned help from His people on a daily basis.

"Besides everything else, I face daily the pressure of my concern for all the churches" (*2 Corinthians 11:28,* NIV).

"But encourage one another daily, as long as it is called 'Today,' so that none of you may be hardened by sin's deceitfulness" (Hebrews 3:13, NIV).

Fellowship is said to be *two or more fellows in the same ship.* The great thing about fellowship is that we are all in the same boat. We have all sinned. We have all failed. We are all dealing with addictions of one kind or another. We are all needing God's mercy and grace each day to continue. So we can all encourage each other in this work. We have a sponsor/accountability partner, meetings that we can attend, or a church that we can become involved in. We can continue with people by staying close to them, praying and studying God's Word.

Some don't want to do this because they can't find the perfect church, meeting, sponsor/accountability partner, or prayer/Bible Study group. There is no such thing. We can still glean much if we are willing. We will continue the word "CONTINUED" in chapter 38.

Dear Lord,

As I continue on this journey, help me to remain humble and poor in spirit. Help me to remember that I am only a step away from stumbling at any moment. Keep me close to You. Let me see the deceitfulness of sin when it tries to consume me with selfishness, pride, and fear. Help me to see You clearly each and every day. You are the light of my salvation. In You will I trust!

In Jesus' Name,

Amen.

Putting it to Work

Answer the following questions in writing and then discuss them with your sponsor/accountability partner.

1. How does the moral of the story in the Tortoise and the hair relate to you?

_____

_____

_____

_____

_____

2. Name some common distractions that keep your addictions operative and how you can better handle them today with the keys given in this chapter.

_____

_____

_____

_____

_____

3. In the acrostic given in this chapter, O stands for "open to correction from God and others." Describe the heart and attitude needed to accomplish this.

_____

_____

_____

_____

_____

4. Discuss with your sponsor how he/she can best help you to continue in keeping on and up with this program of recovery.

_____

_____

_____

_____

_____

Restoring Broken People

Step 10 - We continued to take personal inventory and when we were wrong, promptly admitted it.

"So be careful. If you are thinking, "Oh, I would never behave like that"-let this be a warning to you. For you too may fall into sin" (*1 Corinthians 10:12,* TLB).

We are continuing on with the word "CONTINUED" from Chapter 38.

I - Investing time daily in prayer and Bible study.
We need fellowship with people who share our goals, but we also need personal time with God, alone. Jesus didn't die to give us a religion; *For the Son of Man came to save [make whole in body, soul, and spirit] that which was lost* (*Matthew 18:11,* NASB). He saved us so we could have a personal relationship with Him and to *daily draw near to Him.* (*James 4:8,* NIV). When we draw near to Him, He draws near to us. He wants us to hear what He is saying to us *by His Spirit in our hearts* (*John 14:17*). There is no substitute for spending time alone with God To continue, we have to find time daily to pray, study the Bible, and listen to what God is saying to us by His Spirit in our heart.

N - Navigating life with the leading of the Holy Spirit.
This time with God not only keeps us from falling back into our addictive behavior, it is the means of discovering God's plan for us. God does not write out the whole plan once and then send us on our way. He shows us our path one step at a time one day at a time. This is our inheritance in the Lord.

> *He shows us our path one step at a time, one day at a time. This is our inheritance in the Lord.*

"For all who are led by the Spirit of God are sons of God"
(*Romans 8:14,* ESV).
"But if you are led by the Spirit, you are not under the law"
(*Galatians 5:18*).

God says that He will lead us by His Spirit and that even the difficult and hard times of life will be His tools to help us know the path. The Holy Spirit leads us through all of the dark and difficult days.

"I now rejoice, not that you were made sorrowful, but that you were made sorrowful to the point of repentance; for you were made sorrowful according to the will of God, so that you might not suffer loss in anything through us" (*2 Corinthians 7:9,* NASB)

"Even though I walk through the valley of the shadow of death, I will fear no evil; for you are with me; your rod and your staff, they comfort me"(*Psalm 23:4,* ESV).

U - Understand that God has new lessons for us.

Each day God has something for us to learn. In every circumstance God wants us to see new things. Continuing means that we are staying alert to those lessons and that everything we do is an opportunity for the Holy Spirit to teach us something new. We call the Holy Spirit the Comforter. Comforter means helper, advocate, but it also means teacher. He is our teacher, always wanting us to learn something new about life, God, others, and ourselves. Jesus said the Holy Spirit would guide us into all truth (*John 16:13-14*). He helps us to understand God's love and mercy. He gives us a better understanding of God's ways and how we can prosper in Him. We need to start each day saying to the Lord that we want to hear what He has to say and to learn what He has to teach us.

E - Existing to share God's love with others.

So what is our purpose in life? The Apostle Paul *said that for him to die in Christ was gain* (*Philippians 1:21*). Heaven is a real place and the things that God has prepared for us are so awesome that the blessings of this life cannot compare. Paul had a glimpse of that and knew that death in Christ was a graduation to better things. He was not morbid and depressed. He was full of faith and hope.

However, Paul understood that God has appointed certain days for us to live in this world for His purpose. What did Paul say that purpose is? Two things:

1. *"To live is Christ"* (Philippians 1:21)
2. *"To help others know Christ and to grow in Christ"* (Philippians 1:23-26)

Continuing means that we recognize our true purpose in God. That, like Paul, we live for Christ; that is to please Him and to know Him better. We live to complete our assignment of helping others to know Christ and to grow in Him. That is not just for Apostles and Pastors, it is the call of every human being. *We are to live to know Him and to make Him known* (*Philippians 3:10*).

D - Dealing with our issues daily.

Continuing means that we do not allow our stuff to pile up. When I was kid I was not disciplined to keep my space clean. I used to come in at night and undress, leaving my clothes lay where they landed. Then I would get up the next day and let them stay there and start with another outfit. After a few weeks of that kind of living, my room was a big mess. Mom used to make me clean it when it got too bad. Wow! That became a great dilemma! It was overwhelming. I would cry, throw a fit, and tell my mom how mean she was. I felt like the world was coming to an end because the pile of stuff was so big.

As an adult I have learned to make my bed every morning before I put my feet on the floor. I have learned to hang my clothes up or put them in the laundry when I take them off. I have learned to clean up each mess as I go along the way. It is so much easier to deal with life that way. If we keep it cleaned as we go, then we are ready to take on unexpected visits. The other night a couple came to the door unexpectedly. I was so glad the house was clean and in order. I didn't have to feel embarrassed over piles of messes.

God wants us to look at our hearts daily and deal with the stuff so we can have a sense of His righteousness in our hearts. He wants to help us to stay clean so we can be ready for the unexpected. He wants to keep us healthy and mentally full of life and joy. So, He works with us to daily keep our heart and mind clean. *1 John 1:7* says if we walk in the light as He is the light we have fellowship with God and each other.

Prayer:

Dear Lord,
Thank you for finishing Your course. You completed the mission. By Your work, I am saved from my sins. You are my hope of salvation. Help me to continue in my journey until I finish the course.

In Jesus' Name, Amen.

Putting it to Work

Please answer the following questions in writing then discuss them with you sponsor/accountability partner.

1.   Have you ever had a relapse in your journey? Please describe it and what the circumstances were that led up to it.

_____

_____

_____

_____

_____

2.   How did you feel about yourself when you experienced a relapse?

_____

_____

_____

_____

3.   What are the triggers that lead you back to your addictions?

_____

_____

_____

_____

4.   What can you do to keep from going to the place of relapse?

_____

_____

_____

_____

Step 10 - We continued to take personal inventory and when we were wrong, promptly admitted it.

"So be careful. If you are thinking, 'Oh, I would never behave like that'- let this be a warning to you. For you too may fall into sin" (*1 Corinthians 10:12,* TLB).

Focus is everything. The old Chinese proverb says that if you *aim for nothing that is probably what you will hit.* It is good for us to want to help others. In order to help others we have to listen to them, focus on them, and work with their circumstances to help them improve. However, there is a danger in the effort of helping others. We can become self-righteous and forget that we still need to daily take personal inventory and continually correct our own shortcomings. The key is that we stay balanced which is the key to everything in life.

We, by nature, tend to run in extremes, especially those of us who are addictive personalities. It is our tendency to find a good thing, and then go overboard with it. An example is when I get a new outfit; I like it so much, that I tend to wear it everyday for a year. Wow! That is just not cool. But that is human nature. We need to learn balance. Wear a new outfit once. Get it cleaned and wait a while before wearing it again. That is balance!

In the Bible, the Apostle Paul found the need to correct the Apostle Peter. What a thought. The great Apostle Peter, who was the first General Overseer of the Church and a man who walked on water (with Jesus' help), needed to be corrected in his attitude and actions. That is just amazing. In *Galatians 2,* Paul tells us that Peter became a social snob, an elitist for a season. He said that Peter used to eat pork and beans (unclean according to Jewish custom) with the guys until some of the Jewish Christians from the church in Jerusalem showed up. Then Peter was too embarrassed and feared their rejection, so he separated from the brothers and no longer would fellowship with them. Paul said that he corrected Peter, face-to-face. He didn't go behind Peter's back and talk about him creating a faction. He went to Peter and they talked about it. Apparently Peter recognized his wrong and they were reconciled. Peter grew through the experience and the church as a whole learned a great lesson about prejudice and love.

But the Apostle Paul said that he did not have any righteousness of his own, but that *he was crucified in Christ and that the life he lived was by the faith that he had in Jesus Christ* (*Galatians 2:20*). Balance! Paul understood his need to help someone else, but at the same time saw that his own inconsistencies were ever with him and that he needed to pay attention to his own stuff and keep things right between the Lord and him. We help others, but we have to take a good look at ourselves everyday.

So, even though we have made it this far and we want to help others, we keep our inventory sheets close at hand. Each day we stand before the Lord and ask the Holy Spirit to search our hearts and to see if there be any unclean way in us. We study the Bible and ask the Lord to show us from His Word those things that are not pleasing to Him and that we need to change. We continue to be aware that we are a work in progress, not a finished incorruptible product. At least we are not yet.

The older I get, the more that I realize that keeping Rod Buzzard right is a fulltime job. For some reason, I have to keep working on being more like Jesus every day. I have to take it all personally.

So how do we keep it **"PERSONAL"**?

P -	Prioritize God's Principles in His Word
E -	Evaluate daily events and responses letting God teach us what He wants us to learn
R -	Respond to the Holy Spirit when He leads us or corrects us
S -	Stand on God's Word not our feelings or circumstances
O -	Offer ourselves daily as a living sacrifice unto God
N -	Notice the good that others do and give God and others the credit
A -	Analyze others and recognize our own shortcomings
L -	Let God's Word saturate our thoughts and feelings every day, first thing in the morning.

P - Prioritize God's Principles in His Word

The Bible is more than just a good book or a collection of good or religious sayings. The Bible is a book that lives and breathes. It is God's Word that He has spoken to us. When we read it, think about it, and live by it, life comes into us. We receive power and wisdom from God through His Word. It fills us with joy and peace that comes from knowing God and His love for us. Without this power, we cannot continue on. That is why Dr. Bob and Bill Wilson, founders of AA and authors of the 12 Steps, said that they understood they needed a power greater than themselves to stay sober and not to become abusive dry drunks (more in-depth study in Chap 44). Listen to what God tells us about His Word.

We Live by God's Word

"But he answered, 'It is written, Man shall not live by bread alone, but by every word that comes from the mouth of God.'" (*Matthew 4:4,* ESV).

We receive healing and deliverance by God's Word

"The centurion answered and said, 'Lord, I am not worthy that You should come under my roof. But only speak a word, and my servant will be healed'" (*Matthew 8:8*).

"When evening came, they brought to Him many who were demon-possessed; and He cast out the spirits with a word, and healed all who were ill" (*Matthew 8:16,* NASB).

We grow spiritually by hearing and understanding God's Word

"But he who received seed on the good ground is he who hears the word and understands it, who indeed bears fruit and produces: some a hundredfold, some sixty, some thirty" (*Matthew 13:23*).

We are corrected by God's Word

"And Peter remembered the saying of Jesus, "Before the rooster crows, you will deny me three times." And he went out and wept bitterly" (*Matthew 26:75,* ESV).

We are to share God's Word with Others

"And they went out and preached everywhere, while the Lord worked with them and confirmed the message by accompanying signs" (*Mark 16:20,* ESV).

We receive prosperity from God's Word

"Simon answered, 'Master, we've worked hard all night and haven't caught anything. But because you say so, I will let down the nets'" (*Luke 5:5,* NIV).

We see and understand God through His Word
Jesus is the living Word in human form. The Bible is God's written Word given to us to connect with Him. Studying His Word gives us a revelation of who and what He is. We understand His character, which is love. We become acquainted with His promises which are yes and amen in Him. God wants to hear and answer our prayers. He will keep every promise to us.

"In the beginning was the Word, and the Word was with God, and the Word was God" (*John 1:1*).

"And the Word became flesh and dwelt among us, and we beheld His glory, the glory as of the only begotten of the Father, full of grace and truth" (*John 1:14*).

We receive eternal life through believing His Word
"Most assuredly, I say to you, he who hears My word and believes in Him who sent Me has everlasting life, and shall not come into judgment, but has passed from death into life" (*John 5:24*).

"But you do not have His word abiding in you, because whom He sent, Him you do not believe" (*John 5:38*).

"having been born again, not of corruptible seed but incorruptible, through the word of God which lives and abides forever," (*1 Peter 1:23*).

We become His disciples by abiding in His Word
"Then Jesus said to those Jews who believed Him, 'If you abide in My word, you are My disciples indeed'" (*John 8:31*).

"Jesus answered and said to him, 'If anyone loves Me, he will keep My word; and My Father will love him, and We will come to him and make Our home with him'" (*John 14:23*).

"He who does not love Me does not keep My words; and the word which you hear is not Mine but the Father's who sent Me" (*John 14:24*).

We are made clean by His Word
"You are already clean because of the word which I have spoken to you" (*John 15:3*).

"Sanctify them by Your truth. Your word is truth" (*John 17:17*).

"I do not pray for these alone, but also for those who will believe in Me through their word;" (*John 17:20*).

"that He might sanctify and cleanse her with the washing of water by the word," (*Ephesians 5:26*).

We receive faith by hearing His Word

"So then faith comes by hearing, and hearing by the word of God" (*Romans 10:17*).

"that is, that God was in Christ reconciling the world to Himself, not imputing their trespasses to them, and has committed to us the word of reconciliation" (*2 Corinthians 5:19*).

"In Him you also trusted, after you heard the word of truth, the gospel of your salvation; in whom also, having believed, you were sealed with the Holy Spirit of promise," (*Ephesians 1:13*).

We stand firm on His Word

"And take the helmet of salvation, and the sword of the Spirit, which is the word of God;" (*Ephesians 6:17*).

"who being the brightness of His glory and the express image of His person, and upholding all things by the word of His power, when He had by Himself purged our sins, sat down at the right hand of the Majesty on high" (*Hebrews 1:3*).

"For the word of God is living and powerful, and sharper than any two-edged sword, piercing even to the division of soul and spirit, and of joints and marrow, and is a discerner of the thoughts and intents of the heart" (*Hebrews 4:12*).

"By faith we understand that the worlds were framed by the word of God, so that the things which are seen were not made of things which are visible" (*Hebrews 11:3*).

"But be doers of the word, and not hearers only, deceiving yourselves" (*James 1:22*).

"For if anyone is a hearer of the word and not a doer, he is like a man observing his natural face in a mirror;" (*James 1:23*).

"But the word of the LORD endures forever. Now this is the word which by the gospel was preached to you" (*1 Peter 1:25*).

"as newborn babes, desire the pure milk of the word, that you may grow thereby," (*1 Peter 2:2*).

"He was clothed with a robe dipped in blood, and His name is called The Word of God" (*Revelation 19:13*).

Let me encourage you to read, study, and memorize several or all of the above scriptures. They teach us that God's Word lives and will change us from the inside out. Hearing, understanding, applying, speaking, and living God's Word is the key to overcoming all the temptations of life.

We will continue the thoughts on PERSONAL in the next chapter. To keep it PERSONAL, we have to prioritize God's Word in our hearts and lives. We make it our routine to always be in a Bible Study, to keep notes of the things that God is teaching us from the Word, and to memorize His Word. It will change our thinking and our thinking determines who and what we are as a person. *As a man thinks, so is he (Proverbs 23:7).*

Prayer:

Dear Lord,

Thank you for Your Word. Thank you for keeping Your promises. You are so faithful and dependable. Help me to hide Your word in my heart that I might not sin against You. Help me to study Your word that it might be a lamp unto my feet.

In Jesus' Name, Amen.

Putting it to Work

Answer the following questions in writing and then discuss them with your sponsor/accountability partner.

1.   Why is keeping a balance in all we think and do so important especially when we are attempting to help others with their addictions?

_____
_____
_____
_____
_____

2. According to Dr. Bob and Bill Wilson how can we avoid becoming dry drunks (defined more in Chap 44)?

_____
_____
_____
_____
_____

3.   Name some of the blessings you have received from the Lord since you began this study?

_____
_____
_____
_____
_____

4.   How do you overcome the temptations of life and backsliding into your addiction as stated in the last two paragraphs of this lesson?

_____
_____
_____
_____
_____

Step 10 - We continued to take personal inventory and when we were wrong, promptly admitted it.

"So be careful. If you are thinking, 'Oh, I would never behave like that'- let this be a warning to you. For you too may fall into sin" (*1 Corinthians 10:12*, TLB).

We are continuing with our thoughts on PERSONAL.

E - **Evaluate** daily events and our responses to them, letting God teach us what He wants us to learn

When Samuel was a boy, he was awakened three times hearing a voice calling his name. After going to his spiritual father Eli, Eli realized that the Lord wanted to speak to young Samuel. So Eli said the next time you hear the voice say, *"Speak Lord for your servant hears"* and let God speak to you (*1 Samuel 3:9*). So Samuel did and God began speaking to him.

This little story reminds us that God wants to speak to us. He wants to let us know how we should feel about the events of our day and what He is doing in and through those events. He wants us to respond to Him and follow His voice leading us. As we do, He unfolds His plan to us. He teaches us.

Daily time in His presence, allowing Him to speak to us, gives us the reflection that we need to make each day count. He will direct us to new scriptures and new understandings of His Word.

R - **Respond** to the Holy Spirit when He leads us or corrects us.

God is always speaking. The question is: are we listening? The Lord wants us to be in a continual flow of communion with Him. This is where our wisdom, strength, joy, and understanding come from. Jesus said that the Holy Spirit would be a fountain springing up inside of us. He is a well of water that refreshes us daily and a river that flows through us (*John 4:10-14; 7:38*).

Responding to the Holy Spirit is the key. The Holy Spirit can and will tell us and show us the way, but we have to make the choice to walk in that way. So not only do we take the time to listen, but we make the decision to respond by saying to the Holy Spirit "Yes." It may be that He tells us to change our attitude or to wear different clothes. He may tell us to call someone to encourage him or her or to be in a certain place at a certain time so He can bring someone into our life that will be a blessing or that we are to bless. The Spirit led life is an exciting one.

I heard a missionary speak of a young man who felt called to the mission field. He didn't have any money or support. But the Lord told him to go to South America on a certain day. So, he showed up and stood in line. While standing in line a woman turned to him and said, "Where are you going?" He told her where and why. She said, "The Lord spoke to me to come here today and to buy a ticket for a young man who is going to South America for missions work. You must be him."

The Spirit led life is exciting and filled with God showing up on time and in the right way. Staying focused on Him in our lives keeps us PERSONAL in the walk of Restoration.

S - **Stand** on God's Word not our feelings or circumstances

Our feelings can change so easily. Everything from hormones to the weather conditions can affect them. Feelings are not a good gauge of what God is up to. In *1 Kings 19:11-18,* Elijah became very depressed when Israel didn't respond to God's call to put away idols and to serve Him. He felt like a failure and felt that he was all-alone in this call to serve God. But God showed up with Elijah. First there was a wind, then an earthquake, and then a fire. But God was not in those things. Then a still small voice came to Elijah. It was God. Sometimes we think God will show up in our circumstances and we live by our feelings. Instead we need to listen for the voice of God that comes to us through the Bible and the Holy Spirit. God told Elijah it wasn't as bad as he thought and that God still had a plan for Elijah.

We need to stand on God's Word. He says that, *"being confident of this, that he who began a good work in you will carry it on to completion until the day of Christ Jesus"* (*Philippians 1:6,* NIV). God is not done with us yet. He has a plan and a purpose for us. We need to resist our feelings and stand on His Word to stay PERSONAL in this Restoration.

O - **Offer** ourselves daily as a living sacrifice unto God

Romans 12:1 says that *God wants us to offer ourselves to Him as a living sacrifice.* God does not ask us to die literally for him. Yes there are those who do and will have to die rather than renounce the name of

Jesus, but God's plan for most of us is to live for Him. Living for Jesus always costs us something that is of value and worth to us. It may be our time or a special interest. It may be turning off the TV to spend time with Him in prayer and Bible Study. It may be to not absorb ourselves in our addiction.

Every day we have to make the decision to dedicate our lives to Jesus Christ. It will be reflected in our ambitions, goals, attitude, and life style. It is not seen in what we don't do, but it is seen in what we do. The more we live for Him, the more we find His power and wisdom resting on us. Are we living for Jesus today or do we have some other agenda going?

N - **Notice** the good that others do and give God and others the credit for the good things that happen.

Staying PERSONAL in our inventory will mean that we do all that we can to lift up the Lord and others. Some might say that isn't honest or if we don't promote ourselves, who will? It is always honest to give God the glory for any good thing. The Bible says that, *"all good gifts come from the Father of Lights." (James 1:17)*. It is always right to praise God for good things that happen and come our way. Noticing the good that others do encourages them. What we make happen for others, God will make happen for us *(Ephesians 6:8)*.

A - **Analyze** others and recognize our own shortcomings

In our attempt to help others, we have to be careful that our attitude is correct. Jesus taught that we should *"Judge not, that you be not judged" (Matthew 7:1, ESV)*. God tells us that we are inexcusable when we judge others because we are guilty of breaking the same law. *(Romans 2:1)*. It doesn't matter what the shortcoming is, it all breaks God's law. My sin may not be your sin, but we all have shortcomings. In this context, the word judge means to condemn. So it is not saying that we are not to help others discern how to grow and improve, but we need to watch our attitude that it remains humble and loving. We project support and care rather than impatient or boastful arrogance.

L - **Let** God's Word saturate our thoughts and feelings every day, starting first thing in the morning.

Begin each day in God's Word. Before TV, conversations, rushing off to school or work, take time to get into the Bible. We benefit when we have a Bible study program to follow. I try to read through the Bible every year. It only takes about 15-25 minutes of reading time a day, but it keeps my mind thinking and flowing in the Word of God.

Listening to Christian speakers, teachers, and music all helps to keep us growing personally. This journey is not just for the first year that you get free of your addictions, but it is a pattern for the rest of your life. *"But if we walk in the light as He is the light, and we have fellowship with one another, and the blood of Jesus Christ His Son cleanses us from all sin"* (*1 John 1:7*).

Prayer:

Dear Lord,

Thank You for being so patient with me. It is my desire to stay on track. So, help me to see those things that I need to work on. Let each day be a day of growing closer to You and getting to know You better.

In Jesus' Name, Amen.

Chapter Forty-One ~ Personal 2

Putting it to Work

Please answer the following questions and then discuss them with your sponsor/accountability partner.

1.   When was the last time that you took a personal inventory? How often do you take personal inventory?

_____
_____
_____
_____
_____

2.   What do you believe that God is speaking to you that you need to work on?

_____
_____
_____
_____
_____

3.   What plans of action do you have or want to put in place to address the issues?

_____
_____
_____
_____
_____

4.   How do you see your spiritual growth going over the last six months?

_____
_____
_____
_____
_____

Restoring Broken People

Step 11 - We sought through prayer and meditation to improve our conscious contact with God, praying only for knowledge of His will for us and power to carry that out.

"Let the word of Christ richly dwell within you, with all wisdom teaching and admonishing one another with psalms and hymns and spiritual songs, singing with thankfulness in your hearts to God" (*Colossians 3:16*, NASB).

12 Keys to Prayer- *Matthew 6:5-15*

This step reminds us of prayer and its importance in our lives. God has made many wonderful promises to us, but they are conditioned on prayer. Jesus taught, *"'So I say to you: Ask and it will be given to you; seek and you will find; knock and the door will be opened to you'"* (*Luke 11:9*, NIV). That is in the present continuous tense in the Greek. It literally says to ask and keep asking; seek and keep seeking; knock and keep knocking. God wants us to live a life of prayer relating to Him; trusting Him for all of our needs. In His Sermon on the Mount, Jesus gave us 12 Keys to Prayer.

1.   Right Motives (verse 5) - God does not look on the outward appearance, but the heart. We can't fool God. He knows what we are thinking, feeling, and just why we say and do what we do. God is more interested in our heart than anything else. He knows our motives better than we do. We need to ask Him to show us where our heart is wrong and to help us get it right and keep it right. It will bring God's blessings of answered prayer on us.

2.   Real Faith (verse 6) - Real faith is a knowing that God is real and that He is the One who hears and answers our prayers. *"Now faith is the assurance of things hoped for, the conviction of things not seen. For by it the men of old received divine approval"* (*Hebrews 11:1-2*, NASB). We can commit our request to Him and trust Him to take care of it. Some use prayer as a means to get someone else's sympathy by making sure they hear the prayer, but instead we need to look to God to meet the need.

3.   Refuse to be Religious (verses 7-8) - Tradition and formulas do not impress God. God really doesn't care about the words and the form. He just wants us to have a genuine relationship with Him. Talk to Him like you would any friend. He will be there to help you.

4.   Relate to God as your Father (verse 9a) - The role of a father is to provide, protect, and to lead. Fathers do that out of love for their own. God wants us to know that, as our Creator, He loves us and wants to be Our Father. When we cry, *"Abba! Father!"* (affectionate term meaning Daddy), *it is the Spirit himself bearing witness with our spirit that we are children of God, and if children, then heirs, heirs of God and fellow heirs with Christ. (Romans 8:16-17).* The One who provides, protects, and leads us in every situation is committed to us as a Father. He will not leave us. We may leave Him, but He doesn't leave us. When we do leave Him, He still loves us and wants us to return to Him. We pray to Him as our Father, the Father of all who seek and know Him.

5.   Recognize the Greatness of Your Source (verse 9b) - *"In Heaven"* When we pray, we are tapping in to a resource that is greater than Wall Street, Washington, all the tea in China, or all the gold in S. Africa. Heaven is so rich that they use gold for pavement on the streets. We can't even imagine what God has available for us in Heaven. The Bible says that eye has not seen and ear has not heard the things that God has prepared for those who love Him. There is no limit to His resources. When we pray to God, we tap into His resources and He provides for our needs. Our needs are nothing to Him. He can take care of it. No problem!

6.   Reverence God's Character (verse 9c) - *"Hallowed be Your Name"* God's name reflects His character. God is so awesome that there is not just a single word that can describe Him, so God has many names in the Bible. I won't give all here, but for example He is: Almighty God, All-knowing God, The Lord who sees and provides, The Lord our Righteousness, The Lord our Healer... and many more. He is holy, pure love, goodness, and righteousness. There is none like Him. We need to trust Him and worship Him when we pray. We need to yield to Him because He is holy and good. We can trust Him because He doesn't have false motives. He is the Truth and when we know Him He sets us free.

7.   Refocus on the Big Picture (verse 10a) - *"Your Kingdom Come"* The promise that He would come again and set up His Kingdom on Earth - the phrase is on Earth, not in Earth. We are to pray for God's plan and purpose for this planet to be restored to this place ASAP. The Lord is coming again and He is the answer to all that ails the world - economically, socially, emotionally, healthfully, and politically. The big picture is that we are in a temporary world soon to be replaced by His

Perfect Kingdom. *"Because the creation itself will be set free from its bondage to decay and obtain the glorious liberty of the children of God We know that the whole creation has been groaning in travail together until now;" (Romans 8:21-22).* We need to pray that God will show us how we fit into His greater plan for this planet. For every season in history - God has a plan. In this time, we need to pray that God will show us how He is moving on the earth and how He wants to use us to accomplish His plan. We can't minimize what we do. Remember that every step that we take and every person that we influence is like a ripple in a pond. The event may seem small, but in time the impact touches the total area of the pond. Staying focused on God's will and doing what He shows us to do is more important than anything can we pray for.

8.   Roll off your burdens on the Lord (verse 11) - Cast your cares on Him for He cares for you. Be grateful that He has provided what you need today. He will be there tomorrow for you. God is aware of what is happening to us. He cares and has already made a way for us. Nothing escapes His attention. Don't be filled with anxious thoughts and feelings. Instead when you feel those feelings roll them off on the Lord. We were not created to carry those cares. Give them to the Lord. One of my favorite passages says, *"From the end of the earth I will cry to You, when my heart is overwhelmed; lead me to the rock that is higher than I. For You have been a shelter for me, a strong tower from the enemy" (Psalm 61:2-3).*

God told us to be anxious for nothing. Now that seems like a ridiculous thing to say but if we study it closely we can see that God has a plan to keep us mentally sound. In *Philippians 4:6,* God says, *"to not be anxious for anything but to pray about everything.* Look at how it works:

In Everything	Whatever happens and in every need
With Supplication	Leaving it in God's lap at His throne
And Thanksgiving	With an expectation that He has heard and will take care of it
Make your requests to God	Don't fret, but pray and God will fill you with an awesome peace that will be like a garrison of soldiers guarding your mind from harmful and disturbing thoughts that make you mentally unsound.

Putting it to Work

Answer the following questions in writing and then discuss them with your sponsor/accountability partner.

1.   Have you ever had any hang ups about prayer? Please describe them.

_____

_____

_____

_____

_____

2.   Describe an answer to prayer and how it made you feel.

_____

_____

_____

_____

3.   When you pray, do you ever feel as though you can sense God and hear Him speaking to you? Please describe.

_____

_____

_____

_____

4.   What is your most pressing / greatest prayer request at this time?

_____

_____

_____

_____

Step 11 - We sought through prayer and meditation to improve our conscious contact with God, praying only for knowledge of His will for us and power to carry that out.

"Let the word of Christ richly dwell within you, with all wisdom teaching and admonishing one another with psalms and hymns and spiritual songs, singing with thankfulness in your hearts to God" (*Colossians 3:16*, NASB).

12 Keys to Prayer Continued - *Matthew 6:5-15* (Points 9-12)

9.   Receive God's Mercy (verse 12a) - Mercy is another word for forgiveness. Praying with a sense of being forgiven gives us a sense of freedom in approaching God for our needs. We are told to *"come boldly before the throne of grace to receive help in the time of need"* (*Hebrews 4:16*). The word "boldly" means to come with a sense of confidence and without a fear of being rejected. Have you ever had to ask a favor from someone that you feared would not only say no, but would also ridicule you in the process. God says that He will not do that to you. God says we can come boldly to Him. We come to the throne of grace. We don't come with boldness because we are so deserving and have done nothing wrong, but because God has forgiven us in Christ and wants to favor us. He is gracious and has put His anger for our sins onto Christ. They were nailed to the cross and they are dead, gone, and forgotten in God's mind.

Jesus ascended into Heaven and sits at the right hand of the Father as our High Priest. In the Old Testament, it was the High Priest that would actually go into God's Presence in the Temple once a year to receive forgiveness for the sins of the nation of Israel. Now Jesus, as our High Priest, continually sits in the Presence of the Father and constantly receives forgiveness for all of us who are the citizens of Heaven. It is so good to know that our High Priest understands our weakness and temptation because He was also tempted as we are. He is not interested in putting us down, but in lifting us up. He is a loving and sympathetic High Priest who likes it when we bring our confessions to Him. He instantly obtains forgiveness for us, and Heaven's records of our wrongs are immediately wiped clean. We can feel confident to come to Him in this loving and gracious atmosphere.

We can come boldly because God forgave us already for all of our sins. He provided the payment for by laying them on Jesus. *Hebrews 10:14* says that, *"by a single offering he has perfected for all time those who are being sanctified"* (ESV). He gave His sinless life as a sacrifice for our sins. Now all we have to do is acknowledge our sin and receive His forgiveness. Living in a sense of humility, forgiveness, and God's acceptance of us is the key to inner peace and life flowing from God. Satan tries to keep us separated from God by attacking us and accusing us for our shortcomings. Satan attacked the High Priest named Joshua because his clothes were filthy. But God rebuked Satan and gave Joshua clean clothes (*Zechariah 3:1-5*).

That is what God does for us. We all have sinned and have to fight against its nature every day. But God has had mercy on us. His mercies endure forever. He has cast our sins into the depths of the sea; never to be remembered against us again. Resist the devil. Tell satan that you no longer accept that condemnation because Jesus paid the price. If the debt is paid, it is no longer a debt. God does not want us to dwell in the remorse, but to confess it and then receive His forgiveness and cleansing of our unrighteousness. He wants us to walk through each day free of guilt and shame. He wants us to walk in an awareness of His presence, love, and acceptance.

10.   Release hurts and offenses (verse 12b) - Just as God has forgiven us, we must forgive those who hurt us. Hurt and bitterness is a cancer that will eat us up. Hurt and bitterness is Satan's snare to keep us under his control. Forgiving others is for us, not just for them. Just as Jesus said on the cross, *"Father forgive them"* so we need to pity those who hurt us and forgive them. Hurting people hurt people. We need to ask God to forgive them, heal them, and help them. It will keep us free and release God to bless us and deal with them.

11.   Resist the enemy (verse 13a) - The KJV Bible says deliver us from evil, but in the original it actually says deliver us from the "evil one." This is correctly reflected in the New International Version. In *Ephesians 6* we are told that we don't war against other people, but against spirit beings that want to disrupt God's Kingdom and resist us. Satan and his co-workers are our real enemies. Jesus gave us the keys to the Kingdom and we have power and authority over them. When we resist Satan, he and his demons flee from us. This power is exercised in prayer. Asking the Lord to make us aware of Satan's schemes and temptation and binding his works is a key to prayer.

12. **Reveal God's glory in your life** (verse 13b) - God says that He will not share His glory with any part of His creation. He deserves all the glory because He created us and redeemed us. It is His goodness that works in and through us. Any good that come through us is His goodness at work in us. So He deserves all the glory. Our focus should be to bring glory to God in everything that we say and do. A key to prayer is that we live and do all to God's glory.

I found the following passage in the translation called The Message. I thought the way translators expressed what we call the Lord's Prayer was just awesome. I trust that it is a blessing. God bless you.

Matthew 6:5-15

5."And when you come before God, don't turn that into a theatrical production either. All these people making a regular show out of their prayers, hoping for stardom! Do you think God sits in a box seat?

6."Here's what I want you to do: Find a quiet, secluded place so you won't be tempted to role-play before God. Just be there as simply and honestly as you can manage. The focus will shift from you to God, and you will begin to sense his grace.

7."The world is full of so-called prayer warriors who are prayer-ignorant. They're full of formulas and programs and advice, peddling techniques for getting what you want from God.

8. Don't fall for that nonsense. This is your Father you are dealing with, and he knows better than you what you need.

9. With a God like this loving you, you can pray very simply. Like this: Our Father in heaven, reveal who you are.

10. Set the world right; Do what's best - as above, so below.

11. Keep us alive with three square meals.

12. Keep us forgiven with you and forgiving others.

13. Keep us safe from ourselves and the Devil. You're in charge! You can do anything you want! You're ablaze in beauty! Yes. Yes. Yes.

14. "In prayer there is a connection between what God does and what you do. You can't get forgiveness from God, for instance, without also forgiving others.

15. If you refuse to do your part, you cut yourself off from God's part.

Putting it to Work

Please answer the following questions in writing then discuss them with your sponsor/accountability partner.

1.   Have you ever felt so guilty that you did not feel worthy to pray? Please describe.

_____

_____

_____

_____

_____

2.   Did you find peace and a sense of acceptance in God? Please describe how that felt?

_____

_____

_____

_____

_____

3.   Do you find time to pray daily? Please describe how that works best for you.

_____

_____

_____

_____

_____

4.   What can you do to increase your prayer life?

_____

_____

_____

_____

Step 11 - We sought through prayer and meditation to improve our conscious contact with God, praying only for knowledge of His will for us and power to carry that out.

"Let the word of Christ richly dwell within you, with all wisdom teaching and admonishing one another with psalms and hymns and spiritual songs, singing with thankfulness in your hearts to God" (*Colossians 3:16*, NASB).

Psalm 1:1-6 says, "Blessed is the man who walks not in the counsel of the ungodly, nor stands in the path of sinners, nor sits in the seat of the scornful; But his delight is in the law of the Lord, And in His law he meditates day and night. He shall be like a tree planted by the rivers of water, that brings forth its fruit in its season, whose leaf also shall not wither; And whatever he does shall prosper. The ungodly are not so, But are like the chaff which the wind drives away. Therefore the ungodly shall not stand in the judgment, nor sinners in the congregation of the righteous. For the Lord knows the way of the righteous, But the way of the ungodly shall perish."

Dr. Bob and Bill Wilson understood and developed the power of meditation. It is to be remembered that they came to these discoveries seeking sobriety by attending Christian Bible studies and prayer meetings through the Oxford Group. This was an independent Para-church movement of the 1920's that felt churches overemphasized tradition. These meetings were filled with a true quest to know God better and to get closer to Him on a daily basis. That quest and spiritual desire gave them the power they needed to stay sober. So, we are honoring their lives and discoveries by staying within the parameters in which they walked. They found that we all could find the power we need to overcome addictions by allowing God Almighty to fill us with His power and wisdom. As we turn our lives over to Him, He sets us free and keeps us from the traps of the world. So what is Christian MEDITATION? Let's take a look at this word.

In the chart below, we see there are two Hebrew words that are translated to mean, "meditate." These words form the Biblical basis of meditation.

| Hagah[27] | 1. to moan, growl, utter, muse, mutter, meditate, devise, plot, speak
    1. (Qal)
        1. to roar, growl, groan
        2. to utter, speak
        3. to meditate, devise, muse,
           imagine
    2. (Poal) to utter
    3. (Hiphil) to mutter |
| Siyach[28] | 1. to put forth, mediate, muse, commune, speak, complain, ponder, sing
    1. (Qal)
        1. to complain
        2. to muse, meditate upon, study, ponder
        3. to talk, sing, speak
    2. (Polel) to meditate, consider, put forth thoughts |

The picture of these words is that of a cow eating and digesting its cud. Cows have four stomachs to digest their cud. So they actually chew, regurgitate, and re-chew their cud several times in order to completely digest it. It is said that when a cow stops chewing its cud it is usually sick.

In the same, when we stop meditating on God's law of love we become sick. However, when we meditate on God's law we are blessed. We become like a tree planted by the rivers of waters whose leaf does not wither and who bears fruit in due season.

So what does it mean to MEDITATE?

Here is an acrostic to help us understand this idea.

M Memorization – Making it a part of your being
E Education – Musing over the truth
D Discipline – Being dedicated to study daily
I Inquiry – Asking God for help to understand
T Time spent with God – That says it all
A Attention – Giving God our focus and priority
T Transformation – Allowing it to truly change us
I Inspiration – Being moved by the truth
O Obedience - Doing what God says to do
N New fruit and life – Seeing God produce in us what we can't

M - Memorization – Making it a part of your being

In our last chapter we quoted the scripture *"As a man thinks so is he."* It bears repeating because at issue with all addictions is our thought life. We are born into this world with a clean slate. Then life begins to fill that slate with various experiences creating memories that give way to emotions, imaginations, and beliefs about how life will treat us in the future. Thinking creates who we are and how we will respond to life in the future. In AA, they use the term "stinkin-thinkin" to describe the cause of addictions. When our thinking is skewed due to our past experiences and training, we follow destructive patterns that lead us to our addictions. So, taking control of our thinking is a priority in this work of overcoming addictions.

Since memory forms the basis of our thought life, it is essential that we experi-ence and input positive things for our minds to draw on. Our negative or "stinkin-thinkin" led us into the world of addictions and our positive or good thinking can lead us out. In the book, *Emotional Intelligence,*[29] by Daniel Goleman, we learn that research has determined that IQ (Intelligence Quotient) does not determine the success of a person, but rather EQ (Emotional Quotient) determines a person's success in life. Researchers have found that though our emotional brain does control our initial

> *Our negative or "stinkin-thinkin" led us into the world of addictions and our positive or good thinking can lead us out.*

reactions (for about 2-3 seconds when a new event occurs), it is our reasoning brain that takes over which then determines how we evaluate that event. From this evaluation flows our action to the event. *The standard is to count to 10 before reacting.* Give your reasoning brain time to catch up with your emotional brain and let it take control. Speak from intelligence and reason rather than from emotion.

Memorization gives us an opportunity to introduce new patterns of thinking into our mind. If we walk around all day with thoughts of failure, hurt, pain, sadness, anger, and anxiety, then when something happens, that is how we will react. If we are filled with thoughts of God's love, power, presence, plan, promises, and faithfulness, then that is what will come out during those times of reaction.

A few months ago my pastor, Ken Lichter, taught a simple lesson on love from *1 Corinthians 13*. He handed out the definition of love from that chapter and asked the group to discuss it and then shared some thoughts. On the way home from that Bible study, the Lord spoke to me that I had never memorized those verses, and that if I was to become a more loving person, I needed to have those thoughts in my head constantly. I yielded to the Lord and began the work of memorizing – "*love is patient and kind; it does not envy or boast; it is not arrogant, it is not rude. It does not insist on its own way; it is not irritable or resentful; it does not rejoice at wrongdoing, but rejoices with the truth. Love bears all things, believes all things, hopes all things, endures all things*" (*1 Corinthians 13:4-7*, ESV). Wow! That felt so good to get those thoughts into my psyche.

Then I began to review it several times a day. When I was driving and had a few moments to think, I would think on those things. The more I did it, the more that I found my thinking, demeanor, and feelings were filled with the love of God. I still have to work on it every day because my nature is not to be loving, but when I make that effort love takes over and becomes my character.

God tells us in *Philippians 4:8 "Finally, brethren, whatever is true, whatever is honorable, whatever is right, whatever is pure, whatever is lovely, whatever is of good repute, if there is any excellence and if anything worthy of praise, dwell on these things"* (NASB*).* If we sit around thinking about the injustice of the world, the economy, the things people said or did, or why didn't we get better looks, talents, or opportunities, then we will be filled with strife, bitterness, anger, or depression. That is no way to live. It sets us up for "stinkin-thinkin" and for our addictions. But if we think on those things that God has said, that God has done, that God promises He will do for us and in us, then God honors our faith and we are filled with His peace. We feel so loved and accepted by God that we don't feel a need for our addictions. We will continue these thoughts in the next chapter.

Prayer:

Dear Lord,

You said that You would be with us until the end of this age. Thank You for always being with me. Help me to become more aware of Your presence. Let me hear You speaking to me by Your Holy Spirit, through the Bible, and through others.

In Jesus' Name,

Amen.

Putting it to Work

Please answer the following in writing and then discuss them with your sponsor/accountability partner.

1.   What is your idea of "meditation?"

_____

_____

_____

_____

_____

2.   Have you ever memorized any scriptures? Which ones and why?

_____

_____

_____

_____

3.   Do you feel that you have benefited from memorizing scriptures? Describe how?

_____

_____

_____

_____

_____

4.   What passages of scriptures would you like to memorize in the future?

_____

_____

_____

_____

_____

Step 11 - We sought through prayer and meditation to improve our conscious contact with God, praying only for knowledge of His will for us and power to carry that out.

"Let the word of Christ richly dwell within you, with all wisdom teaching and admonishing one another with psalms and hymns and spiritual songs, singing with thankfulness in your hearts to God" (*Colossians 3:16*, NASB).

    2 Corinthians 10:3-6 says, "The world is unprincipled. It's dog-eat-dog out there! The world doesn't fight fair. But we don't live or fight our battles that way - never have and never will. The tools of our trade aren't for marketing or manipulation, but they are for demolishing that entire massively corrupt culture. We use our powerful God-tools for smashing warped philosophies, tearing down barriers erected against the truth of God, fitting every loose thought and emotion and impulse into the structure of life shaped by Christ. Our tools are ready at hand for clearing the ground of every obstruction and building lives of obedience into maturity." (The Message).

    We are continuing the thoughts on "**MEDITATION.**" Meditation is memorization of God's Word and truth to make it a part of our daily thinking. We memorize so we have those good, true, noble, lovable, pure, and just thoughts floating around in our mind and filling our hearts. We don't just memorize it once then forget about it. We memorize it then remember it over and over again to keep it in our thinking as our standard of belief and response to life situations.

E - Education – Musing over the truth
    Meditation is not some practice of emptying our brain to let just anything occupy it. That is the basis of addictions. We don't like the effects of our thoughts, so we turn to addictions to get rid of our thoughts and feelings. That life leaves us empty, out of control, and open to Satan and his traps. It fills us with contempt, anger, and hatred for self and for others. It makes us destructive and unproductive.
    Meditation is a very purposeful effort to learn the truth and then to stay focused on it so that our hearts and lives are governed by that truth.

Education is also a part of meditation. By education we mean taking some classes from a Bible college or at our church. We mean that we attend Bible studies on a regular basis. We mean that we attend a local church and carry a Bible, notebooks, and pen so that we can studiously take notes. So we encourage you to find a church that teaches and speaks from the Bible as God's Word. We make going to church not only for worship and prayer, but we make it a time for education in God's Word. We meditate on the truth so we can be that person who is like the tree planted by the rivers of water whose leaf does not wither.

D - Discipline – Being dedicated to study daily

Jesus made disciples. We have all heard that from the Bible. He calls us to make disciples of Him. The word "discipline" comes from the word "disciple." Discipline is a prescribed way to follow certain guidelines with motivations built in to keep a person involved in following. A disciple is one who follows in the way. Jesus gave us a pattern or way that we should follow. *"He is the way, the truth and the life that lead to the Father in Heaven"* (*John 14:6*). When we receive Jesus Christ as our Lord and Savior, we have the truth living in us. We dedicate ourselves to following Him and being His disciples. To be disciplined, we must be diligent to follow the Lord and to practice what we know to be true in Christ. We don't just study and meditate for a season, but we study and meditate on Christ for a lifetime. *We daily pick up our cross and follow Him.* We pay the price everyday and stay in His Word following His will and plan for our lives.

I - Inquiry – Asking God for help to understand

God's Word interprets itself. It is not open for private interpretations. Listen to what God says about this: *"The main thing to keep in mind here is that no prophecy of Scripture is a matter of private opinion. And why? Because it's not something concocted in the human heart. Prophecy resulted when the Holy Spirit prompted men and women to speak God's Word"* (*2 Peter 1:20-21*, The Message).

When we go with our own interpretations we open ourselves to deception. Our own heart will deceive us. Satan and his demons will attempt to deceive us. So we need an anchor of truth that is not based on our whims and feelings, but is based on truth. Jesus said that the wise man built his house on the rock and when the storm came, that house

278

stood. But the foolish man built his house on the sand and when the storm came that house fell (*Matthew 7:24-29*). Both houses experienced a storm, but only the one built on the rock withstood the storm. Storms of life will come. We need to build our house (our mental life including our thoughts, emotions, and decisions) on the rock of Jesus Christ. Jesus said that His Words are the rock on which we are to build. When we do so we lay a firm foundation that will withstand every storm.

Meditation will involve our seeking out those who are educated in God's Word and experienced at living the Christian life and staying sober. We have to give up our "know it all" attitudes to meditate.

T -   Time spent with God – That says it all

Nothing can replace time spent with a person in the nurturing and development of a relationship. When a couple falls in love and marries, it is for the purpose of communing together. This is literally day and night. Yes, they may go to work for 8 or so hours a day, but for the marriage to be good and satisfying there has to be a connecting in conversation, love, and enjoyment of one another on a daily basis. It is no good when a couple drifts apart and just share a roof over their heads living separate lives. They need constant communion for their marriage to be satisfying.

The same is true of God and us. Jesus gave Himself to make for Himself a bride (the church). God wants to share life with us on a daily basis. That life is shared when we make time for God and put our focus on Him. The Psalmist said it this way: *"Be still, and know that I am God; I will be exalted among the nations, I will be exalted in the earth!"* (*Psalm 46:10*).

David understood that in a world that is ravaged with war, hatred, injustice, and a total disregard for God and His love, that we can stop and put things in perspective. God is still God. Relax and let your mind focus on God's greatness and goodness. Focus on the fact that He has everything under control. Focus on the fact that God is not threatened by the world and its chaos. Focus on the fact that God knows how it will end and that in the end God will cause all nations to come and worship at His feet in love and holiness. Then focus on the fact that God knows us, loves us, knows what we need, and has promised to take care of us. Meditate by being still and know that He is God.

Get into God's presence in prayer and Bible study. Spend time singing songs of worship to Him. This is good in groups, but do it on your own as well. What we do in a group is only as real as what we do on our own. If the only time I pray is with other people, then my prayers don't mean anything. That is just religion. My prayer life begins with what happens just between God and me. We spend time with Him getting to know Him personally and intimately. We don't just pray, but we spend time asking the Lord to speak to us.

There are many people that we are acquainted with, but there are some people that we are so close to that we know what they are thinking before they say it. That is how God wants us to know Him.

Prayer:

Dear Lord,

Help me to develop a hunger for Your Word. It is called milk and meat for our spiritual lives. Let me hunger and thirst for it even more than natural food.

In Jesus' Name,

Amen.

Putting it to Work

Please answer the following in writing and then discuss it with your sponsor/accountability partner.

1.   Have you ever taken a Bible class or attended a Bible study? Please describe.

_____

_____

_____

_____

_____

2.   How did you benefit or could you benefit from taking classes on Bible topics?

_____

_____

_____

_____

_____

3.   What is your favorite book and passage in the Bible? Describe how it has impacted your life.

_____

_____

_____

_____

_____

4.   Do you carry a Bible and notebook to church? Do you study your notes through the week? Does it or would it be a help to you?

_____

_____

_____

_____

Restoring Broken People

Step 11 - We sought through prayer and meditation to improve our conscious contact with God, praying only for knowledge of His will for us and power to carry that out.

"Let the word of Christ richly dwell within you, with all wisdom teaching and admonishing one another with psalms and hymns and spiritual songs, singing with thankfulness in your hearts to God" (*Colossians 3:16*, NASB).

Ephesian 1:17-23:
    "...that the God of our Lord Jesus Christ, the Father of glory, may give to you the spirit of wisdom and of revelation in the knowledge of him, having the eyes of your heart enlightened; that you may know what is the hope to which he has called you, what are the riches of his glorious inheritance in the saints, and what is the immeasurable greatness of his power toward us who believe, according to the working of his great might that he worked in Christ when he raised him from the dead and seated him at his right hand in the heavenly places, far above all rule and authority and power and dominion, and above every name that is named, not only in this age but also in the one to come. And he put all things under his feet and gave him as head over all things to the church, which is his body, the fullness of him who fills all in all" (ESV).

    God tells us that *when we draw near to Him He draws near to us* (*James 4:7*). God has a desire to fill us up with an understanding of who He is and of the spiritual truth. God wants us to see the victory that is ours as a free gift through Jesus Christ. God wants us to be able to operate in the power of the resurrection of Jesus Christ. God wants us to know *"that we truly can do all through Christ who strengthens us"* (*Philippians 4:13*). The Apostle Paul tells us that God will pour out on us a spirit of wisdom and revelation in the knowledge of Him.
    God cannot be known through education alone. In order for us to really know God we must have a "revelation" that comes from Him. In order to know Him better and to grow in Him we have to continually and regularly have a "revelation" of Him that comes from Him. When we meditate we position ourselves to receive that revelation from God. God says that *"eye has not seen and ear has not heard the things that He has*

prepared for us in Christ Jesus" (1 Corinthians 2:9). So God wants to show them to us by the work of the Holy Spirit in us.

A - Attention – Giving God our focus and priority

In order to meditate we have to concentrate on God, His Word, His voice, and His will for our lives. Focus is everything in life. In order to hit a target we have to focus. I have learned in playing golf that I have to see the target in my mind when I hit the ball. My eye is on the ball to hit it square, but my target is in my mind to move the ball in the right direction.

That is how it is in God. We have to have our eyes on this life, in this world to take the steps we are to take, but we have to have our Heavenly target in mind to move ourselves in the right direction. Meditation brings our mind into contact with God. He is our goal. Knowing Him and being like Him is our goal. Making Him known to others is our goal. So while we are eating, working, playing, and living in this world, our mind needs to be filled with an awareness of His presence and knowledge of His will in order for us to move and act in the way that He wants us to go.

T - Transformation – Allowing it to truly change us

God tells us *"not to be conformed to this world but to be transformed by the renewing of our minds" (Romans 12:2).* The word "transform" comes from the Greek word that means "metamorphous." It is the idea of a caterpillar becoming a beautiful butterfly. That is what God says that meditating on His Word does for us. It transforms us into the image of His Son, Jesus Christ. Listen to how God says that looks in our lives.

"And we all, who with unveiled faces contemplate the Lord's glory, are being transformed into his image with ever-increasing glory, which comes from the Lord, who is the Spirit" (2 Corinthians 3:18, NIV).

The more time we spend with people, the more we take on their traits. Several years ago some of my Indiana friends moved to Tennessee. After a few years I met with them and noticed that they had picked up a Tennessee accent. It was cute and we joked about it. Living around and hanging out with people from that part of the country was rubbing off on them.

In the same way, our meditation on the Lord and His law of love rubs off on us. We become more like Him. As the passage says above, each time we meet with the Lord we receive more of His image on us. It becomes a part of our being and character. We are not transformed in a day, but over a lifetime one day at a time.

I - Inspiration – Being moved by the truth

Inspired means that we are moved upon by someone or something that results in becoming or doing something new or different. A writer may hear a story that inspires him or her to write a book or play. An artist may see a scene or object that inspires a painting, sculpture, etc.

The word "inspire" means to be "in the spirit of" something. In the Bible it is used of godly people being "in the Holy Spirit" and moved to do God's will and work. That is what happened in the writing of the Bible. *2 Timothy 3:16-17* reminds us that *"All Scripture is given by inspiration of God, and is profitable for doctrine, for reproof, for correction, for instruction in righteousness, that the man of God may be complete, thoroughly equipped for every good work."*

The Apostle Peter said that the Holy Men of old were moved upon by the Holy Spirit to write the Bible. They were inspirited to write God's Word. It is God's book and they were just the instruments that He used to write it.

God wants to use us as well. He does that by moving on us and filling us with knowledge of His will for our lives. He does that by giving us a vision and showing us the path that He wants us to walk. That happens as we commune with Him and meditate on Him. He does that by giving us an understanding of His Word. As we read, study, memorize and think on His Word, His Spirit moves on us to do the will of God. We are inspired.

O - Obedience - Doing what God says to do

It is one thing to mediate and get a glimpse of God, a greater understanding of Him and knowledge of His will. It is another to do what He shows us to do. King Saul and King David both heard from God and had a revelation of God's will, but Saul was rejected as the king and God said that David was a man after His own heart. What was the difference? Saul did not obey what God told him to do, but David did. David was yielded to the Lord and was interested in pleasing God more than anything or anyone else. Yes David made some big mistakes and had his days of failings, but at the end of the day he would repent and do the will of God. God told Saul, *"obedience is better than sacrifice"* (*1 Samuel 15:22*). So our religious acts and spirituality don't bring us blessing unless we sincerely put it to work in our lives. Hearing God and obeying God bring His wisdom and power on us.

N - New fruit and life – Seeing God produce in us what we can't
The product of MEDITATION is that we will be like a tree planted by the rivers of water whose leaf does not wither. God wants us to study Him and His love so that we can see *"the height, the depth, the width, and the length of His love"* (*Ephesians 3:18-19*). The result of seeing this is that *God will do exceedingly abundantly above all that we ask or think for us in our lives"* (*Ephesians 3:20*). We will prosper in Him. That is God's desire for us. He really loves us and wants to bless us. He says that when we meditate on Him and His law of love, that He will bless us way beyond our wildest dreams.

Prayer:

Dear Lord,

Today I draw close to You by spending time with You. Help me to be free of the distractions of this world that I might be more aware of You.

In Jesus' Name.

Amen.

Putting it to Work

Please answer the following in writing and then discuss your answers with your sponsor/accountability partner.

1. What are some of the things that you have learned about God through meditation?

_____

_____

_____

_____

_____

2. What is the most important transformation that you have experienced by your meditating?

_____

_____

_____

_____

_____

3. Have you ever felt inspired by the Holy Spirit to do or change something in your life? How did that look?

_____

_____

_____

_____

_____

4. How has meditation benefited you in your desire to stay free from addictions?

_____

_____

_____

_____

Restoring Broken People

Chapter Forty-Seven ~ Experience

Step 12 - Having had a spiritual experience as the result of these steps, we try to carry this message to others and to practice these principles in all our affairs.

"Dear brothers, if a Christian is overcome by some sin, you who are godly should gently and humbly help him back onto the right path, remembering that next time it might be one of you who is in the wrong" (*Galatians 6:1*, TLB).

Freedom from addictions happens when we experience the Twelve Steps. The experience is a *spiritual journey* in God. This spiritual journey experience happens when we truly know and interact with God Himself through Jesus Christ. Theory, religion, and self-reform doesn't make it happen. A personal revelation of God from Him through prayer, Bible Study, and worship makes it happen. It is not riding on someone's coat tails that makes it happen. God does not have any grandchildren, only children. He meets with us personally, never indirectly. God tells us that there is only One Mediator between God and Man. That Mediator is Jesus Christ. He gave Himself to pay for all of our sins: past, present, and future; and now offers us a personal relationship with God through His blood (*1 Timothy 2:5-6*).

Long distance relationships never satisfy. God did not wind up the universe and remove Himself from it leaving us on our own. He created the world and immediately entered into to it to have fellowship with us. *Genesis 3:7-8* tells us that God walked in the garden in the cool of the day to have fellowship with His creation and that He was looking for Adam and Eve so that He could hang out with them. When they hid themselves out of a sense of guilt and shame, which is the fear of being rejected, God persisted. God did not want separation. He wanted connection and communion and friendship.

Hebrews 13:8 says that *God has not changed*. He still desires friendship and communion with all of us. Figuratively we were all in Adam when God called out and God still calls out to us daily saying, "Where are you? I want to hang out with you today. I have things to discuss with you. Draw near to me and I will draw near to you" (*James 4:8*). He says that when we come to Him that He will never leave us nor forsake us (*Hebrews 13:5*). God says that we can look to Him daily to be our helper (*Hebrews 13:6*).

Experience means that real life happens between God and us. Positive thinking results, but alone does not cut it. When we experience God, positive thinking is a result. The more we experience God, the more positive we become in our thinking. We see God in His love, power, and faithfulness towards us. So we can be positive knowing that God is with us and that He will take care of us today and in whatever we will go through. God makes us positive thinkers.

DRY DRUNK

Have you ever met a "dry drunk?" What is that? A "dry drunk" is someone who is sober but they are mean as a "junk yard dog." They have achieved sobriety from drugs, alcohol, eating disorders, but have replaced it with unforgiveness and bitterness. They are proud and brutal people. This is not the goal of sobriety. God has something much better for us. He has a life that is filled with love, joy, peace, and a sense of God's righteousness and presence in our hearts. *Romans 14:17* says that, *"For the kingdom of God is not a matter of eating and drinking but of righteousness and peace and joy in the Holy Spirit"* (ESV). Sobriety alone does not cut it. God promises an abundant life that will fill our hearts and minds.

When we are negative in our thinking, we have *"stinkin-thinkin."* This kind of thinking leads us back to our addictions. Those *addictions* are our *idols* that we use to try to fill in the spot that is created for God to occupy. Instead of going back to our *addictions*, when we hear *"stinkin-(negative)-thinkin"* in our brain, we need to let it trigger us to get close to *God*. It means that we have wandered off and have lost the *sense of His Presence* that we need to be a fulfilled and happy person.

> *This kind of thinking ("stinkin-thinkin") leads us back to our addictions.*

A CLOSE LOOK AT OUR EXPERIENCE

In this step we need to take a close look at our experience. What are we experiencing? Is it just sobriety? Or have we really come into a spiritual experience with God? Do we really know God on a personal level, one on one? Are we getting to know God better every day? Is Jesus our best friend or just an acquaintance that we acknowledge as the Lord of the Universe? Is restoration and recovery just another religion or club, or has it resulted in a true personal relationship with the Lord that makes us aware of His presence in our lives every day. Do we possess *the joy of the Lord that is our strength*? (*Nehemiah 8:10*). Do we know what it is to roll our cares off on Him knowing that He cares for us? Do we walk in a sense of His peace in our hearts? Do we know what it is to be anxious for nothing because in everything that happens we make it a matter of prayer? With thanksgiving do we leave our worries in God's hands? Are we filled with His peace guarding our minds from destructive and stressful thoughts (*Philippians 4:6*)? What are we experiencing?

THE REAL THING THAT HELPS OTHERS

Before we can help others, we need to make sure that we have the *real thing*, not just sobriety or some form of positive thinking. We need to have a true spiritual experience with God. We need to make sure that we have been cleansed of our bitterness, unforgiveness, pride, strife, vengeful anger, jealousy, envy, lusts, and desire to control others.

So, it is time to thank God for what He has done for us and to do a check up. It is time to look at the map and see just where we are on this "spiritual journey." What is our experience? Do we have true sobriety or do we have a "dry drunk?" Do we truly experience God on a daily basis in our lives? Are we allowing Him to guide us and to have control of our hearts? Have we yielded our minds to Him believing that He causes all things to work together for our good, even the evil that others intend?

This is important because the Twelfth Step is graduation time to becoming the one who leads others to the spiritual experience that will give them the power to achieve true sobriety. We can only give to others what we have. If we have a cold, we give people a cold. If we have the flu, we give people the flu. So, what do we really have? Do we have a program that keeps us sober, or do we have a true spiritual experience with God through Jesus Christ that has made us into the person that God created us to be? What do we have? As we consider these questions, listen to what our Lord Jesus Christ says to us.

"And to the angel of the church in Laodicea write: 'The words of the Amen, the faithful and true witness, the beginning of God's creation. "'I know your works: you are neither cold nor hot. Would that you were either cold or hot! So, because you are lukewarm, and neither hot nor cold, I will spit you out of my mouth. For you say, I am rich, I have prospered, and I need nothing, not realizing that you are wretched,

pitiable, poor, blind, and naked. I counsel you to buy from me gold refined by fire, so that you may be rich, and white garments so that you may clothe yourself and the shame of your nakedness may not be seen, and salve to anoint your eyes, so that you may see. Those whom I love, I reprove and discipline, so be zealous and repent. Behold, I stand at the door and knock. If anyone hears my voice and opens the door, I will come in to him and eat with him, and he with me. The one who conquers, I will grant him to sit with me on my throne, as I also conquered and sat down with my Father on his throne. He who has an ear, let him hear what the Spirit says to the churches"' (*Revelation 3:14-22,* ESV).

Prayer:

Dear God,

Let me be aware of the "stinkin-thinkin" that would try to pull me back to the bondage of my addictions and compulsions. Help me to know when the "old person" wants to take control. Help me to remember that the "old me" makes my life confusing, miserable, and unmanageable. Help me to be alert to the enemy who wants to destroy me.

In Jesus' Name,

Amen.

Chapter Forty-Seven ~ Experience

Putting it to Work

Please answer the following in writing and then discuss your answers with your sponsor/accountability partner.

1.   Do you have a true spiritual experience with God through Jesus Christ as your Lord, Savior, and best friend? Please describe.

_____
_____
_____
_____
_____

2.   Where are you at in your spiritual journey with God? How does it look to you?

_____
_____
_____
_____
_____

3.   Do you daily experience a sense of God's presence and peace in your heart? How does that look?

_____
_____
_____
_____
_____

4.   How will your spiritual experience with God help you to help others?

_____
_____
_____
_____

Restoring Broken People

Chapter Forty-Eight ~ Message

Step 12 - Having had a spiritual experience as the result of these steps, we try to carry this message to others and to practice these principles in all our affairs.

"Dear brothers, if a Christian is overcome by some sin, you who are godly should gently and humbly help him back onto the right path, remembering that next time it might be one of you who is in the wrong" (*Galatians 6:1*, TLB).

This message defines our role from this point on. Once we possess sobriety through a true spiritual experience, once we experience a true relationship with God through Jesus Christ that gives us the power we need to be the person that God created us to be, we turn to sharing this with others. Jesus said to us freely you have received, now freely give.

"Heal the sick, raise the dead, cleanse those who have leprosy, drive out demons. Freely you have received; freely give" (Matthew 10:8, NIV).

Jesus said this to His disciples when He sent them out on their first ministry journey. He says the same to us today. He has given us the gift of His love, salvation, power to overcome, and a sense of His presence in our lives. All of it is free to us. But it is not just for us; it is for everyone. It is a gift of healing, cleansing, deliverance, and resurrection power. God came into our hearts and set us free from the bondage of addiction and the world's "stinkin-thinkin." He has made New Creations of us. He did not charge us. As a matter of fact, He paid for it with the blood of His own dear Son. He says now we have a debt to pay. We owe others who need the same thing. We need to carry this message to them as well. The Apostle Paul said it this way:

"I am obligated both to Greeks and non-Greeks, both to the wise and the foolish. That is why I am so eager to preach the gospel also to you who are in Rome." (Romans 1:14-15, NIV).

In the same way there are those in our lives who need this message of faith, hope, and love. They need to know that there is a way out of the pit that the world has thrown them into and that we are witnesses because God lifted us up out of that pit.

295

"He lifted me out of the slimy pit, out of the mud and mire; he set my feet on a rock and gave me a firm place to stand" (*Psalm 40:2,* NIV).

God wants to use us to help others. Our life experiences are the tools that God uses to touch others. We who have experienced addictions can relate to those who are still caught in the bonds of addictions. We are the ones who can win their trust more easily and lead them to the steps that will cause them to have a spiritual experience in Christ that will set them free. God tells us that He *"comforts us in all our tribulation, that we may be able to comfort those who are in any trouble, with the comfort with which we ourselves are comforted by God"* (*2 Corinthians 1:4*).

So what is this MESSAGE?

M	Meekness brings wholeness
E	Exchange addictions for communion with God
S	Seeing your mistakes gives you cleansing
S	Sorrow brings a change that heals us
A	Atonement comes through Christ's blood alone
G	God is your only hope
E	Extend your life to others

M- Meekness brings wholeness

Meekness means to yield power to the control of a greater source. Picture a stallion being bridled by the trainer here. We are meek when we acknowledge that we are created with talents, gifts, abilities, and powers, but that those powers are wasted and useless until we let God have control of them. We don't have the wisdom and power needed to manage our own lives. Doing that led to addictions. So we begin by acknowledging our need for God. We admit that we need Jesus Christ to be our higher power that takes control of our out-of-control lives. When we do, He makes us whole in body, soul, and spirit.

Chapter Forty-Eight ~ Message

E – Exchange addictions for communion with God

Addictions artificially fill a hole that God put in us that He alone is to occupy. He is the only thing that can fill that void successfully. Everything else, drugs, sex, porn, alcohol, rage and bitterness, eating disorders, success, money, knowledge, or whatever else will leave us feeling empty and without a purpose. We were created to know God and worship Him. Only that relationship with God will fill the hole in our heart. The good news is that God loves us and wants to fill us with His Spirit and give us the love, joy, and peace that we seek. Jesus died to make that possible. Now all we have to do is ask God to come into our heart and He will. He will instantly cleanse us and start us on a new path that will lead to freedom and wholeness.

S – Seeing your mistakes gives you cleansing

Humbling ourselves to God with confession of our shortcomings and weaknesses results in receiving God's forgiveness and cleansing from all of our unrighteousness. God has already forgiven us and paid for our transgressions in the death of Jesus Christ. The question is not will God forgive, but will we receive His forgiveness? Humble confession frees us from all guilt and removes shame. We receive an assurance from God that we are His children and that He accepts us in Christ. This acceptance frees us to be the person that God created us to be.

S – Sorrow brings a change that heals us

Our cleansing will come through a sorrowful time of self-examination. Such sorrow motivates us to change and to make amends with others. This change and making of amends heals both them and you. God causes all things to work for His good as we follow Him.

A – Atonement comes through Christ's blood alone

None of our efforts for the good can make us right with God. Our righteousness is like filthy rags. The only thing that can make us right with God is the blood of Jesus Christ. His blood is the only sacrifice for our sins. When we receive Christ as our Lord and Savior, God makes us a part of His family with all the privileges of family. You cannot earn God's love. He already loves you enough that He sent Jesus to die for your sins.

G – God is your only hope

      The only way we can have hope is through God. Hope means a confident expectation. To have a confidence that in all things it will work for the good is to believe that God is the rewarder of those that diligently seek Him. This hope gives us confidence for this life and for an eternal life with God in Heaven.

E – Extend your life to others

      God created us and has a plan for us. He wants to use us. First of all He saves us and makes us whole. He sets us free from the world and its bondages. He doesn't just set us free to sit around and enjoy the ride or to be a spectator. God wants to use us to help others to know Him and to have freedom from the addictions of this world. God wants to use our lives and testimonies to touch someone else. So we continue in Him and let Him use us to touch somebody else. It is our choice. How will we live our lives? Will it be for us or for God and others?

Prayer:

Dear Lord Jesus,

Thank You so much for Your blood. It is Your blood that has paid the debts for all of my sins and shortcoming. Help me to share with others what You have done for them.

In Jesus' Name,

Amen.

Chapter Forty-Eight ~ Message

Putting it to Work

Please answer the following in writing and then discuss your answers with your sponsor/accountability partner.

1.   Do you remember who was there to help you begin your journey in the 12 Step experience? Describe how that happened.

_____

_____

_____

_____

2.   How do you feel about that person who helped and encouraged you in your journey in these steps?

_____

_____

_____

_____

3.   Do you feel a desire to want to give these steps to others and to be like those who helped you?

_____

_____

_____

_____

4.   Do you have any hang ups about being a helper to others in this 12 Step journey?

_____

_____

_____

_____

Restoring Broken People

Step 12 - Having had a spiritual experience as the result of these steps, we try to carry this message to others and to practice these principles in all our affairs.

"Dear brothers, if a Christian is overcome by some sin, you who are godly should gently and humbly help him back onto the right path, remembering that next time it might be one of you who is in the wrong." (*Galatians 6:1*, TLB).

Practice makes Perfect. We have heard this all of our lives. It is to be noted that the saying does not mean that those who practice are perfect. None of us are flawless. We are all prone to mistakes and failure. As a matter of fact that is why we have to "practice" our faith. We are not without flaw. We do make mistakes and even sometimes fail miserably. The good news is that God knows that and has already decided that He loves us and that He has and will overlook our flaws, inconsistencies, and our failures.

We need to know that we are practicing in order to grow. We are not there yet. When will we be perfected? The Bible says that when the Lord returns that we shall be like Him. God says it this way:

"What marvelous love the Father has extended to us! Just look at it - we're called children of God! That's who we really are. But that's also why the world doesn't recognize us or take us seriously, because it has no idea who he is or what he's up to. But friends, that's exactly who we are: children of God. And that's only the beginning. Who knows how we'll end up! What we know is that when Christ is openly revealed, we'll see him - and in seeing him, become like him. All of us who look forward to his Coming stay ready, with the glistening purity of Jesus' life as a model for our own" (*1 John 3:1-3*, The Message).

When we say that we "practice" we are saying that we have set Jesus Christ as our model. We want to be like Him and continue to strive to be like Him. We work at it each day and become a little more like Him.

Our good friends in the medical world are a great example. They often fail in their attempts to help people medically. Sometimes they lose patience. But they don't quit. They keep showing up to work every day and try again. Because they do, they experience successes. They provide medicines that often cure and many times save the lives of their patients. They are *practicing* medicine.

It is with this concept of practice that we walk this spiritual journey in Christ. We are a work in progress. We have learned some things that we know are right and we emulate being like Jesus and showing His love to others. There are other things that we are attempting to learn or maybe don't even know about yet, and we stumble around. But we keep going and living in Christ knowing that as we walk forward the Lord will teach us how to be more like Him, and to be of further help to others. In this process the Lord is loving, patient, kind, and encouraging. He has no thought of condemning us. He wants to help us each day learn and comfort us when we feel that we have failed. He said that if we would come to Him for wisdom that He would give it to us without chiding or chastising us. He is gracious and loving to us. He said we can count all our trials as joy because He will patiently use them to help us learn from our challenges and to become more like Him (*James 1:1-5*).

So what does it mean to PRACTICE?

P	Putting knowledge to work
R	Relying on God for the results
A	Accepting our weaknesses
C	Confessing God's Word
T	Trying out new ways of living in God
I	Increasing our understanding
C	Caring about God, others, and ourselves
E	Eternally enjoying God's presence

Putting knowledge to work

The 12 Steps are principles that Dr. Bob and Bill Wilson discovered through Bible Study and Prayer. They are spiritual principles that come from the Bible. That is why they work. God tells us that when we look up to Him, and trust in Him, that we begin the path of wisdom. Dr. Bob and Bill Wilson discovered that wisdom in studying the Bible and in spending time in prayer. The principles worked because they were studying the Bible and Praying.

Chapter Forty-Nine ~ Practice

This is a spiritual journey. David said *"I will look unto the hills from where does my help come? My help comes from the LORD, who made heaven and earth"* (*Psalm 121:1-2*, ESV). This passage is a rhetorical question of David referring to the places in the hills where the Baal and local fertility gods were worshipped. He was saying that the gods of this world system offer no help. That God who made Heaven and Earth is the only hope that we have.

Sometimes we are tempted to look at the high places of the world system and to think that those high places will provide our help and security. We get addicted to those things and they begin to take over our thought life. We find ourselves living for those things. Then we wake up and find out that they destroyed us. David said that instead of relying on the high places of the world, he had learned to trust in the Lord and that the Lord would make the difference for Him.

It is not the program and principles that make us better. The key in PRACTICE is God. We are walking a living, vital, spiritual journey with God Himself. He is our help and our guide. He is the maker of heaven and earth and knows the way for us each and every day. It is not enough to just have a program. We have to have God to make this work. Without Him we are just "Dry Drunks." He is the One who gives us love, joy, peace, and life more abundantly.

There is a move in AA, at the time that I am writing this, to take God out of the 12 Steps. To do so will bring ruin to the work of AA. So many people that I have spoken to in the medical and psychological field have said that they have no lasting answers to keep people free of their addictions. They know how to detoxify them and get them over those symptoms of withdrawal, but they don't have a pill that cures the addictions. AA has worked for many because it presents a power that is higher than this world to help people. That power is God in Jesus Christ. When Christ enters us and makes us know His love, we experience the power that satisfies us at a higher level than any drug or addiction ever could or ever will. He heals our pleasure centers and causes us to be able to enjoy the world in Him. The joy of the Lord is our strength. Anything less than this is a "Dry Drunk" and we will not truly know sobriety.

So PRACTICE means to put to work these principles resulting in a spiritual experience and journey with God. This is everyday for the rest of our lives. God has great things in store for us in this exciting journey in Him.

Relying on God for the Results

To PRACTICE we have to recognize that we are not responsible for the results, only the efforts to show up and do what we know to do each day. Life presents so many twists and turns that there is no way that we can guarantee that we will always be right and always succeed. The only one who can do that is God. He alone can be called the Righteous One. So, we lean on Him. We look to Him to lead us, comfort us, direct us, and to motivate us to go with His plan. As we walk according to His principles, we learn that He knows how to have us in the right place at the right time. As we say and do what He tells us, we find Him using us in ways that we could have never imagined. We become helpers of the others to know the love and joy of the Lord. We see others experiencing the peace of God that passes all understanding.

We start our day with God and His Word. We pray that God will lead us in our day. We take our concerns to Him and leave them with Him, trusting Him to take care of those concerns. We confess that He is trustworthy and we rely on His Word. The faith journey is filled with miracles and events, which we know are orchestrated by God. We see God's hand moving in ways that we didn't realize could happen. God shows us His ways. He is awesome and never fails us. We rely on Him and He comes through for us. We will continue these thoughts on PRACTICE in the next chapter.

Prayer:

Dear Lord Jesus,

Help me to practice Your presence everyday. Let me be so full of You, that wherever I go, people will sense Your presence in my life. Help me share with others what You have done for me. Help me be a fountain of hope for others who need to begin their journey with You.

In Jesus' Name,

Amen.

Putting it to Work

Please answer the following in writing and then discuss your answers
with your sponsor/accountability partner.

1.	Have you ever had to practice for something such as sports,
music, speech, etc.? What was it? How did it work?

_____

_____

_____

_____

_____

2.	Do you ever have hang ups with feelings like you are not good
enough or you won't make it? Please describe.

_____

_____

_____

_____

_____

3.	Have you ever thought that you would quit and relapse? How did
that feel? What happened?

_____

_____

_____

_____

_____

4.	Why have you stayed with this spiritual journey?

_____

_____

_____

_____

Restoring Broken People

Step 12 - Having had a spiritual experience as the result of these steps, we try to carry this message to others and to practice these principles in all our affairs.

"Dear brothers, if a Christian is overcome by some sin, you who are godly should gently and humbly help him back onto the right path, remembering that next time it might be one of you who is in the wrong" (*Galatians 6:1*, TLB).

P	Putting knowledge to work
R	Relying on God for the results
A	Accepting our weaknesses
C	Confessing God's Word
T	Trying out new ways of living in God
I	Increasing our understanding
C	Caring about God, others, and ourselves
E	Eternally enjoying God's presence

In our last chapter we looked at the first two points of PRACTICE. Now we will look carefully at the rest of the truths about PRACTICE.

Accepting our weaknesses

As we discussed in the first section of this book, we struggle with the idea of personal weakness. We want to believe that we are immortal, invincible; that we have our own answers and can make our own way. That syndrome leads us to addictions, because we aren't that strong so we look for something that will take away the pain and the shame. Now, we are operating without the addictions, but we can still have the attitude. PRACTICE means that we accept that we are weak in ourselves and that we need the Lord to help us everyday. We do have weaknesses and practice means that we accept that fact and begin to live life aware of our weaknesses. We ask God to help us to know when those weaknesses are eroding away at our lives and to ask God to take over. We don't graduate as those who have no weaknesses. No, we have the same weaknesses that we had when we came into this program. We have the same weaknesses that we had when we began this spiritual experience and journey. We accept that they are a part of our natural man and ask the Lord to help us to guard against them.

James said that a person is considered perfect (mature) when he/she can control his/her tongue (*James 3:2*). Then James said that no man can control it (*James 3:8*). In other words, we all stumble with words at some point in time. We are all weak. This was so real to David that he prayed that God would put a guard over his lips to warn him when he was about to say something that he shouldn't.

"I said, 'I will guard my ways, Lest I sin with my tongue; I will restrain my mouth with a muzzle, While the wicked are before me'" (*Psalm 39:1*).
"Set a guard, O Lord, over my mouth; Keep watch over the door of my lips" (*Psalm 141:3*).
That is what we have to do. We have to recognize that we have, in the natural, weaknesses that are with us everyday. We have to take them to the Lord and be ever conscious of them. Then we have to ask God to warn us when we are about to allow those weaknesses to take hold and control us. God has put the Holy Spirit in us and He will warn us. If we will listen, He will keep us from falling.

Confessing God's Word
"Faith comes from hearing, and hearing through the Word of Christ" (*Romans 10:17,* ESV). What we listen to will determine our faith level. If we listen to someone's doubt and believe it, my faith level will go down. We lose confidence in God and ourselves. Everything becomes chaotic. Our life goes out of control. So, we want to mingle with those who doubt in order to reach out to them, but we have to be careful to not allow them to infect us with their doubts.

Our self-talk determines our faith level. When we speak God's Word in confidence, and confess that we believe that God is trustworthy and will keep His Word, then our faith level grows. If we mutter around and grump about how things are going then our faith level begins to go down. We PRACTICE by confessing God's Word. Keeping a guard on our mouth so we don't speak out doubt, fear, anger, depression, and bad reports about others and ourselves keeps us from moving into the realm of unbelief and fear. Speaking out our beliefs in a positive way builds faith in others and in us.

Chapter Fifty ~ Practice 2

Peter learned this when he and his friends had worked all night to catch fish and caught none. They were professionals and could not find the fish. Then Jesus came by and called out to Peter to throw out his net on the other side of the boat. Peter said they had tried all night. Peter was about to lose out on the Lord's blessing and the revelation that the Lord wanted to give to him. Then he remembered whom he was talking to and said, *"But nevertheless at your Word."* Peter was saying it doesn't make sense in the natural, but I know that you are wiser than I am. I trust your Word, Lord. When he confessed God's Word, Peter brought in a catch that was so big it almost sank the boat. PRACTICE means we Confess God's Word daily.

Trying out new ways of living in God

One of the greatest enemies of growth is resistance to change. We, by nature, resist change. It is always a problem when we say "We have never done it this way before" or "We do it this way because we have always done it this way." These phrases are the death knoll to growth in us. God wants us to be fruitful, but in order to bear fruit we have to allow Him to bring change into our lives. Growth brings changes. It makes us uncomfortable because those changes move us outside of our comfort zone. When we sense that, we resist change and growth stops.

If we are to PRACTICE, we have to continue through all the changes that God brings into our lives. After the Lord told Peter how to catch a greater load of fish than he ever imagined, He told Peter that it was time to change. The Lord told Peter that he would no longer catch fish, but that he would fish for souls. Jesus wanted Peter to grow and to bear more fruit. In order for that to happen, Peter had to see the potential of following the Lord. Jesus demonstrated what could happen when he would obey God's Word. Then the Lord changed Peter's life and moved him into His calling. Peter went on to be a great fisher of men, but he had to be willing to follow the Lord and change at any cost (*Luke 5:10-11*).

In order for us to practice this spiritual experience and journey, we have to be willing to change whatever the Lord wants us to change. It may be as simple as a phrase of speech that we use, or a habit that we have. It may be our jobs or our appearance. To PRACTCICE we have to be like Mary the mother of Jesus and say, *"Let it be to me according to your word"* (*Luke 1:38,* ESV).

The songwriter Adelaide A. Pollard wrote, *"Have thine own way*

Lord, have thine own way. Thou art the potter and I am the clay. Mold me and make me after thine will, while I am waiting yielded and still." We are the clay and He is the potter. We have to know that He sees great potential in us, but we have to be ready and willing to change.

When my ex-wife decided to leave me, it threw me into a tailspin. My world totally changed. I found myself alone, lonely, and without a church to pastor. None of it made sense. But the Lord spoke to me and said that He had allowed this (didn't cause it) because He wanted to re-position me to use me in a new way. He began to put a new vision in my heart to touch people around the world with the good news of His love. This book is part of that new thing. I decided that I wasn't going to give up and go back, but that I wanted to continue on my spiritual journey in Christ. It has been exciting to see how God has used this change to grow me, and to use me in ways that I never thought possible. To PRACTICE, we have to be moldable, pliable, and ready to try new things in God, no matter what the cost. We will continue these thoughts in the next chapter.

Prayer:

Dear God,

Just as the song says, have Your way in me. You are the potter and I am the clay. So mold me and make me according to Your will. Thank you God for making me Your child and allowing me to know You. Let Your plans and purposes unfold in me.

In Jesus' Name,

Amen.

Putting it to Work

Please answer the following in writing and then discuss your answers with your sponsor/accountability partner.

1.   What are the character traits that surface as your weaknesses? What are you doing about those traits?

_____
_____
_____
_____
_____

2.   Have you had occasion when your weaknesses got the best of you and hurt others or you? Describe.

_____
_____
_____
_____

3.   What does faith look like in your life? Are you believing for things that look impossible?

_____
_____
_____
_____

4.   How has God changed you? How is He changing you now?

_____
_____
_____
_____

Restoring Broken People

Step 12 - Having had a spiritual experience as the result of these steps, we try to carry this message to others and to practice these principles in all our affairs.

"Dear brothers, if a Christian is overcome by some sin, you who are godly should gently and humbly help him back onto the right path, remembering that next time it might be one of you who is in the wrong" (*Galatians 6:1*, TLB)

P	Putting knowledge to work
R	Relying on God for the results
A	Accepting our weaknesses
C	Confessing God's Word
T	Trying out new ways of living in God
I	Increasing our understanding
C	Caring about God, others, and ourselves
E	Eternally enjoying God's presence

In our last two chapters we looked at the first five points of PRACTICE.

Putting knowledge to work
Relying on God for the results
Accepting our weaknesses
Confessing God's Word
Trying out new ways of living in God

Now we will look carefully at the rest of the truths about PRACTICE.

Increasing our understanding

My dad was a schoolteacher for 35 years. It was not just a profession for him; it was a calling. He was passionate about teaching and helping his students understand their lessons. He knew that what he taught them would give them skills to take care of their families and make them prosperous in their future. In 50 years of living in the area where I was raised, it never failed that when I was out with my dad someone would stop and say to him that he had been their teacher. Then that person would say, "You know you changed my life by teaching me to..." then they would fill in the sentence. They would go on to tell what kind of benefits his teaching had brought into their lives and how they used the things that they learned. One thing that I discovered about teachers, they never stop teaching.

God tells us that He is our teacher. Jesus was called "rabbi," which is another word for "teacher." Jesus told us that the Holy Spirit would teach all things that we would need to know and understand. God is a teacher and is always teaching us. God calls us to be His disciples. The idea of a disciple is that of being a student to someone. They are the mentor and we are the one being mentored.

One of the great privileges that I had in my life was that the bishop of our churches used to call me to be his traveling companion when he would go to places to share. We would travel in cars and sometimes by airplane to places all over the country and world. During those times he would always seem to be teaching me. It wasn't a classroom. He was there and things would happen that created discussion, questions, and then he would have an observation or even a lesson that would come out of it. I loved those trips because I was always learning so much from him. We did that for so many years, that I now feel like he deposited something in me that defines who I am and how I think.

That is who Jesus wants to be to us. He is the "Rabbi," "Master," or "Teacher," and we are the disciples. He wants us to journey with Him and be with Him each day. He wants us to experience life with Him and as we do there will be discussion and questions that create new and better understandings of God, life, and others. There is always something more for us to learn. He has greater understanding to give us. To PRACTICE means that we will be His students forever. One million years from now we will still be traveling with Him, maybe in a distant galaxy zapping through outer space, and He will still be showing us new and wonderful things.

So to PRACTICE we stay in a place of learning. We never stop being a student of God, His Word, abundant life, faith, and the spiritual journey that we are on. We continue to find new truths and to learn all that we can. We realize that there is something to learn from every event, experience, and person that comes into our lives. We stay humble and continually ask the Lord to show us what He wants us to learn in each new chapter in the book of our lives.

Chapter Fifty-One ~ Practice 3

Caring about God, others, and ourselves

Jesus warned the church in Laodicea about being lukewarm. Give me a drink that is hot or cold, but not one that is tepid, room temperature. Jesus was trying to let us know that we have to have passion. We have to be passionate about life, God, others, and who we are. We can't be like the guy who was asked what the word apathy meant. He looked at the questioner with disgust for asking the question and bothering him and said, "I don't know and I don't care!"

We have to care to PRACTICE. We have to care everyday about everyone, everything, and all that God allows to come into our lives. We have to see it as a gift from Him that gives us an opportunity to be a blessing or to receive a blessing. Caring is the essence of life. Addictions took away our passion. They distracted us and allowed us to escape our caring. They made us lukewarm and apathetic people. It is no wonder that Jesus was speaking to the church of this time in history and warned against apathy (*Revelation 3:14-22,* ESV). We are so full of riches, things, and self-satisfaction that we are easily distracted from really caring about God and His plan for us.

We have to care about others. It can't be enough that we were set free from our addictions; we have to care about the others who need to be set free. We all have a role to play in making that happen. We are a team and each player has a role. Each role is essential to winning the game. The game is to see others come aboard this ship and begin a spiritual journey based on a relationship with God through Jesus Christ. Their addictions are telling them that they need this spiritual journey. If we don't get them on the boat, their addictions will ruin their lives, families, careers, and their souls. We have to care about them. We can't just say, "I don't know them and I don't care." We have to say, "Lord show me who you want me to help today." You gave me a gift; now show me who I can give it to. Show me what role you want me to play on this team. Then with passion we have to listen and let God use us.

Eternally enjoying God's presence

This spiritual journey is not just for a little time to get sober. This is an eternal experience that will take us to heaven to be with Jesus Christ forever. When we make the decision to receive Jesus Christ and turn our lives over to Him as our Lord and Savior, we begin this eternal journey.

When will it stop? Never! It never comes to an end. His mercies endure forever. Forever we will be with Him and He with us. We will be together with Him forever in heaven. So we better learn to forgive each other now and to get along, because we have to be neighbors forever and ever.

Heaven is a wonderful place. God tells us that it is a joyful place that is full of pleasures (*Psalm 16:11*). Heaven is our eternal home. Jesus is making a place for each of us in heaven that will be our home eternally. We will live with Him forever (*John 14:1-3*).

In the now, we can enjoy a taste of Heaven. As believers we can be both on earth and in heaven at the same time. This happens when we pray, worship, and become aware of God's presence. He has a way of allowing our spirit man to commune with Him in heavenly places while our human feet are still on the ground. I read a post from a friend on Facebook recently that said that they wished they didn't have to leave their secret place with the Lord. They were so enjoying His presence that they didn't want to go out of that place and deal with the natural things of life. It is not a burden to pray and spend time with the Lord. It is a pleasure. It is enjoyable.

To PRACTICE we have to turn this whole thing into a pleasure. We have to really enjoy God, His Word, His Presence, His People, His Plan, Purposes, and His Person. Let me encourage you to enjoy the journey!

Prayer:

Dear God,

As I continue this journey with You, help me to keep in focus my destiny. Thank You for the hope of heaven. Let me always live for the day when I will see You face-to-face. Let me be so full of Your joy that I will never feel the need for my addictions and compulsions again. I give You all the glory for all that You have done for me.

In Jesus' Name,

Amen.

Putting it to Work

Please answer the following in writing and then discuss your answers with your sponsor/accountability partner.

1.   Can you think of some truth that God has recently taught you? Please describe.

_____

_____

_____

_____

_____

2.   What is your passion in God? How is God using you today?

_____

_____

_____

_____

3.   Who do you feel the Lord wants you to reach with these principles of a spiritual journey? How will you go about doing that?

_____

_____

_____

_____

4.   Do you enjoy God, His Word, and His People? Please describe how that looks for you.

_____

_____

_____

_____

_____

Restoring Broken People

Bibliography

1. Baker, John. Stepping out of Denial and into God's Grace. Grand Rapids: Zondervan, 2012.
2. "Alcohol Facts and Statistics." National Institute on Alcohol Abuse and Alcoholism. Revised June 2016. NIAAA. https://www.niaaa.nih.gov/alcohol-health/overview-alcohol-consumption/alcohol-facts-and-statistics
3. "Admit." Def 1, 2. *Dictionary.cambridge.org.* Cambridge Dictionary, 1995. 2008.
4. a. Begley, Sharon. "How Behavior Can Change Your DNA." Newsweek. The Newsweek Daily Beast. Jan. 13, 2011.
   b. Bliss, Stasia. "DNA Affected by Love Praise and Gratitude-Studies Say." Liberty Voice. Guardian Liberty Voice. July 27, 2013.
5. Various Authors. Touchstones: A book of Daily Meditations for Men. Center City: Hazelden Foundation, 1991. May 24 entry.
6. "Powerless." Def 1a. *Webster-dictionary.org.* Merriam-Webster. 1806. 2008.
7. BibleStudyTools.com. 2008. Strong's Exhaustive Concordance. http://www.biblestudytools.com/concordances/strongs-exhaustive-concordance/
8. Ibid
9. Comiskey, Joel. "The Filling of the Holy Spirit. *"* Christian Broadcast Network. http://www1.cbn.com/biblestudy/the-filling-of-the-holy-spirit
10. "Michael Phelps." *Wikipedia.* Wikipedia Foundation, Inc. July 2016. Web. Aug 2008. https://en.wikipedia.org/wiki/Michael_Phelps
11. Young, William P., *The Shack.* Newbury Park: Windblown Media, 2007. pg 174
12. "Sounding Board." Def 1-4. *Kdictionaries-online.com.* Random House Dictionary. 2008, 2010.
13. "Moral." Def 1-4. *Webster-dictionary.org.* Merriam-Webster. 1806. 2008.
14. BibleStudyTools.com. 2008. Strong's Exhaustive Concordance. http://www.biblestudytools.com/concordances/strongs-exhaustive-concordance/
15. Dake, Jennings Finis. Dake's Annotated Reference Bible. South Carolina: Ministry Helps, 1991.
16. Ibid
17. Ibid
18. Ibid
19. Ibid

20. Ibid
21. Ibid
22. Ibid
23. BibleStudyTools.com. 2008. Strong's Exhaustive Concordance. http://www.biblestudytools.com/concordances/strongs-exhaustive-concordance/
24. "Remove." Def 1-4. *Webster-dictionary.org*. Merriam-Webster. 1806. 2008.
25. "Forgive." Def 1a-2. *Webster-dictionary.org*. Merriam-Webster. 1806. 2008.
26. Alcoholics Anonymous World Services, Inc. Big Book. Riverside Drive, NY: Alcoholics Anonymous World Services, Inc., 2013.
27. BibleStudyTools.com. 2008. Strong's Exhaustive Concordance. http://www.biblestudytools.com/concordances/strongs-exhaustive-concordance/
28. Ibid
29. Goleman, Daniel. Emotional Intelligence. New York, NY: Bantum Books, 1995.

We do pray that this book will be a blessing to many people and a help to those who find themselves broken from the hurts of life.

For bulk orders please contact us at Light for Life Ministries, Inc. at the above address.